Lecture Notes in Computer Science   7172

Commenced Publication in 1973
Founding and Former Series Editors:
Gerhard Goos, Juris Hartmanis, and Jan van Leeuwen

Editorial Board

David Hutchison
  Lancaster University, UK
Takeo Kanade
  Carnegie Mellon University, Pittsburgh, PA, USA
Josef Kittler
  University of Surrey, Guildford, UK
Jon M. Kleinberg
  Cornell University, Ithaca, NY, USA
Alfred Kobsa
  University of California, Irvine, CA, USA
Friedemann Mattern
  ETH Zurich, Switzerland
John C. Mitchell
  Stanford University, CA, USA
Moni Naor
  Weizmann Institute of Science, Rehovot, Israel
Oscar Nierstrasz
  University of Bern, Switzerland
C. Pandu Rangan
  Indian Institute of Technology, Madras, India
Bernhard Steffen
  TU Dortmund University, Germany
Madhu Sudan
  Microsoft Research, Cambridge, MA, USA
Demetri Terzopoulos
  University of California, Los Angeles, CA, USA
Doug Tygar
  University of California, Berkeley, CA, USA
Gerhard Weikum
  Max Planck Institute for Informatics, Saarbruecken, Germany

Sølvi Ystad   Mitsuko Aramaki
Richard Kronland-Martinet Kristoffer Jensen
Sanghamitra Mohanty (Eds.)

Speech, Sound and Music Processing: Embracing Research in India

8th International Symposium, CMMR 2011
20th International Symposium, FRSM 2011
Bhubaneswar, India, March 9-12, 2011
Revised Selected Papers

 Springer

Volume Editors

Sølvi Ystad
Mitsuko Aramaki
Richard Kronland-Martinet
Centre National de la Recherche Scientifique
Laboratoire de Mécanique et d'Acoustique
31 Chemin Joseph Aiguier
13402 Marseille Cedex 20, France
E-mail: {ystad, aramaki, kronland}@lma.cnrs-mrs.fr

Kristoffer Jensen
Aalborg University Esbjerg
Niels Bohr Vej 8
6700 Esbjerg, Denmark
E-mail: krist@create.aau.dk

Sanghamitra Mohanty
North Orissa University
Sriram Chandra Vihar, Takatpur
Baripada, Orissa 757003, India
E-mail: sangham1@rediffmail.com

ISSN 0302-9743   e-ISSN 1611-3349
ISBN 978-3-642-31979-2   e-ISBN 978-3-642-31980-8
DOI 10.1007/978-3-642-31980-8
Springer Heidelberg Dordrecht London New York

Library of Congress Control Number: 2012942225

CR Subject Classification (1998): J.5, H.5, C.3, H.5.5, G.3, I.5

LNCS Sublibrary: SL 3 – Information Systems and Application, incl. Internet/Web and HCI

Typesetting: Camera-ready by author, data conversion by Scientific Publishing Services, Chennai, India

Printed on acid-free paper

Springer is part of Springer Science+Business Media (www.springer.com)

Preface

The Computer Music Modeling and Retrieval (CMMR) 2011 conference was the 8th event of this international series, and the first that took place outside Europe. Since its beginnings in 2003, this conference has been co-organized by the Laboratoire de Mécanique et d'Acoustique in Marseille, France, and the Department of Architecture, Design and Media Technology (ad:mt), University of Aalborg, Esbjerg, Denmark, and has taken place in France, Italy, Spain, and Denmark. Historically, CMMR offers a cross-disciplinary overview of current music information retrieval and sound modeling activities and related topics, such as human interaction, perception and cognition and much more. CMMR built its strength on its open and multidisciplinary approach to these fields and the interaction of researchers with expertise in the CMMR areas. As such, CMMR evolves with the researchers and their openness to new trends and directions within the related fields of interest.

Frontiers of Research in Speech and Music (FRSM) has been organized in different parts of India every year since 1991. Previous conferences were held at ITC-SRA Kolkata, NPL New Delhi, BHU Varanasi, IIT Kanpur, Lucknow University, AIISH Mysore, IITM Gwalior, Utkal University, Bhubaneswar, Annamalai University, and IIDL Thiruvananthapuram to promote research activities covering many interdisciplinary research areas such as physics, mathematics, speech, musicology, electronics and computer science and their practical application. Through this symposium indigenous speech technologies applicable for Indian languages get an appropriate platform for their advancement. Indian music is multicategorical in nature in this country of multilingualism. It has rich classical music at one end and numerous ethnic and folk music at the other end. At FRSM, different aspects of Indian classical music and its impact in cognitive science are the focus of discussion. Eminent scientist from the USA, Japan, Sweden, France, Poland, Taiwan, India and other European and Asian countries have delivered state-of-the-art lectures in these areas every year at different places providing an opportunity to researchers, academicians and industrialists to enhance their knowledge and to interact with each other to share their knowledge and experience in the latest developments in the fields. Participation in FRSM has always encouraged researchers to contribute toward achieving the objectives of the symposium effectively.

This year the two conferences merged for the first time into the FRSM/CMMR-2011 symposium that took place in Bhubaneswar, Orissa, India, during March 9–12, 2011. The conference was organized by the Resource Centre For Indian Language Technology Solution, Department of Computer Science and Application, Utkal University, together with LMA and INCM (CNRS, France) and ad:mt, Aalborg University Esbjerg (Denmark). The conference featured prominent keynote speakers working in the area of music information retrieval and automatic speech recognition, and the program of CMMR 2011 included paper sessions, panel discussions, posters, and cultural events. We are pleased to announce that in light of the location in India there was a special focus on Indian speech and music. The melting pot of the FRSM and CMMR events gave rise to many interesting meetings with a focus on the field from different cultural perspectives.

The proceedings of previous CMMR conferences were published in the *Lecture Notes in Computer Science* series (LNCS 2771, LNCS 3310, LNCS 3902, LNCS 4969, LNCS 5493, LNCS 5954 and LNCS 6684), and the present edition follows the lineage of the previous ones, including a collection of 17 papers on the topics of CMMR. These articles were specially reviewed and corrected for this proceedings volume. The current book is divided into four main chapters that reflect the high quality of the sessions of CMMR 2011, the collaboration with FRSM 2011, and the Indian influence on the topics of Indian music, music information retrieval, sound analysis synthesis and perception and speech processing of Indian languages. The Indian focus provided many interesting topics related to the Raga, from a music theory point of view to the instruments and the specific ornamentation of Indian classical singing. Another particular topic that reflects the participation of FRSM is related to the speech of different Indian languages. We are pleased to present this work of FRSM/CMMR 2011 that brings forward both fundamental research in these important areas and research with a special focus from an Indian perspective, and gives a splendid opportunity to keep up to date on these issues.

We would like to thank the Program Committee members for their valuable paper reports and thank all the participants who made CMMR 2011 an exciting and original event. In particular, we would like to acknowledge the organizers and participants in FRSM 2011 for their participation. Finally, we would like to thank Springer for accepting to publish the CMMR 2011 proceedings in their LNCS series.

April 2012

Sølvi Ystad
Mitsuko Aramaki
Richard Kronland-Martinet
Kristoffer Jensen
Sanghamitra Mohanty

Organization

The 8th International Symposium on Computer Music Modeling and Retrieval (CMMR2011) was co-organized with the 20th international Symposium on Frontiers of Research on Speech and Music (FRSM2011) by the Resource Centre For Indian Language Technology Solution, Department of Computer Science and Application, Utkal University (Orissa, India), Aalborg University Esbjerg (Denmark), and Laboratoire de Mécanique et d'Acoustique/Institut de Neurosciences Cognitives de la Méditerrannée (Centre National de la Recherche Scientifique), Marseille (France).

FRSM Symposium Co-chairs

A.K. Datta   Society for Natural Language Technology
                               Research (SNLTR), Kolkata, India
Sanghamitra Mohanty   Utkal University, Orissa, India
S. Ray Chaudhury   ITC SRA, Kolkata, India
Phalguni Gupta   IIT Kanpur, India

CMMR Symposium Co-chairs

K. Jensen   Aalborg University, Esbjerg, Denmark
M. Aramaki   INCM-CNRS, Marseille, France
R. Kronland-Martinet   LMA-CNRS, Marseille, France
S. Ystad   LMA-CNRS, Marseille, France

Organizing Committee

A.K. Datta   SNLTR, (Chair), India
Sanghamitra Mohanty   Utkal University (Convenor), India
Sølvi Ystad   LMA-CNRS, France
Anupam Shukla   ABV-IIITM, Gwalior, India
S.R. Savithri   AIISH, Mysore, India
Shyamal Das Mandal   IIT, Khatagpur, India
A. Deb   Jadavpur University, Kolkata, India
N. Dey   ITC SRA, Kolkata, India
R. Sengupta   Jadavpur University, Kolkata, India
S. Ray Chaudhury   ITC SRA, Kolkata (Co-convenor), India
M. Chakraborty   ITC SRA, Kolkata, India

Program Committee

Phalguni Gupta   IIT Kanpur (Chair), India
Richard Kronland-Martinet   LMA-CNRS, France
Mitsuko Aramaki   INCM-CNRS, France

D. Ghosh	Jadavpur University, Kolkata, India
B. Gupta	Jadavpur University, Kolkata, India
Sanghamitra Mohanty	Utkal University, India
Anupam Shukla	ABV-IIITM, Gwalior, India
R. Sengupta	JU, Kolkata, India
N. Dey	ITC SRA, Kolkata, India

Local Organizing Committee

Ajay Kumar Bisoi	Utkal University
Bikram Keshari Ratha	Utkal University
Prafulla Kumar Behera	Utkal University
Sohag Sundar Nanda	Utkal University
Sampa Chaupattanaik	Utkal University
Soumya Mishra	Utkal University
Suman Bhattacharya	TCS, Bhubaneswar

Table of Contents

Part III: Sound Analysis-Synthesis and Perception

Part IV: Speech Processing of Indian Languages

Objective Assessment of Ornamentation
in Indian Classical Singing

Chitralekha Gupta and Preeti Rao

Department of Electrical Engineering, IIT Bombay, Mumbai 400076, India
chitralekha85@gmail.com, prao@ee.iitb.ac.in

Abstract. Important aspects of singing ability include musical accuracy and voice quality. In the context of Indian classical music, not only is the correct sequence of notes important to musical accuracy but also the nature of pitch transitions between notes. These transitions are essentially related to *gamakas* (ornaments) that are important to the aesthetics of the genre. Thus a higher level of singing skill involves achieving the necessary expressiveness via correct rendering of ornamentation, and this ability can serve to distinguish a well-trained singer from an amateur. We explore objective methods to assess the quality of ornamentation rendered by a singer with reference to a model rendition of the same song. Methods are proposed for the perceptually relevant comparison of complex pitch movements based on cognitively salient features of the pitch contour shape. The objective measurements are validated via their observed correlation with subjective ratings by human experts. Such an objective assessment system can serve as a useful feedback tool in the training of amateur singers.

Keywords: singing scoring, ornamentation, Indian music, polynomial curve fitting.

1   Introduction

Evaluation of singing ability involves judging the accuracy of notes and rendering of expression. While learning to sing, the first lessons from the guru (teacher) involve training to be in *sur* or rendering the notes of the melodic phrase correctly. In the context of Indian Classical music, not only is the sequence of notes critical but also the nature of the transitions between notes. The latter, related to *gamaka* (ornamentation), is important to the aesthetics of the genre. Hence the next level of singing training involves specific note intonation and the formation of *raga*-dependent phrases linking notes all of which make the singing more expressive and pleasing to hear. The degree of virtuosity in rendering such expressions provides important cues that distinguish a well-trained singer from an amateur. So incorporating expression scores in the singing evaluation systems for Indian music in general is expected to increase its performance in terms of its accuracy with respect to perceptual judgment. Such a system will be useful in singing competition platforms that involve screening out better singers from large masses. Also such an evaluation system could be used as a feedback tool for training amateur singers.

S. Ystad et al. (Eds.): CMMR/FRSM 2011, LNCS 7172, pp. 1–25, 2012.

The aim of this work is to formulate a method for objective evaluation of singing quality based on perceived closeness of various types of expression rendition of a singer to that of the reference or model singer. The equally important problem of evaluating singing quality in isolation is not considered in the present work. The present work is directed towards computational modeling of the perceived difference between the test and reference pitch contour shapes. This is based on the hypothesis that the perceived quality of an ornament rendered in singing is mainly determined by the pitch contour shape although it is not unlikely that voice quality and loudness play some role as well.   This hypothesis is tested by subjective listening experiments presented here. Next, several methods to evaluate a specific ornament type based on the pitch contour extracted from sung phrases have been explored. The objective measures obtained have been experimentally validated by correlation with subjective judgments on a set of singers and ornament instances.

2   Related Work

Past computational studies of Indian classical music have been restricted to scales and note sequences within melodies. There has been some analysis of ornamentation, specifically of the ornament *meend* which can be described as a glide connecting two notes. Its proper rendition involves the accuracy of starting and ending notes, speed, and accent on intermediate notes [2 - 3]. Perceptual tests to differentiate between synthesized singing of vowel /a/ with a pitch movement of falling and rising intonation (concave, convex & linear) between two steady pitch states, 150 and 170 Hz, using a second degree polynomial function, revealed that the different types of transitory movements are cognitively separable [4]. A methodology for automatic extraction of meend from the performances in Hindustani vocal music described in [5] also uses the second degree equation as a criterion for extracting the meend. Also automatic classification of meend attempted in [6] gives some important observations like descending meends are the most common, followed by the rise-fall meends (meend with kanswar). The meends with intermediate touch notes are relatively less frequent. The duration of meend is generally between 300 - 500 ms. The transition between notes can also be oscillatory with the pitch contour assuming the shape of oscillations riding on a glide. Subramanian [7] reports that such ornaments are common in Indian classical music and he uses Carnatic music to demonstrate, through cognitive experiments that pitch curves of similar shapes convey similar musical expression even if the measured note intervals differ.

In Indian classical singing education, the assessment of progress of music learners has been a recent topic of research interest [1]. In the present work, two ornaments have been considered viz., glide and oscillations-on-glide. The assessment is with respect to the "model" or ideal rendition of the same song. Considering the relatively easy availability of singers for popular Indian film music, we use Hindustani classical music based movie songs for testing our methods. The previous work reported on glide has been to model it computationally. In this work, computational modeling has been used to assess the degree of perceived closeness between a given rendition and a reference rendition taken to be that of the original playback singer of the song.

3   Methodology

Since we plan to evaluate a rendered ornament with respect to an available reference audio recording of the same ornament, we need to prepare a database accordingly. Due to the relatively easy availability of singers for popular music, we choose songs from old classical music based Hindi film songs that are rich in ornamentation. Next, both reference and test audio files are subjected to pitch detection followed by computation of objective measures that seek to quantify the perceptually relevant differences between the two corresponding pitch contour shapes.

3.1   Reference and Test Datasets

The dataset consisting of polyphonic audio clips from popular Hindi film songs rich in ornament, were obtained as the reference dataset. The ornament clips (300 ms – 1 sec.) were isolated from the songs for use in the objective analysis. Short phrases (1 – 4 sec. duration) that include these ornament clips along with the neighboring context were used for subjective assessment. The ornament clips along with some immediate context makes it perceptually more understandable.

The reference songs were sung and recorded by 5 to 7 test singers. The test singers were either trained or amateur singers who were expected to differ mainly in their expression abilities. The method of 'sing along' with the reference (played at a low volume on one of the headphones) at the time of recording was used to maintain the time alignment between the reference and test songs.

The polyphonic reference audio files as well as the monophonic test audio files are processed by a semi-automatic polyphonic pitch detector [8] to obtain a high time-resolution voice pitch contour (representing the continuous variation of pitch in time across all vocal segments of the audio signal). It computes pitch every 10 ms interval throughout the audio segment.

3.2   Subjective Assessment

The original recording by the playback singer is treated as the model, with reference to which singers of various skill levels are to be rated. The subjective assessment of the test singers was performed by a set of 3 - 4 judges who were asked either to rank or to categorize (into good, medium or bad classes) the individual ornament clips of the test singers based on their closeness to the reference ornament clip.

Kendall's Coefficient. Kendall's W (also known as Kendall's coefficient of concordance) is a non-parametric statistic that is used for assessing agreement among judges [9]. Kendall's W ranges from 0 (no agreement) to 1 (complete agreement).

3.3   Procedure for Computational Modeling and Validation

- From the reference polyphonic and test monophonic audio files, first the pitch is detected throughout the sung segments using the PolyPDA tool [8]. The pitch values are converted to a semitone (cents) scale to obtain the pitch contour.

- The ornament is identified in the reference contour and marked manually, and the corresponding ornament segment pitch is isolated from both the reference and the test singer files for objective analysis. Also a slightly larger segment around the ornament is extracted from the audio file for the subjective tests so as to incorporate the melodic context.
- Model parameters are computed from the reference ornament pitch.
- Subjective ranks/ratings of the ornaments for each test token compared with the corresponding reference token are obtained from the judges. Those ornament tokens that obtain a high inter-judge agreement (Kendall's W>0.5) are retained for use in the validation of objective measures.
- The ranks/ratings are computed on the retained tokens using the objective measures for the test ornament instance in comparison to the reference or model singer ornament model parameters.
- The subjective and objective judgments are then compared by computing a correlation measure between them.
- Glide and oscillations-on-glide ornament pitch segments obtained from the datasets are separately evaluated.

3.4   Subjective Relevance of Pitch Contour

Since all the objective evaluation methods are based on the pitch contour, a comparison of the subjective evaluation ranks for two versions of the same ornament clips - the original full audio and the pitch re-synthesized with a neutral tone, can reveal how perceptual judgment is influenced by factors other than the pitch variation. Table 1 shows inter – judge rank correlation (Kendall Coefficient W) for a glide segment. Correlation between the two versions' ranks for each of the judges ranged from 0.67 to 0.85 with an average of 0.76 for the glide clip. This high correlation between the ratings of the original voice and resynthesized pitch indicate that the pitch variation is indeed the major component in subjective assessment of ornaments. We thus choose to restrict our objective measurement to capturing differences in pitch contours in various ways.

Table 1. Agreement of subjective ranks for the two versions of ornament test clips (original and pitch re-synthesized)

Ornament Instance	No. of Test Singers	No. of Judges	Inter-judges' rank agreement (W) for		Avg. correlation between original and pitch re-syn. judges' ranks (W)
			Original	Pitch re-synthesized	
Glide	5	4	0.86	0.76	0.76

4   Glide Assessment

A glide is a pitch transition ornament that resembles the ornament *meend*. Its proper rendition involves the following: accuracy of starting and ending notes, speed, and accent on intermediate notes [2]. Some types of glide are shown in Fig.1.

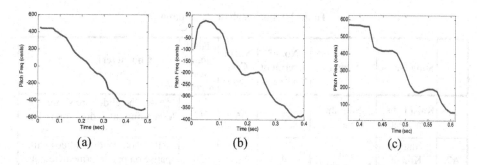

Fig. 1. Types of *Meend* (a) simple descending (b) pause on one intermediate note (c) pause on more than one intermediate notes

4.1 Database

This section consists of the reference data, test singing data and the subjective rating description.

Reference and Test Dataset. Two datasets, A and B, consisting of polyphonic audio clips from popular Hindi film songs rich in ornaments, were obtained as presented in Table 2. The pitch tracks of the ornament clips were isolated from the songs for use in the objective analysis. The ornament clips (1 - 4 sec) from Dataset A and the complete audio clips (1 min. approx.) from Dataset B were used for subjective assessment as described later in this section. The reference songs of the two datasets were sung and recorded by 5 to 9 test singers (Table 2).

Subjective Assessment. The original recording by the playback singer is treated as ideal, with reference to which singers of various skill levels are to be rated.

Dataset A. The subjective assessment of the test singers for Dataset A was performed by 3 judges who were asked to rank the individual ornament clips of the test singers based on their closeness to the reference ornament clip. The audio clips for the ornament glide comprised of the start and end steady notes with the glide in between them. The judges were asked to rank order the test singers' clips based on perceived similarity with the corresponding reference clip.

Dataset B. The subjective evaluation of the test singers for Dataset B was performed by 4 judges who were asked to categorize the test singers into one of three categories (good, medium and bad) based on an overall judgment of their ornamentation skills as compared to the reference by listening to the complete audio clip. The inter-judge agreement was 1.0 for both the songs' test singer sets.

Table 2. Glide database description

	Song Name	Singer	No. of ornament clips	No. of Test singers	Total no. of test tokens	Characteristics of the ornaments
A1.	Kaisi Paheli (Parineeta)	Sunidhi Chauhan	3	5	15	All the glides are simple descending (avg. duration is 1 sec approx.)
A2.	Nadiya Kinare (Abhimaan)	Lata Mangeshkar	4	5	20	All are descending glides with pause on one intermediate note (avg. duration is 0.5 sec approx.)
A3.	Naino Mein Badra (MeraSaaya)	Lata Mangeshkar	3	6	18	All are simple descending glides (avg. duration is 0.5 sec approx.)
A4.	Raina Beeti Jaye (Amar Prem)	Lata Mangeshkar	4	7	28	First and fourth instances are simple descending glides, second and third instances are complex ornaments (resembling other ornaments like murki)
B1.	Ao Huzoor (Kismat)	Asha Bhonsle	4	9	36	All are simple descending glides
B2.	Do Lafzon (The Great Gambler)	Asha Bhonsle	4	8	32	All are simple descending glides

4.2   Objective Measures

For evaluation of glides, two methods to compare the test singing pitch contour with the corresponding reference glide contour are explored: (i) point to point error calculation using Euclidean distance and (ii) polynomial curve fit based matching.

Euclidean Distance between Aligned Contours. Point to point error calculation using Euclidean distance is the simplest approach. Euclidean distance (ED) between pitch contours p and q (each of duration n samples) is obtained as below where p_i and q_i are the corresponding pair of time-aligned pitch instances

$$d(p,q) = \sqrt{\sum_{i=1}^{n}(p_i - q_i)^2} \tag{1}$$

But the major drawback of this method is that it might penalize a singer for perceptually unimportant factors because a singer may not have sung 'exactly' the same shape as the reference and yet could be perceived to be very similar by the listeners.

Polynomial Curve Fitting. Whereas the Euclidean distance serve to match pitch contours shapes in fine detail, the motivation for this method is to retain only what may be the perceptually relevant characteristics of the pitch contour. The extent of fit of a 2nd degree polynomial equation to a pitch contour segment has been proposed as a criterion for extracting/detecting *meends* [5]. This idea has been extended here to evaluate test singer glides. It was observed in our dataset that 3rd degree polynomial gives a better fit because of the frequent presence of an 'inflection point' in the pitch contours of glides as shown in Fig. 2. An inflection point is a location on the curve where it switches from a positive radius to negative. The maximum number of inflection points possible in a polynomial curve is n-2, where n is the degree of the polynomial equation. A 3rd degree polynomial is fitted to the corresponding reference glide, and the normalized approximation error of the test glide with respect to this polynomial is computed. The 3rd degree polynomial curve fit to the reference glide pitch contour will be henceforth referred to as 'model curve'.

An R-Square value measures the closeness of any two datasets. A data set has values y_i each of which has an associated modeled value f_i, then, the total sum of squares is given by,

$$SS_{tot} = \sum_i \left(y_i - \bar{y} \right)^2 \tag{2}$$

where,

$$\bar{y} = \frac{1}{n} \sum_i^n y_i \tag{3}$$

The sum of squares of residuals is given by,

$$SS_{err} = \sum_i \left(y_i - f_i \right)^2 \tag{4}$$

and,

$$R^2 = 1 - \frac{SS_{err}}{SS_{tot}} \tag{5}$$

which is close to 1 if approximation error is close to 0.

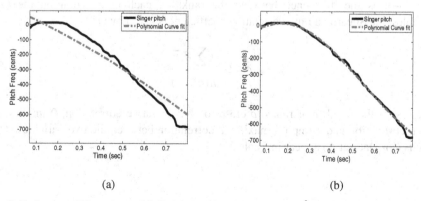

(a)   (b)

Fig. 2. Reference glide polynomial fit of (a) degree 2; $P_1(x) = ax^2+bx+c$; R-square = 0.937 (b) degree 3; $P_2(x) = ax^3+bx^2+cx+d$; R-square = 0.989

In Dataset B, the average of the R-square values of all glides in a song was used to obtain an overall score of the test singer for that particular song.

In this work, three different methods of evaluating a test singer glide based on curve fitting technique have been explored. They are:

i.   Approximation error between test singer glide pitch contour and reference model curve (Fig.3(a))
ii. Approximation error between test singer glide 3rd degree polynomial curve fit and reference model curve (Fig.3(b)).

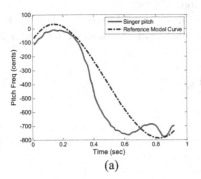 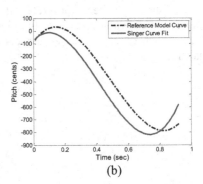

(a)   (b)

Fig. 3. (a) Test singer pitch contour and reference model curve (b) Test singer polynomial curve fit and reference model curve

4.3   Validation Results and Discussion

A single overall subjective rank is obtained by ordering the test singers as per the *sum* of the individual judge ranks. Spearman Correlation Coefficient (ρ), a nonparametric (distribution-free) rank statistic that is a measure of correlation between subjective and objective ranks, has been used to validate the system. If the ranks are x_i, y_i, and $d_i = x_i - y_i$ is the difference between the ranks of each observation on the two variables, the Spearman rank correlation coefficient is given by [10]

$$\rho = 1 - \frac{6\sum d_i^2}{n(n^2 - 1)} \tag{6}$$

where, n is the number of ranks. ρ close to -1 is negative correlation, 0 implies no linear correlation and 1 implies maximum correlation between the two variables. The results (for Dataset A) appear in Table 3.

Table 3. Inter-Judges' rank agreement (W) and correlation (ρ) between judges' avg. rank and objective measure rank for the ornament instances for Dataset A. Objective Measure 1: ED, Measure 2: 3rd degree Polynomial fit with best shift for glide: (i) Test glide pitch contour and model curve (ii) Test glide 3rd deg. polynomial curve fit and model curve (iii) ED between polynomial coefficients of the test glide curve fit and the model curve.

Type of Ornament	Instance no.	Inter-judges' rank agreement (W)	Correlation between Judges' avg. rank &		
			Obj. measure 1 rank (ρ)	Obj. measure 2 rank (ρ)	
				(i)	(ii)
Simple Descending Glide	1	0.99	0.75	0.65	0.65
	2	0.98	0.35	0.15	0.05
	3	0.82	0.77	0.66	0.66
	4	0.87	0.48	0.5	0.5
	5	0.88	0.94	0.94	0.94
	6	0.84	0.93	0.61	0.54
	7	0.65	0.67	0.63	0.59
Complex Descending Glide	1	1	0.5	0.6	0.6
	2	0.95	0.48	0	0.2
	3	0.96	0.65	0.65	0.55
	4	0.73	0.58	0.52	0.87
	5	0.70	0.87	0.94	0.94

Dataset A. We observe that out of 12 instances with good inter-judges' agreement (W>0.5), both ED and 3rd degree Polynomial Curve fit measures give comparable number of instances with a high rank correlation with the judges' rank ($\rho >= 0.5$) (Table 4). Methods i. and ii. for Measure 2 (Polynomial Curve Fit) show similar performance, but method i. is computationally less complex. In the case of simple glides, Measure 1 (ED) performs as well as Measure 2 (Polynomial Curve Fit) (methods i. and ii.). ED is expected to behave similar to polynomial modeling methods because there is not much difference between the real pitch and the modeled pitch. For simple glides, ED and modeling methods differ in performance only when there occurs pitch errors like slight jaggedness or a few outlier points in the pitch contour. Such aberrations get averaged out by modeling, while ED gets affected because of point-to-point distance calculation.

In case of complex glides however, point-to-point comparisons may not give reliable results as the undulations and pauses on intermediate notes may not be exactly time aligned to the reference (although the misalignment is perceptually unimportant) but ED will penalize it. Also, the complex glides will have a poor curve fit by a low degree polynomial. A lower degree polynomial is able to capture only the overall trend of the complex glide, while the undulations and pauses on intermediate notes that carry significant information about the singing accuracy (as observed from the subjective ratings) are not appropriately modeled as can be seen in Fig.4.

Table 4. Summary of performance of different measures for the ornament glide in Dataset A

Measures		No. of instances that have $\rho >= 0.5$	
		Simple Glides (out of 7 with judges' rank agreement)	Complex Glides (out of 5 with judges' rank agreement)
1 - Euclidean Distance		5	4
3 - 3rd degree Polynomial curve fit	(i)	6	4
	(ii)	6	4

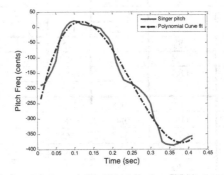

Fig. 4. Complex glide (reference) modeled by a 3rd degree polynomial

Dataset B. The overall ornament quality evaluation of the singer as carried out on Dataset B has good inter-judge agreement for almost all singers for both the songs in this dataset. The most frequent rating given by the judges (three out of the four judges) for a singer was taken as the subjective ground truth category for that singer. The cases of contention between the judges (two of the four judges for one class and the other two for another class) have not been considered for objective analysis.

The R-square value of the curve fit measure (i.e. error between reference model curve and test glide pitch contour) is used for evaluating each of the glide instances for the songs in Dataset B. A threshold of 0.9 was fixed on this measure to state the detection of a particular glide instance. For a test singer, if all the glide instances are detected, the singer's overall objective rating is "good"; if the number of detections is between 75 – 100% of the total number of glide instances in the song, the singer's overall objective rating is "medium"; and if the number of detections is less than 75%, the singer's overall objective rating is "bad". The above settings are empirical. Table 5 shows the singer classification confusion matrix. Though no drastic misclassifications between good and bad singer classification is seen but the overall correct classification is very poor (31.25%) due to large confusion with the "medium" class. One major reason for this inconsistency was that the full audio clips also contained complex glides and other ornaments that influenced the overall subjective ratings while the objective analysis was based solely on the selected instances of simple glides. This motivates the need of objective analysis of complex ornaments so as to come up with an overall expression rating of a singer.

Table 5. Singer classification confusion matrix for Dataset B

Objectively→ Subjectively↓	G	M	B
G	0	3	0
M	2	0	4
B	0	2	5

5   Assessment of Oscillations-on-Glide

The ornament 'oscillations-on-glide' refers to an undulating glide. Nearly periodic oscillations ride on a glide-like transition from one note to another. The oscillations may or may not be of uniform amplitude. Some examples of this ornament appear in Fig. 5. While the melodic fragment represented by the pitch contour could be transcribed into a sequence of notes or scale intervals, it has been observed that similar shaped contours are perceived to sound alike even if the note intervals are not identical [7]. From Fig. 5, we see that prominent measurable attributes of the pitch contour shape of the undulating glide are the overall (monotonic) trajectory of the underlying transition, and the amplitude and rate of the oscillations. The cognitive salience of these attributes can be assessed by perceptual experiments where listeners are asked to attend to a specific perceptual correlate while rating the quality. Previous work has shown the cognitive salience of the rate of the transition of synthesized *meend* signals [4].

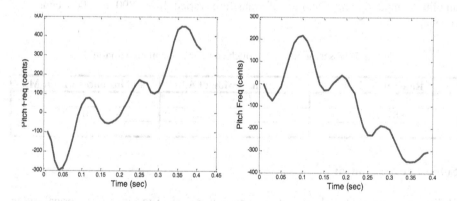

Fig. 5. Fragments of pitch contour extracted from a reference song: (a) ascending glide with oscillations (b) descending glide with oscillations

5.1   Database

Reference and Test Dataset. The reference dataset, consisting of polyphonic audio clips from popular Hindi film songs rich in ornaments, were obtained as presented in Table 6. The pitch tracks of the ornament clips were isolated from the songs for use in the objective analysis. Short phrases containing the ornament clips (1 - 4 sec) were used for subjective assessment as described later in this section. The reference songs were sung and recorded by 6 to 11 test singers (Table 6).

Table 6. 'Oscillations-on-glide' database description

Song No.	Song Name	Singer	No. of ornament clips	No. of Test singers	Total no. of test tokens	Characteristics of the ornaments
1.	Ao Huzoor (Kismat)	Asha Bhonsle	3	6	18	All three instances are descending oscillations-on-glide. Duration: 400 ms (approx.)
2.	Nadiya Kinare (Abhimaan)	Lata Mangeshkar	3	8	24	All three instances are ascending oscillations-on-glide. Duration: 380 - 450 ms (approx.)
3.	Naino Mein Badra (Mera Saaya)	Lata Mangeshkar	13	11	143	All thirteen instances are ascending oscillations-on-glide. Duration: 300 - 500 ms (approx.)

Observations on Pitch Contour of Oscillations-on-Glide. This ornament can be described by the rate of transition, rate of oscillation and oscillation amplitude which itself may not be uniform across the segment but show modulation (A.M.). Rate of oscillations is defined as the number of cycles per second. The range of the oscillation rate is seen to be varying from 5 to 11 Hz approximately as observed from the 19 instances of the reference ornament. Some observations for these 19 reference instances are tabulated in Table7. 11 out of the 19 instances are within the vibrato range of frequency, but 8 are beyond the range. Also 7 of the instances show amplitude modulation. The rate of transition varied from 890 to 2000 cents per second.

Table 7. Observations on the pitch contour of oscillations-on-glide

Rate range (Hz)	# of instances without A.M.	# of instances with A.M.
5 – 8	5	6
8 – 10	6	0
10 – 12	1	1

Subjective Assessment

Holistic Ground-Truth. Three human experts were asked to give a categorical rating (Good (G), Medium (M) and Bad (B)) to each ornament instance of the test singers. The most frequent rating given by the judges (two out of the three judges) for an instance was taken as the subjective ground truth category for that ornament instance. Out of the total of 185 test singers' ornament tokens (as can be seen from 6), 105 tokens were subjectively annotated and henceforth used in the validation experiments. An equal number of tokens were present in each of these classes (35 each). Henceforth whenever an ornament instance of a singer is referred to as good/medium/bad, it implies the subjective rating of that ornament instance.

Parameter-Wise Ground-Truth. Based on the kind of feedback expected from a music teacher about the ornament quality, a subset of the test ornament tokens (75 test tokens out of 105) were subjectively assessed by one of the judges separately for each of the three attributes: accuracy of the glide (start and end notes, and trend), amplitude of oscillation, and rate (number of oscillations) of oscillation. For each of these parameters, the test singers were categorized into good/medium/bad for each ornament instance. These ratings are used to investigate the relationship between the subjective rating and individual attributes.

5.2   Modeling Parameters

From observations, it was found that modelling of this ornament can be divided into 2 components with 3 parameters in all:

    i.   **Glide**
   ii.   **Oscillation**
           a.   **Amplitude**
           b.   **Rate**

Glide represents the overall monotonic trend of the ornament while transiting between two correct notes. **Oscillation** is the pure vibration around the monotonic glide. Large amplitude and high rate of oscillations are typically considered to be good and requiring skill. On the other hand, low amplitude of oscillation makes the rate of oscillation irrelevant, indicating that rate should be evaluated only after the amplitude of oscillation crosses a certain threshold of significance.

5.3   Implementation of Objective Measures

Glide. Glide modeling, as presented in Section 4.2, involves a 3rd degree polynomial approximation of the reference ornament pitch contour that acts as a model to evaluate the test ornament. A similar approach has been taken to evaluate the glide parameter of the ornament oscillations-on-glide. The 3rd degree polynomial curve fit is used to capture the underlying glide transition of the ornament. Since the glide parameter of this ornament characterizes the trend in isolation, the following procedure is used to assess the quality of the underlying glide.

- Fit a "trend model" (3rd degree polynomial curve fit) in the reference ornament (Fig.6(a))
- Similarly fit a 3rd degree curve into the test singer ornament (Fig.6(b))
- A measure of distance of the test singer curve fit from the reference trend model evaluates the overall trend of the test singer's ornament.

As in Section 5, the R-square value is the distance measure used here; R-sq close to 1 implies closer to the trend model (reference model) (Fig. 6(c)). This measure is henceforth referred to as *glide measure.*

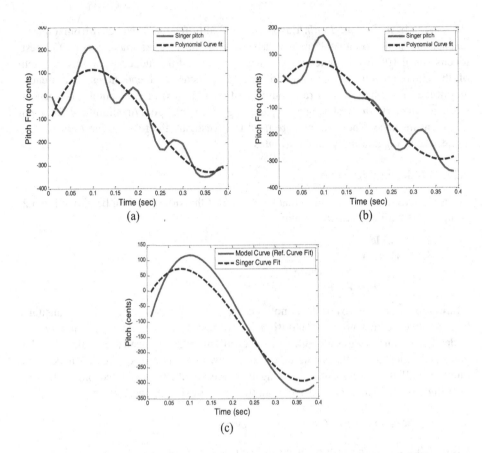

Fig. 6. (a) 'Trend Model'; 3rd degree curve fit into reference ornament pitch (b) 3rd degree curve fit into test singer ornament pitch (c) Trend Model and Test curve fit shown together; R-square = 0.92

Oscillations. To analyze the oscillations component of the ornament, we need to first subtract the trend from it. This is done by subtracting the vertical distance of the lowest point of the curve from every point on the pitch contour, and removing DC offset, as shown in Fig.7.

The trend-subtracted oscillations, although similar in appearance to vibrato, differ in following important ways:

i. Vibrato has approximately constant amplitude across time, while this ornament may have varying amplitude, much like amplitude modulation, and thus frequency domain representation may show double peaks or side humps

ii. The rate of vibrato is typically between 5 - 8 Hz [11]while the rate of this oscillation may be as high as 10 Hz.

These oscillations are, by and large, characterized by their amplitude and rate, both of which are studied in the frequency and time domain in order to obtain the best parameterization.

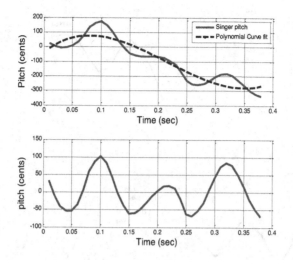

Fig. 7. Trend Subtraction

Frequency Domain Attributes

- *Amplitude.* Ratio of the peak amplitude in the magnitude spectrum of test singer ornament pitch contour to that of the reference. This measure is henceforth referred to as *frequency domain oscillation amplitude feature (FDOscAmp).*

$$FDOscAmp = \frac{\max\left(\left|Z_{test}(k)\right|\right)}{\max\left(\left|Z_{ref}(k)\right|\right)} \tag{7}$$

where $Z_{test}(k)$ and $Z_{ref}(k)$ are the DFT of the mean-subtracted pitch trajectory $z(n)$ of the test singer and reference ornaments respectively.

- *Rate.* Ratio of the frequency of the peak in the magnitude spectrum of the test singer ornament pitch contour to that of the reference. This measure is henceforth referred to as *frequency domain oscillation rate feature (FDOscRate).*

The ratio of energy around test peak frequency to energy in 1 to 20 Hz may show spurious results if the test peak gets spread due to amplitude modulation (Fig.8). Also it was observed that amplitude modulation does not affect the subjective assessment. Thus the scoring system should be designed to be insensitive to the amplitude modulation. This is taken care of in frequency domain analysis by computing the sum of the significant peak amplitudes (3 point local maxima with a threshold of 0.5 of the maximum on the magnitude) and average of the corresponding peak frequencies and computing the ratio of these features of the test ornament to that of the reference ornament.

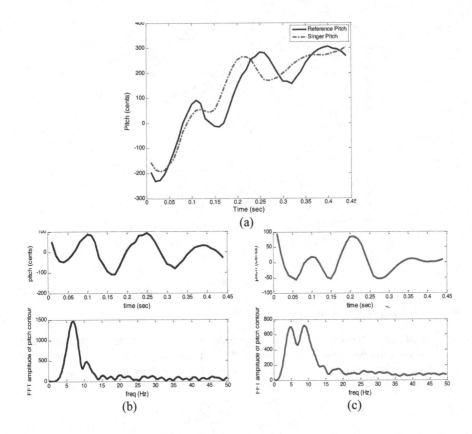

Fig. 8. (a) Reference and Test ornament pitch contours for a "good" test instance, (b) Trend subtracted reference ornament pitch contour and frequency spectrum, (c) Trend subtracted test singer ornament pitch contour and frequency spectrum

Time Domain Attributes. Due to the sensitivity of frequency domain measurements to the amplitude modulation that may be present in the trend-subtracted oscillations, the option of time-domain characterization is explored. The pitch contour in time domain may sometimes have jaggedness that might affect a time domain feature that uses absolute values of the contour. Hence a 3-point moving average filter has been used to smoothen the pitch contour (Fig. 9)

- *Amplitude.* Assuming that there exists only one maxima or minima between any two zero crossings of the trend subtracted smoothened pitch contour of the ornament, the amplitude feature computed is the ratio of the average of the highest two amplitudes of the reference ornament to that of the test singer ornament. The average of only the highest two amplitudes as opposed to averaging all the amplitudes has been used here to make the system robust to amplitude modulation (Fig. 9). This measure is henceforth referred to as *time domain oscillation amplitude feature (TDOscAmp).*

- *Rate.* The rate feature in time domain is simply the ratio of the number of zero crossings of ornament pitch contour of the test singer to that of the reference (Fig. 9). This measure is henceforth referred to as *time domain oscillation rate feature (TDOscRate)*.

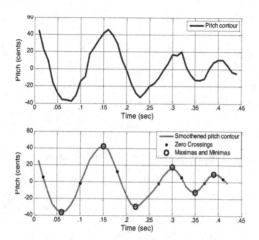

Fig. 9. Trend subtracted pitch contour and smoothened pitch contour with zero crossings and maxima and minima marked

5.4   Results and Discussion

This section first describes the performance of the different measures of each of the modelling parameters using the **parameter-wise ground truths** for validation. Then the different methods of combining the best attributes of the individual model parameters to get a holistic objective rating of the ornament instance have been discussed.

Glide Measure. In the scatter plot (Fig.10), the objective score is the glide measure for each instance of ornament singing that are shape coded by the respective subjective rating of glide (parameter-wise ground-truth). We observe that the "bad" ratings are consistently linked to low values of the objective measure. The "medium" rated tokens show a wide scatter in the objective measure. The medium and the good ratings were perceptually overlapping in a lot of cases (across judges) and thus the overlap shows up in the scatter plot as well. A threshold of 0.4 on the objective measure would clearly demarcate the bad singing from the medium and good singing. It has been observed that even when the oscillations are rendered very nicely, there is a possibility that the glide is bad (Fig.11). It will be interesting to see the weights that each of these parameters get in the holistic rating.

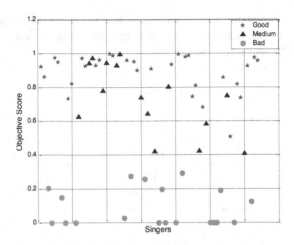

Fig. 10. Scatter Plot for Glide Measure

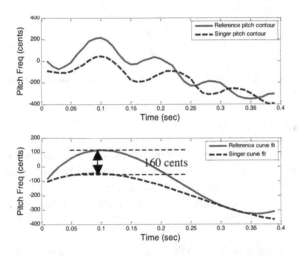

Fig. 11. Reference and singer ornament pitch contour and glide curve fits

Oscillation Amplitude Measures. In the scatter plot (Fig.12), the objective score is the oscillation amplitude measure for each instance of ornament singing that are shape coded by the respective subjective rating of oscillation amplitude (parameter-wise ground-truth). As seen in the scatter plot, both frequency and time domain features by and large separate the good and the bad instances well. But there are a number of medium to bad misclassification by the frequency domain feature assuming a threshold at objective score equal to 0.4. A number of bad instances are close to the threshold, this happens because of occurrence of multiple local maxima in the spectrum of the bad ornament that add up to have a magnitude comparable to that of the reference magnitude, and hence a high magnitude ratio (Fig.13). Also a few of the good instances are very close to this threshold in frequency domain analysis. This happens because of the occurrence of amplitude modulation that reduces the magnitude of the peak in the magnitude spectrum (Fig.14).

The number of misclassifications by the time domain amplitude feature is significantly less. The mediums and the goods are clearly demarcated from the bads with a threshold of **0.5** only with a few borderline cases of mediums.

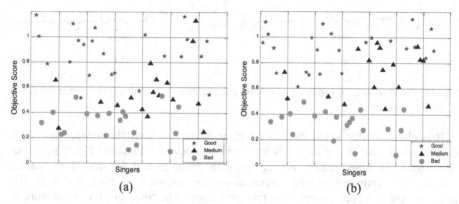

(a)   (b)

Fig. 12. Scatter plot for Oscillation Amplitude measure in (a) Frequency domain (b) Time domain

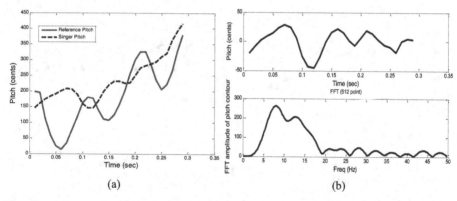

(a)   (b)

Fig. 13. (a) Bad ornament pitch along with reference ornament pitch (b) Trend subtracted bad ornament pitch from (a) and its magnitude spectrum

Oscillation Rate Measures. It is expected that perceptually low amplitude of oscillation makes the rate of oscillation irrelevant; hence the instances with bad amplitude (that do not cross the threshold) should not be evaluated for rate of oscillation.

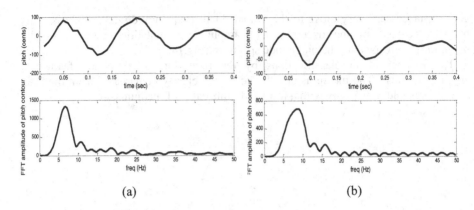

Fig. 14. Trend subtracted ornament pitch and magnitude spectrum of (a) Reference (b) Good ornament instance

It is observed that while there is no clear distinction possible between the three classes when rate of oscillation is analyzed in frequency domain (Fig. 15(a)), but interestingly in time domain, all the instances rated as bad for rate of oscillation already get eliminated by the threshold on the amplitude feature and only the mediums and the goods remain for rate evaluation. The time domain rate feature is able to separate the two remaining classes reasonably well with a threshold of **0.75** on the objective score that result in only a few misclassifications (Fig. 15(b)).

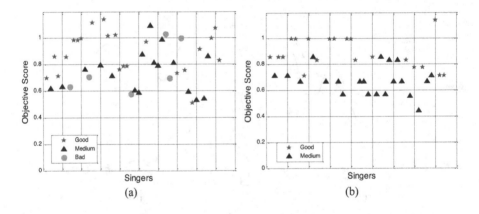

Fig. 15. Scatter plot for Oscillation Rate measure in (a) Frequency domain (b) Time domain

Obtaining Holistic Objective Ratings. The glide measure gives a good separation between the bad and the good/medium. Also the time domain measures for oscillation amplitude and rate clearly outperform the corresponding frequency domain measures. Thus the glide measure, TDOscAmp and TDOscRate are the three attributes that will be henceforth used in the experiments to obtain holistic objective ratings.

A 7-fold cross-validation classification experiment is carried out for the 105 test tokens with the holistic ground truths. In each fold, there are 90 tokens in train and 15 in test. Equal distribution of tokens exists across all the three classes in both train and test sets. Two methods of obtaining the holistic scores have been explored, a purely machine learning method and a knowledge-based approach.

While a machine learning framework like Classification and Regression Trees (CART) [12] (as provided by The MATLAB Statistics Toolbox) can provide a system for classifying ornament quality from the measured attributes of glide, TDOscAmp and TDOscRate, it is observed that a very complex tree results from the direct mapping of the actual real number values of these parameters to ground-truth category. With the limited training data, this tree has limited generalizability and performs poorly on test data. So, we adopt instead simplified parameters obtained by the thresholds suggested by the scatter plots of Figs. 10, 12 and 15 which is consistent with the notion that human judgments are not finely resolved but rather tend to be categorical with underlying parameter changes.

From the thresholds derived from the observations of the scatter plots and combining the two time domain features for oscillation using the parameter-wise ground-truths, as explained earlier, we finally have two attributes – the glide measure and the combined oscillation measure. Glide measure gives a binary decision (0, 1) while the combined oscillation measure (TDOsc) gives a three level decision (0, 0.5, 1). Using the thresholds obtained, we have a decision tree representation for each of these features as shown in Fig. 16. Each branch in the tree is labeled with its decision rule, and each terminal node is labeled with the predicted value for that node. For each branch node, the left child node corresponds to the points that satisfy the condition, and the right child node corresponds to the points that do not satisfy the condition. With these decision boundaries, the performance of the individual attributes is shown in Table 8.

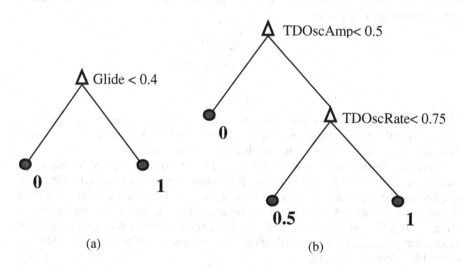

(a)   (b)

Fig. 16. Empirical threshold based quantization of the features of (a) Glide (b) Oscillation

Table 8. Summary of performance of the chosen attributes with empirical thresholds and parameter-wise ground-truths

Attribute →	Glide Measure		TDOsc Measure		
Threshold→ Subjective Category↓	1	0	1	0.5	0
G	41	0	0	5	28
M	15	0	3	16	4
B	0	19	19	0	0

Once the empirical thresholds are applied to the features to generate the quantized and simplified features **Glide Measure** and **TDOsc Measure**, the task of combining these two features, for an objective holistic rating for an ornament instance has been carried out by two methods:

- *Linear Combination.* In each fold of the 7-fold cross-validation experiment, this method searches for the best weights for linearly combining the two features (glide measure and TDOsc measure) on the train dataset by finding the weights that maximizes the correlation of the objective score with the subjective ratings.

The linear combination of the features is given by

$$h = w_1 g + (1 - w_1) o \qquad (8)$$

Where w_1 and $(1 - w_1)$ are the weights, g and o are the glide and oscillation features respectively and h is the holistic objective score. The holistic subjective ratings are converted into three numeric values (1, 0.5, 0) corresponding to the three categories (G, M, B). The correlation between the holistic objective scores and numeric subjective ratings is given by

$$corr = \frac{\sum_i (h_i \cdot GT_i)}{\sqrt{\sum_i h_i^2 \sum_i GT_i^2}} \qquad (9)$$

where h_i and GT_i are the holistic objective score and numeric holistic ground truth (subjective rating) of an ornament token i. Maximizing this correlation over w_1 for the train dataset gives the values of the weights for the two features.

The glide attribute got a low weighting (0.15 – 0.19) as compared to that of the oscillation attribute (0.85 – 0.81). The final objective scores obtained using these weights on the test data features lie between 0 and 1 but are continuous values. However, clear thresholds are observed between good, medium, and bad tokens as given in Fig.17 and Table 9. With these thresholds, the 7-fold cross-validation experiment gives 22.8% misclassification. The performance of the linear combination method is shown in Table 10.

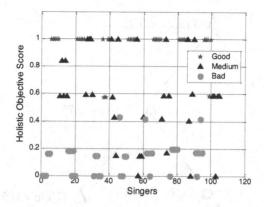

Fig. 17. Scatter plot of the holistic objective score obtained from Linear Combination method

Table 9. Thresholds for objective classification on holistic objective score obtained from Linear Combination method

Holistic Objective Score	Objective classification
>= 0.8 0.35 – 0.8 <0.35	G M B

Table 10. Token classification results of 7-fold cross-validation with Linear Combination method

Objectively→ Subjectively↓	G	M	B
G	32	3	0
M	11	17	7
B	0	3	32

• *Decision Boundaries Using CART.* Another method of obtaining a holistic objective rating of an ornament instance is to obtain decision boundaries from a classification tree trained on the two quantized features Glide measure and TDOsc measure. A 7-fold cross-validation experiment has been carried out and testing in each of the folds has been done once with the full tree and next with the pruned tree. Both full and pruned tree cross-validation experiments gave 22.8% misclassifications. A full tree for the entire dataset (105 tokens) is shown in Fig. 18. Because of the simplified nature of the features, the full tree itself is a short tree with a few nodes and branches and hence mostly the best level of pruning comes out to be zero implying that the tree remains un-pruned and thus no difference in performance. Also it was observed that misclassification rate in this case is same as that in linear combination. The token classification confusion matrix is also same for both the cases (Table 10). This suggests that the simple weighted linear combination of attributes provides an adequate discrimination of quality.

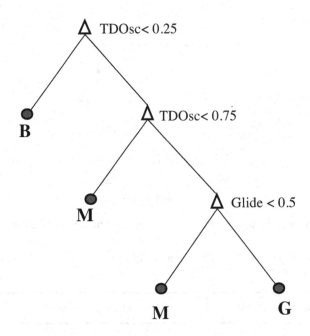

Fig. 18. Full tree by machine learning using thresholded features

6   Conclusion

Pitch contour shapes are shown to be sufficient in the characterization of the perceived similarity between a reference and test rendering of an ornament in vocal music. Modelling the pitch contour shape by polynomial curve fitting has given encouraging results in objective assessment. Out of 7 simple glides (that closely resemble the Indian classical music ornament *meend*), the objective ratings obtained from 3rd degree polynomial curve approximation method for 6 of these show high correlation with the subjective ratings. The complex ornament termed 'oscillations-on-glide' (similar to the Indian classical music ornament *Gamak*) has been modelled in terms of individual cognitively salient attributes. Various frequency and time domain features were explored for the oscillation modelling. The time domain features for oscillation perform better than the corresponding frequency domain features. With 23% misclassification in the 3-category quality rating, there were no confusions observed between the two extreme categories. Since this ornament is a critical differentiator between a good and a bad singer, a fair automatic assessment of this ornament will be very useful in singing scoring systems.

Further, an attempt (not reported here) was made to get an overall judgment of a singer's ornamentation skills from the complete audio clip (not just the individual instances) based on objectively evaluated vibratos and glides of the audio clip. This too gave encouraging results clearly indicating the feasibility of objective assessment of singers based on their ornamentation skills.

Future work will target a framework more suited to the Indian classical vocal music performance where the test singer's rendition may not be time aligned with that of the ideal singer. An ornament assessment system in such a scenario demands reliable automatic detection of ornaments. In the context of purely improvised Indian classical music, the task of evaluation becomes even more challenging as it demands evaluation without a copycat reference and hence the need for more universal computational models.

References

1. Datta, A., Sengupta, R., Dey, N.: On the possibility of objective assessment of students of Hindustani Music. Ninaad Journal of ITC Sangeet Research Academy 23, 44–57 (2009)
2. Bor, J., Rao, S., Meer, W., Harvey, J.: The Raga Guide, A survey of 74 Hindustani Ragas. Wyastone Estate Limited (2002)
3. ITC Sangeet Research Academy: A trust promoted by ITC Limited, http://www.itcsra.org/alankar/alankar.html
4. Datta, A., Sengupta, R., Dey, N., Nag, D., Mukherjee, A.: Perceptual evaluation of synthesized 'meends' in Hindustani music. In: Frontiers of Research on Speech and Music (2007)
5. Datta, A., Sengupta, R., Dey, N., Nag, D.: A methodology for automatic extraction of 'meend' from the performances in Hindustani vocal music. Ninaad Journal of ITC Sangeet Research Academy 21, 24–31 (2007)
6. Datta, A., Sengupta, R., Dey, N., Nag, D.: Automatic classification of 'meend' extracted from the performances in Hindustani vocal music. In: Frontiers of Research on Speech and Music, Kolkata (2008)
7. Subramanian, M.: Carnatic RagamThodi – Pitch Analysis of Notes and Gamakams. Journal of the Sangeet Natak Akademi XLI(1), 3–28 (2007)
8. Pant, S., Rao, V., Rao, P.: A melody detection user interface for polyphonic music. In: NCC 2010, IIT Madras (2010)
9. Kendall, M.G.: Rank Correlation Methods, 2nd edn. Hafner Publishing Co., New York (1955)
10. Spearman, C.: The proof and measurement of association between two things. Amer. J. Psychol. 15, 72–101 (1904)
11. Nakano, T., Goto, M., Hiraga, Y.: An automatic singing skill evaluation method for unknown melodies using pitch interval accuracy and vibrato features. In: Interspeech 2006, Pittsburgh (2006)
12. Steinberg, D., Colla, P.: CART: Tree-Structured Nonparametric Data Analysis. In: Salford Systems, San Diego, CA (1995)

Optimized Neural Architecture
for Time Series Prediction Using Raga Notes

Moujhuri Patra[1], Soubhik Chakraborty[2], and Dipak Ghosh[3]

[1] Department of MCA, Netaji Subhash Engineering College,
Kolkata-700152, India
`moujhuri@gmail.com`
[2] Department of Applied Mathematics,
B.I.T. Mesra, Ranchi- 835215, India
`soubhikc@yahoo.co.in`
[3] C V Raman Centre for Physics and Music,
Jadavpur University, Kolkata-700032, India
`deegee111@gmail.com`

Abstract. This paper represents a neural model for multilayer perceptron networks in predicting raga notes. In modeling multilayer perceptrons for time series prediction in musicology, the present algorithm chooses the optimal architecture on the basis of minimum of minimum squared error among one, two and three hidden layered architecture .The study related to a sequence of notes in raga Bhupali. The algorithm measures the performance of the neural network evaluated by the minimum squared error at various time instance of the predicted output.

Keywords: Time series prediction, raga, multilayer perceptron topology, optimal architecture.

1 Introduction

Digital note forecasting is a well-known problem in musicology and Artificial Neural Network (ANN) is an important tool for solving a forecasting problem. The purpose of this paper is twofold. The first objective is to develop a neural model which can perform a one step ahead prediction based on linear basis function on forecasting the note sequence which comes at every time instance and the second is to measure the performance of our model evaluated by the minimum squared error at every time instance of the predicted output. Our study related to a sequence of notes in raga Bhupali and the letters S, R, G, M, P, D and N stand for Sa, Sudh Re, Sudh Ga, Sudh Ma, Pa, Sudh Dha and Sudh Ni respectively. The letters r, g, m, d, n represent Komal Re, Komal Ga, Tibra Ma, Komal Dha and Komal Ni respectively. Normal type, italics or bold type indicates that the note belongs to the middle octave or to the lower octave or higher octave respectively. Sa, the tonic in Indian music, is taken at C. Corresponding Western notation is also provided. The terms "Sudh", "Komal" and "Tibra" imply, respectively, natural, flat and sharp. We start by giving some general feature of Raga Bhupali:

S. Ystad et al. (Eds.): CMMR/FRSM 2011, LNCS 7172, pp. 26–33, 2012.
© Springer-Verlag Berlin Heidelberg 2012

Thaat (a specific way of grouping ragas according to scale): Kalyan
Aroh (ascent): S R G P, D, S
Awaroh (descent): S, D P, G, R, S
Jati: Aurabh-Aurabh (5 distinct notes allowed in ascent and 5 in descent)
Vadi Swar (most important note): G
Samvadi Swar (second most important note): D
Anga: Poorvanga pradhan (first half more important)
Prakriti (nature): Restful
Pakad (catch): G, R, S, D, S R G, P G, D P G, R, S
Speciality: Meend (glide) from S to D (or S to D) and from P to G
Nyas Swar (Stay notes): G, P and D   Time of rendition: First phase of night (6 PM to 9 PM)

The following table (Table 1) gives the numbers representing pitches in different octaves.

Table 1. Numbers representing pitch of notes (Adiloglu, Noll and Obermayer [1])

	C	Db	D	Eb	E	F	F#	G	Ab	A	Bb	B
Lower	S	r	R	g	G	M	m	P	d	D	n	N
Octave	-12	-11	-10	-9	-8	-7	-6	-5	-4	-3	-2	-1
Middle	S	r	R	g	G	M	m	P	d	D	n	N
Octave	0	1	2	3	4	5	6	7	8	9	10	11
Higher	S	r	R	g	G	M	m	P	d	D	n	N
Octave	12	13	14	15	16	17	18	19	20	21	22	23

The paper is organized as follows: Section 2 gives a brief outline on neural network and music. Section 3 describes the ANN approach to time series modeling. Here, Subsection 3.1 describes the prediction model while Subsection 3.2 gives the prediction algorithm. Section 4 gives the preliminary data analysis and empirical results. In this section, Subsection A describes the data preprocessing tasks while Subsection B describes the neural architecture. Section 5 gives the main results followed by a discussion. Finally, Section 6 draws the conclusion with suggestions for future work.

2   Neural Network and Music

The disadvantage of the traditional Von Neumann algorithm-based concept is that the processing rules must be clearly specified. In art, especially when it is extempore such as Indian classical music, a better option is to use neural networks where instead of following the traditional pre-programmed layout (which would mean we must specify how to create a certain artwork; in most cases we may not be knowing this "how part" or cannot write explicitly even if we know), here we would train the network examples of what we want and having the network produce new examples maintaining the style as "learned from the examples" [2].There is a huge application of neural networks in music. Musical structures can be 'learnt' without needing to formalise rules. Networks can 'compose' based on structures learnt during training[3].We acknowledge the works of Todd, Jenkins, Sano, Bharucha, Desain, Honing, Gjerdingen and Mozer to name a few, adding the recent use of hybrid neural network (HNN) in artificial composition in Indian classical music by Sinha [4].

3   Artificial Neural Network Approach to Time Series Modeling

The basic idea of forecasting is to find an approximation of mapping between the input and output data in order to discover the implicit rules governing the observed movements. In time series forecasting problem, the inputs are typically the past observations of the data series and the output is the future value. The ANN performs the following functional mapping $y_{t+1} = f(y_t, y_{t-1}, ..., y_{t-i})$, where y_t is the output (observation) at time t. The ANN is equivalent to the nonlinear autoregressive model for time series forecasting problems. In current forecasting problems, the most widely used network model in feed-forward neural network model is multilayer perceptron (MLP). An MLP is typically composed of several layers, each layer consisting of several numbers of nodes. The first or the lowest layer is an input layer where the past information is received. The last or the highest layer is an output layer where the solution is obtained. The input layer and the output layer are separated by one or more intermediate hidden layers. A multilayer perceptron is a sequential network of interconnected neurons as diagramed below (Fig 1):

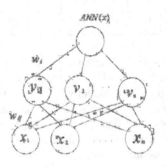

Fig. 1. Schematic diagram of multilayer perceptron (MLP)

The output of neuron i, one circle, is $v_i = f(\sum_j w_{ij} x_n + b_i)$, where the following terms apply: f is the nonlinear transformation, x_n is the nth input of neuron i, w_{ij} is the connection strength to neuron i from neuron x_j, b_i is the bias of neuron i.

The output of the perceptron is a nonlinear transformation applied to a weighted sum of inputs. The nonlinear transformation is often a sigmoid function

$$f(x) = \frac{1}{(1 + e^{-x})}$$

If we let x_n as the n-th input, the above figure (with one output) can be written as:

$$ANN(\vec{x}) = f\left(\sum_i w_i f\left(\sum_j w_{ij} x_j + b_i\right) + b\right)$$

3.1   Prediction Model

Here we are interested to build a model for one step ahead prediction and the variable which is used as an input is the pitch value, where P_t is the pitch value at time instance t. A simple time series prediction is of the form

$$P_{t+1} = f(P_t, P_{t-1}, \ldots, P_{t-n+1}) \tag{1}$$

In equation (1) the pitch value at time instance (t+1) is a function of the pitch values at previous time instances, t, (t-1), (t-2), and so on. Therefore at a point in time t, a one step ahead forecast P_{t+1} is computed using observations $P_t, P_{t-1}, \ldots, P_{t-n+1}$ from n preceding points in time t with n denoting the number of inputs in MLP. In our model forecasting the output of a perceptron can be depicted in the following way:

$$P_t = w_0 + \sum_{i=1}^{j} w_i P_{t-i}, \tag{2}$$

where R_t is the output and R_{t-i} are the lagging variables, $i = 1, \ldots, j$, where j is the maximum number of lags and w_i, for $i = 1, \ldots, j$, are the connection weights for the j inputs representing by j lag variables and w_0 is the bias, which is equivalent to a constant. We suppose, the input, the hidden and the output layers are as $\{X, H, Z\}$, respectively. Here the input layer has m number of neurons, the hidden layer H has n number of neurons and the output layer Z has only k output values. Let $w^{(L)}$ denote the weights at level L. Let (x_p, y_p), $p = 1, 2, \ldots, P$, be the set of given input/output vectors for training the neural network. For each input x_{pi}, the neurons H_{pj} and Z_{pk} are calculated according to the following equations:

$$H_{pj}(w^{(1)}) = f^{(1)}\left(\sum_{i=0}^{m} x_{pi} w_{ij}^{(1)}\right), j = 1, 2, \ldots, n \tag{3}$$

$$Z_{pk}(w^{(1)}, w^{(2)}) = f^{(2)}(\sum_{j=0}^{n} H_{pj} w^{(1)}) w_{jk}^{(2)}), k = 1, 2, ..., K \tag{4}$$

Here, the transfer function $f^{(1)}$ from the input to the hidden layer is the sigmoid function $y = \dfrac{1}{(1+e^{-x})}$, and the transfer function $f^{(2)}$ from the hidden layer to the output layer is the linear function $y = x$ .The training of the neural network is done by feeding the set of input-output vectors (x_p, y_p) to the neural networks and by minimizing the following objective function:

$$g(w) = \frac{1}{p \times k} \sum_{p=1}^{P} \sum_{k=1}^{K} \left[y_{pk} - z_{pk}(w) \right]^2 , \tag{5}$$

where $w = w^{(1)} \cup w^{(2)}$ represents the weight of the neural network. The error function g defined by (5) is the mean squared error (MSE).

3.2   Prediction Algorithm

The prediction algorithm finds out the optimal architecture i.e., minimum number of neurons at various layers by learning and training a single layer, two layers and three layers network simultaneously.

1. Initialize the maximum number of neurons (mn) and maximum lags (mlg), assuming total number of hidden layers to be 3
2. For each hidden layer network:
   initialize n=1 lg=1
   create a feedforward back propagation network and continue until n = mn and lg=mlg
3. Training:
   train and simulate each network with logsig transfer function and calculate the minimum squared error. Set n1, n2, n3 as the number of neurons in each hidden layer network.
4. Compute the performance in each case. Set pf1, pf2, pf3 as the performance of a single layer, a two layer and a three hidden layer network.
5. Post Processing:
   Compute minpf=min(min(pf1),min(min(min(pf2))),min(min(min(min(pf3)))))
   If pf3 ( ) ==minpf
   set optimum neurons at layer 3=n3
   optimum neurons at layer 2=n2
   optimum neurons at layer 1=n1
   else if pf2( )==minpf

```
set optimum neurons at layer 2=n2
optimum neurons at layer 1=n1
else if pf1( )==minpf
set optimum neurons at layer 1=n1
endif
endif
endif
```

4   Preliminary Data Analysis

We define a raga, the nucleus of Indian Classical music, as a melodic structure with fixed notes and a set of rules characterizing a certain mood conveyed by performance. Here we take a sequence of 157 notes of raga Bhupali taken from a standard text [6]. Here Pt values are pitch of the raga notes which are a function of time (the instance t of realization of musical notes are here the serial numbers 1, 2, 3....157).

4.1   Data Preprocessing

Before we use the data into the models, the data series have been applied to feed forward models by dividing them into training and a testing set, where the training set comprises of 70% of the corresponding data and the testing set has the remaining 30% of the data series. So the process of data scaling is necessary. When log sigmoid or tan sigmoid neurons are used then scaling is a necessary step. If the data set is not scaled to a reasonable interval, such as [0, 1] or [-1, 1], then the neurons will set reasonably large (low) values to 1 (0 for log sigmoid or -1 for tan sigmoid neurons). Scaling has been done in this way. As highest pitch value in the third octave value is 23 and the lowest in the first octave is -12 we have, a=-12, b=23 to compute Pitch = (2y-a-b) / (b-a). Now the scaled pitch values will be in [-1, 1].

4.2   Network Architecture

Here the feed forward network has been simulated by means of simple iterations and the transfer function used was log sigmoid. Iterations have been done for a maximum number of three layers and in each layer the maximum number of neurons is five. The iterations were also used for determining the lag structure.

5   Result and Discussions

By comparing the graphical plot for the actual pitch series versus the predicted pitch series, as shown in Figure 2 it is quite evident from visual inspection of the plot that the chosen model is adequate, as the predicted series is very close to the observed series.

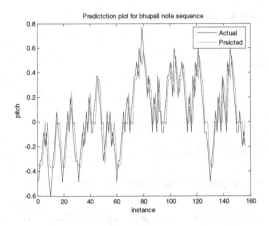

Fig. 2. Predicted pitch vs. observed pitch

5.1   Mean Square Error of the Predicted Output

In Table 2, the number of nodes is optimum in each layer, the minimum number of neurons in each hidden layer which makes the architecture optimal as 5, 5 and 1 respectively where the learning rate is 0.1 and number of epochs we take is 100. The table also shows the training and testing error for Bhupali note sequence.

Table 2. Output results

Raga Notes	No of nodes in each hidden layer	Training Error	Testing Error
Bhupali	5-5-1	0.0208753	0.0285645

6   Conclusion

We have proposed an algorithm which selects an optimal architecture based on a given selection rule such as lowest error on the validation set. Further extensions of our experiments will incorporate additional modeling on degrees of freedom i.e.; different activation functions in hidden and output layers, different learning paradigms etc. and the heuristics to analyze the validity of the selection criteria in more detail.

Acknowledgement. We thank an anonymous referee for helping us bring the paper to its final form.

References

1. Adiloglu, K., Noll, T., Obermayer, K.: A Paradigmatic Approach to Extract the melodic Structure of a Musical Piece. Jour. of New Music Research 35(3), 221–236 (2006)
2. Shukla, R.K., Chakraborty, S.: On an Ethical Use of Neural Networks: A Case Study on a North Indian Raga. Annals. Computer Science Series VII(Fasc. 2), 41–56 (2009)
3. Todd, P.M., Loy, D.G. (eds.): Music and Connectionism. MIT Press, Cambridge (1991)
4. Sinha, P.: Artificial Composition; An Experiment on Indian Music. Journal of New Music Research 37(3), 221–232 (2008)
5. Cortez, P., Rocha, M., Neves, J.: Time Series Forecasting by Evolutionary neural Networks. In: Rabunal, J.R., Dorado, J. (eds.) Artificial Neural Networks in Real Life Applications, pp. 47–70. Idea Group Publishing (2006)
6. Dutta, D.: Sangeet Tattwa (Pratham Khanda), 5th edn., Brati Prakashani (2006) (Bengali)

Meter Detection from Audio for Indian Music

Sankalp Gulati, Vishweshwara Rao, and Preeti Rao

Department of Electrical Engineering
Indian Institute of Technology Bombay, Mumbai 400076, India
sankalp.gulati@gmail.com, {vishu,prao}@ee.iitb.ac.in

Abstract. The meter of a musical excerpt provides high-level rhythmic information and is valuable in many music information retrieval tasks. We investigate the use of a computationally efficient approach to metrical analysis based on psycho-acoustically motivated decomposition of the audio signal. A two-stage comb filter-based approach, originally proposed for double/ triple meter estimation, is extended to a septuple meter (such as 7/8 time-signature) and its performance evaluated on a sizable Indian music database. We find that this system works well for Indian music and the distribution of musical stress/accents across a temporal grid can be utilized to obtain the metrical structure of audio automatically.

Keywords: Meter detection, Indian music, complex meter, comb filtering.

1   Introduction

All music, across geographies and cultures, comprises of events occurring at regular time intervals. Meter is a hierarchical temporal framework consisting of pulses at different levels (time-scales), where pulses represent regularly occurring musical events [1]. Perception of meter is an innate cognitive ability in humans. Meter provides useful rhythmic information essential in understanding musical structure and is useful in various music retrieval tasks like similarity based music classification [2], beat tracking and tempo estimation of music [3]. In this study we investigate automatic meter detection for Indian music.

1.1   Previous Work on Meter Detection

Considerable research has been directed towards extraction of low-level rhythmic information like onset detection and beat tracking [4]. However, relatively less attention has been paid to higher-level metrical analysis. Most of the earlier work on meter analysis concentrated on symbolic data (MIDI). The system proposed by Goto and Muraoka [8] is considered as being the first to achieve a reasonable accuracy for the meter analysis task on audio signal. Their system was based on agent based architecture, tracking competing meter hypotheses and operated in real time. Meter detection requires tempo independent information about the rhythmic structure. And hence tempo normalization becomes a crucial stage in the meter detection system. In the

S. Ystad et al. (Eds.): CMMR/FRSM 2011, LNCS 7172, pp. 34–43, 2012.

approach proposed by Gouyon and Herrera [9] the beat indices are manually extracted and then an autocorrelation function, computed on chosen low level features (energy flux, spectral flatness, energy in upper half of the first bark band) is used to detect meter type. Also, in this approach the meter detection problem was simplified by restricting the result to double (2/4, 4/4) and triple (3/4, 6/8) meter. Metrical analysis of non-Western music using the scale transform for the tempo normalization is proposed by Holzapfel and Stylianou [2]. A more detailed description of previous work on meter analysis from audio can be found in [1].

1.2   Meter in Indian Music

Meter, from a perspective of Indian music, is discussed in depth by Clayton[10]. Rhythmic organization in Indian Classical Music is described by the Tāl system [10]. Tal can be viewed as a hierarchical structure organized on three temporal levels, the smallest time unit 'matra', the section 'vibhag' and the complete rhythmic cycle 'avart'. Matra may be interpreted as the beat in most cases. Automatic metrical analysis from audio of Indian music is a relatively unexplored area despite the well established Tal framework of rhythmic organization. There are multiple Tals containing a given number of beats in a rhythmic cycle but which differ from each other in terms of sectional divisions and distribution of stressed/unstressed beats. In the current work we do not discriminate between the different possible sectional structures within a cycle but restrict ourselves to obtaining higher metrical level information by mapping the number of beats in a cycle to a meter type. This is similar to considering 3/4 and 6/8 metrical structure to both belong to triple meter [11].

In the current work, we implement the meter detection system proposed by Schuller, Eyben, and Rigoll[11] in which the tatum duration is extracted to establish the temporal grid on which metrical analysis is then implemented. Tatum can be defined as that regular time division which coincides most highly with all notes onsets [12]. This approach does not explicitly use any knowledge about the note onsets, beat positions or downbeat locations. We evaluate the above system on a previously used database of ballroom dance music and also a new database of Indian music. The latter, in addition to songs having double or triple meter, also includes songs in a complex meter, in this case septuple meter (7 beats in a cycle).

2   System Implementation

The meter detection system is described in Figure 1. The method relies on finding the tatum duration and how well the integer multiple of this duration resonates with the sizable segment of the song. We follow the implementation procedure described in [11]. As can be seen in Figure 1 whole system can be divided into three stages. The implementation of each of these stages is described next.

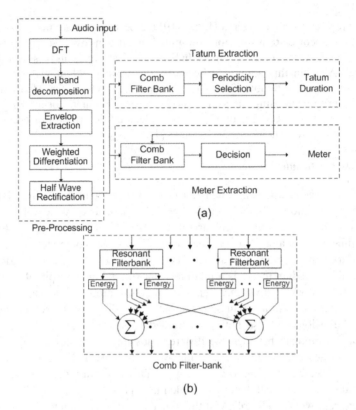

Fig. 1. (a) Block diagram of meter detection system, (b) Comb filter bank

2.1   Pre-processing

The input audio signal is down sampled to 16 kHz and converted to mono channel. The data is split into 32 ms frames with a hop size of 5 ms and corresponding frame rate of 200 Hz. A Hamming window is applied to each frame and a 512-point FFT is computed. By using 12 overlapping triangular filters, equidistant on the Mel-Frequency scale, these DFT frequency bins are reduced to 12 non-linear frequency bands. The temporal evolution of amplitude of each of these 12 bands can be seen as band envelop with sampling frequency of 200Hz (frame rate). The band envelope is then converted to log scale (dB) and subsequently low pass filtered by convolving with a half-wave raised cosine filter of length 15 frames (75 ms). This filters out the noise and high frequencies in the envelope signal without diminishing the fast relevant transient attacks. From this envelope a weighted differential d_{wtd} is computed according to Eq. 1.

$$d_{wtd}(i) = (o_i - \bar{o}_{i,l}) \cdot \bar{o}_{i,r} \qquad (1)$$

where, o_i is the sample at position (frame) i, $\bar{o}_{i,l}$ is the moving average over one window of 10 samples to the left of the sample and $\bar{o}_{i,r}$ of the window of 20 samples to the right of the sample o_i. This step is perceptually motivated as it tries to incorporate the fact that a human listener perceives a note onset louder if that is preceded by a long note or silence. Also, the note accent depends upon the following note energy and note duration, which is taken care of by the right mean $\overline{O}_{i,r}$.

2.2   Tatum Extraction

Tatum can be defined as that regular time division which coincides most highly with all notes onsets [12]. It is the lowest metrical level of the song. The tatum extraction method used by [11] uses a comb filter bank based approach, originally proposed by Scheirer[13]. In the current implementation, the comb filter bank is implemented with delay varying from 0.1-0.6 sec consisting of 100 filters. The comb filter bank processes the extracted differential signal d_{wtd} for each Mel band separately. The total energy corresponding to a particular comb filter delay is computed by summing the output of the comb filer banks at this delay for every Mel band. This is clearly shown in the Figure 1(b), where the input is the differential signal extracted for each Mel band and the output is the summed energy corresponding to each comb filter bank delay. These output values for each delay form the tatum vector. The location of the maximum peak of this function is the delay corresponding to the tatum duration.

2.3   Meter Extraction

The meter vector $\vec{m}$ is also computed from the extracted differential signal d_{wtd} by setting up narrow comb filter banks around integer multiples of tatum duration. The number of comb filters implemented per filter bank is equal to twice the integer multiple of the tatum duration plus one to compensate for the round off factor of the tatum duration. For each filter bank that filter (i.e. with particular delay value) with the highest output energy is selected and the total energy of this filter over all Mel bands is taken as the salience value in the meter vector at the position of that integer multiple. In the current implementation multiples from 1-19 are considered. An example of meter vectors for different meters is shown in Figure 2.

$$S_2 = [\vec{m}(4) + \vec{m}(8) + \vec{m}(16)] \cdot \tfrac{1}{3} \tag{2}$$

$$S_3 = [\vec{m}(3) + \vec{m}(6) + \vec{m}(9) + \vec{m}(18)] \cdot \tfrac{1}{4} \tag{3}$$

$$S_7 = [\vec{m}(7) + \vec{m}(14)] \cdot \tfrac{1}{2} \tag{4}$$

The final meter value is determined from $\vec{m}$ using a simple rule based approach. For each possible meter i.e. double, triple and septuple, we calculate a salience value as in Eq. 2, 3, 4 respectively. The maximum of S2, S3, and S7 determines the final meter of the song.

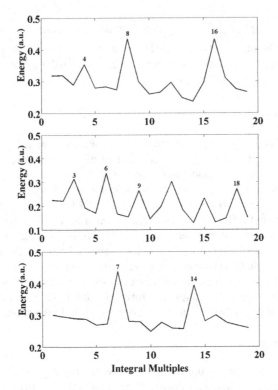

Fig. 2. Meter vector example for (a) double meter, (b) triple meter and (c) septuple meter

3   Experimental Evaluation

3.1   Database

We have used two databases in the evaluation of the above system. The first is the well-known ballroom dance database containing 698 30-sec duration audio clips [14]. The audio is categorized by 8 different ballroom dance styles (Jive, Quickstep, Tango, Waltz, Viennese Waltz, Samba, Cha chacha and Rumba). Each of these styles belongs to either double or triple meter categories. We have annotated them as such. The total duration of this database is 5 hrs 49 min.

The second database includes 620 30-sec duration audio clips from Indian film songs. Most of the songs from old Indian films tend to rigidly follow the tal frame- work and use mostly acoustic instruments whereas the songs from new movies also contain drum loops and electronic instrumentation. In this database we have included an equal number of popular songs from both old as well as new films. These audio clips belong to three different metrical structures most commonly found in Indian film music. 470 clips belong to double meter (4/4, 2/4 time signature), 109 triple meter (3/4, 6/8) and 41 follow septuple meter (7/8 time signature). The total duration of the database is 5 hrs 10 min. The ground truth meter values for the database have been annotated by the authors.

3.2   Evaluation and Results

The performance accuracy of the meter detection system for both databases Indian music database (IMDB) and ballroom dance database (BDDB) is summarized in Table 1 in the form of a confusion matrix. It is to be noted that although database 1 did not have any audio clips in the septuple meter category, this category was still included as a possible output of the meter detection system. Removing this category from the system naturally increases system accuracy for this dataset.

We note that although the overall accuracies for both datasets are quite high, the performance of the system for the triple meter for both datasets is quite low. The performance for the double meter, for both databases, and the complex meter (septuple), for database 2, are equally high. The overall accuracy for the meter extraction over both databases is 87.1%.

Table 1. Confusion matrix for meter detection and performance accuracies for both the databases BDDB and IMDB

Database	Annotated Meter	Detected			Overall Accuracy (%)
		Double	Triple	Septuple	
BDDB	Double	482	24	17	92.16
	Triple	33	116	26	66.29
	Septuple	-	-	-	-
	Total				85.67
IMDB	Double	443	25	2	94.26
	Triple	39	69	1	63.3
	Septuple	3	0	38	92.68
	Total				88.7

3.3   Discussion

As seen from Table 1 the maximum number of errors is encountered in the detection of triple meter with large confusion between triple and double meters in both datasets. An analysis of the misclassified cases revealed that for many songs the error was due to incorrect estimation of tatum duration. Such errors in tatum estimation for triple meter songs are more often found to occur in songs with fast tempo. Here periodicity at metrical levels higher than the tatum, such as half-rhythm cycle, fall within the search range of tatum delays (0.1-0.6 sec). Peaks in the tatum vector at such locations have saliences comparable to that at the true tatum duration leading to incorrect tatum detection. It is mainly the octave errors in tatum estimation that lead to incorrect meter detection.

This phenomenon can be observed in Figure 3, which shows a spectrogram of a song in triple meter. In this figure we notice that the percussion strokes at periodicity of half rhythm cycle duration are more prominent than the ones at tatum duration. This prominence is also manifested in the comb filter output as high peak at half cycle duration, which for this song is within the search range for tatum duration (relatively fast song). Thus, we end up estimating incorrect tatum duration. If we make this kind of octave error in the tatum estimation, naturally we will get prominent peaks in meter vector at the multiples of 4, 8, 16 of this duration (which corresponds to integer multiples of rhythm cycle duration which is highly periodic.) and finally a wrong meter value for the song.

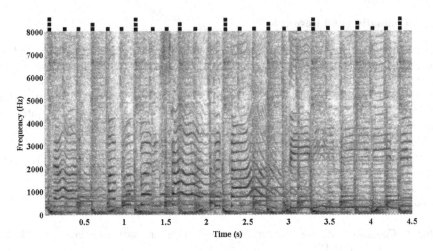

Fig. 3. Spectrogram of a song in triple meter. Rhythm cycle boundaries are indicated on top boundary by three boxes, half cycle by two and tatum boundaries by single box.

For the double meter songs also we encounter errors in tatum estimation, but for most of these cases even if we incorrectly estimate tatum duration as half or quarter rhythm cycle, we get correct meter value because the prominent strokes are indeed at the multiples of 4,8,16 of this duration (coinciding with rhythm cycle boundaries).

In the case of septuple meter, we found that the tatum estimation errors were very few. One reason for this is that these songs are typically of low tempo values, so less possibility of encountering half cycle duration within tatum search range. Secondly, as the rhythm cycle for the songs in septuple meter is such that it doesn't have any intra cycle repetition of sections (even in term of beat locations if not timbre), we don't get a prominent peak in comb filter output corresponding to any subsection duration of the rhythm cycle. Figure 4 shows the spectrogram of a song in septuple meter, we can notice that no intra cycle repetition exist (which is expected as 7 is a prime number.

To verify that incorrect tatum estimation is the reason for erroneous meter estimation in most of the triple meter songs, we consider the same triple meter song as in Figure 3, for which meter was incorrectly estimated as double meter and manually correct the tatum duration value to the ground truth value. Figure 5.a. and Figure 5.b. display the meter vectors computed from an incorrectly estimated tatum duration value (half-cycle duration) and the true tatum duration respectively. Clearly the salience of the double meter (S2) is high for figure 5.a. and that of the triple meter (S3) is high for Figure 5.b.

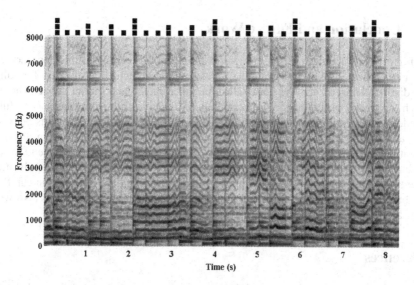

Fig. 4. Spectrogram of a song in septuple meter. Rhythm cycle boundaries are indicated by three boxes, sectional divisions by two boxes and tatum by single box. This rhythm structure is of type 3+2+2.

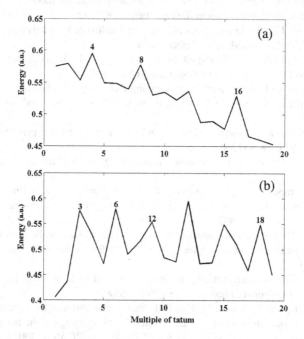

Fig. 5. Meter vector of a song from Indian music dataset in triple meterfrom (a) incorrectly estimated tatum (b) true tatum duration

4   Conclusion and Future Work

The high overall accuracy 87 % in meter classification reveals that this approach for accent extraction from audio is suitable for the automatic detection of meter for culturally distinct datasets, viz. Western ballroom dance music and Indian music. The approach, originally proposed for simple meters like double and triple, was successfully extended to determining complex meters like septuple. However confusions between triple and double meters are found to occur resulting from incorrect tatum duration estimation. Further work is needed to reduce these confusions. We also intend to test the above system on other complex meters like 5/8 and 9/8 and extend its application to the task of tal detection in Indian music where time signature information can be a useful input. The automatic segmentation of music by rhythmic structure is also worthy of future investigation.

References

1. Klapuri, A., Eronen, A.J., Astola, J.T.: Analysis of the meter of acoustic musical signals. IEEE Transactions on Acoustics Speech and Signal Processing 14(1), 342–355 (2006)
2. Holzapfel, A., Stylianou, Y.: Rhythmic similarity in traditional turkish music. In: Proceedings of International Conference on Music Information Retrieval (2009)
3. Gulati, S., Rao, P.: Rhythm Pattern Representation for Tempo Detection in Music. In: Proceedings of the First International Conference on Intelligent Interactive Technologies and Multimedia, Allahabad, India (December 2010)
4. Dixon, S.: Onset Detection Revisited. In: Proceedings of the International Conference on Digital Audio Effects (DAFx 2006), Montreal, Canada (2006)
5. Klapuri, A.: Sound Onset Detection by Applying Psychoacoustic Knowledge. In: Proceedings of the IEEE International Conference on Acoustics, Speech, and Signal Processing (March 1999)
6. Dixon, S.: Automatic extraction of tempo and beat from expressive performances. J. New Music Res. 30(1), 39–58 (2001)
7. Ellis, D.P.: Beat tracking by dynamic programming. J. New Music Res. 36(1), 51–60 (2007)
8. Goto, M., Muraoka, Y.: Music Understanding at the Beat Level Real-time Beat Tracking for Audio Signals. In: Proceedings of IJCAI 1995 Workshop on Computational Auditory Scene Analysis, p. 6875 (1995)
9. Gouyon, F., Herrera, P.: Determination of the meter of musical audio signals: Seeking recurrences in beat segment descriptors. In: 114th Audio Engineering Society Convention (March 2003)
10. Clayton, M.: Time in Indian music: rhythm, metre, and form in North Indian rāg performance. Oxford University Press Inc., New York (2000)
11. Schuller, B., Eyben, F., Rigoll, G.: Fast and robust meter and tempo recognition for the automatic discrimination of ballroom dance styles. In: Proceedings of the IEEE International Conference on Acoustics, Speech and Signal Processing (ICASSP 2007), Honolulu, Hawaii, USA, pp. 217–220 (April 2007)

12. Gouyon, F.: A computational approach to rhythm description – Audio features for the computation of rhythm periodicity functions and their use in tempo induction and music content processing. PhD dissertation, Music Technology Group, PompeuFabra University (2005)
13. Scheirer, E.: Tempo and beat analysis of acoustic musical signals. J. Acoust. Soc. Amer. 103(1), 588–601 (1998)
14. Gouyon, F., Dixon, S., Pampalk, E., Widmer, G.: Evaluating rhythmic descriptors for musical genre classification. In: Proceedings. AES 25th Int. Conf., New York, pp. 196–204 (2004)

Assessment of Level of Recovery
of Cognitive Impairment in the Cerebrovascular
Accident and Head Injuries Cases:
Therapeutic Impact of North Indian Ragas

Shashi Bhushan Singh[1], Soubhik Chakraborty[2], and Keashav Mohan Jha[3]

[1] Department of Preventive and Social Medicine,
Rajendra Institute of Medical Sciences, Ranchi, India
sbsingh2011@yahoo.com
[2] Department of Applied Mathematics, Birla Institute of Technology,
Mesra, Ranchi-835215, India
soubhikc@yahoo.co.in
[3] Department of Neuro-Surgery, Rajendra Institute of Medical Sciences,
Ranchi-834009, India
drkmjha@gmail.com

Abstract. This paper briefs the ongoing statistical study on the therapeutic effects of some north Indian ragas on cerebrovascular accident and diffuse head injury cases being conducted at Rajendra Institute of Medical Sciences, Ranchi, India in collaboration with Birla Institute of Technology, Mesra, Ranchi.

Keywords: music therapy, ragas, cerebrovascular accident, diffuse head injury, statistics.

1   Introduction

This paper briefs the ongoing statistical study on the therapeutic effects of some North Indian ragas on cerebrovascular accident and diffuse head injury cases being conducted at Rajendra Institute of Medical Sciences (RIMS), Ranchi in collaboration with Birla Institute of Technology, Mesra, Ranchi. This study is supposed to establish the therapeutic effect of music especially ragas in the treatment of CVA and brain injured patients and if found efficacious, can be of great help to medical sciences and ultimately the society.

Music therapy is a scientific method for effective treatment of disease through the power of music. It restores, maintains and improves emotional, physiological and psychological well being. A raga, in Indian classical music, is a melodic structure comprising of fixed notes and a set of rules that characterizes a certain mood which the artist conveys through performance. There are specific times for rendering ragas. To get the specific benefits from ragas, one should follow the corresponding suitable rendition time (e.g morning for Bhairav and evening for Yaman). Depending on their nature, a raga could induce or intensify joy, sorrow, peace etc. and it is this quality

S. Ystad et al. (Eds.): CMMR/FRSM 2011, LNCS 7172, pp. 44–52, 2012.

which forms the basis of therapeutic application. Thus ragas are not just for entertainment but their vibrations touch one's interiors as a healing medicine. By activating brain wave patterns, ragas could be used as a powerful tool for alleviating the most common ailments such as blood pressure, depression, stress, sleep disorder etc.

Keeping the aforementioned considerations in mind, the objectives of the present study are to assess and monitor cognitive impairment of the patients at different prescribed time interval, and to estimate various cognitive and behavioral disturbances as well as brain dysfunction for the patients under investigation at different prescribed time interval.

2   Literature Review

Although there is an extensive literature on music therapy applications, there is a general absence of valid clinical research material from which substantive conclusions can be drawn. An article by D. Aldridge is a good source of review on music therapy literature [1]. Regarding raga therapy, the book by T. V. Sairam titled Raga Therapy and the references cited therein can be referred [2]. Music therapy has been reviewed in medical & nursing press; the principle emphasis is on the soothing ability of music & the necessity of music as antidote to an overly technological medical approach. Most of these articles are concerned with passive music therapy and playing of prerecorded music to patients emphasizing the necessity of healthy pleasures like music, fragrance and beauty sights for the reduction of stress and the enhancement of well being. The overall expectation is that the recreational, emotional and physical health of the patients is improved [3]. After the Second World War music therapy was intensively developed in American hospitals [4]. Since then some hospitals, particularly in mainland Europe, have incorporated music therapy carrying on a tradition of European hospital-based research and practice [5-6]. Continental Europe has encouraged the use of music particularly in terms of individual and group psychotherapy to encourage awakening of the patient's emotions to cope with unconscious intrapsychic conflicts [7-15].

In many cases neurological diseases become traumatic because of their abrupt appearance resulting in physical and/or mental impairment [16]. Music appears to be a key in the recovery of former capabilities in the light of what at first can be seen like a hopeless neurological devastation [17-19]. For some patients with brain damage following head trauma, the problem may be temporary in the loss of speech (aphasia). Music therapy can play valuable role in the aphasia rehabilitation [20].

3   Experiment

This study is a prospective one in nature and it has been conducted at Neurosurgery Department, RIMS, Ranchi (for music therapy) and Applied Mathematics Department, BIT Mesra, Ranchi (for statistical analysis).

3.1 Participants

Inclusion Criteria

- Patients above 18 years of age & resident of Ranchi district.
- Patients suffering from diffuse head injury and cerebrovascular accident.

— who were stabilized from life threatening medical & neurological complication.
— whose medical & clinical status, level of consciousness and social & environmental factors were also considerable.

Exclusion Criteria

- Patients less than 18 years of age & not resident of Ranchi district.
- Those suffering from acute illnesses.

Mode of Selection of Subjects

Patients of diffuse head injury and cerebrovascular accident, meeting the above criteria, were chosen after establishing rapport and receiving written informed consent from the patients or head of his/her family. Patients in intervention group (Case group) i.e music group and the patients in control group were allocated randomly by the method of draw of lots as a process of randomization to minimize the unknown bias. Patients in the intervention group were subjected to both medicine and prerecorded north Indian music while the control group of patients were given medicine only.

3.2 Stimuli

The following ten ragas were used as intervening stimuli:

	Time period of a day for intervention
• Ragas Bhairav and Ahir Bhairav:	05 AM to 08 AM
• Raga Bilaval:	06 AM to 09 AM
• Raga Todi:	09 AM to 12 AM
• Rgas Bhimpalashree and Pilu :	01 PM to 03 PM
• Raga Multani:	03 PM to 06 PM
• Ragas Yaman and Bhairavi:	06 PM to 09 PM
• Raga Bageshree :	09 PM to 12 PM

The strategy behind the choice of aforementioned ragas in the experiment is that the benefits of some of these ragas were explored in earlier studies [2]. For example, Ahir Bhairav relieves stress related disorders. Bhairav helps in anger management, bringing down the excitement. Bageshree works well in sleep disorder. Yaman, being a restful raga, brings relaxation. Todi has been found to be useful in the treatment of hysteria while Bhairavi works well for a number of maladies from sinusitis to cancer. Pilu tackles depression. The present study was expected to re-confirm the utilities of all these seven ragas as well as explore the other three, namely, Bilaval, Bhimpalashree and Multani for possible therapeutic effects on the patients.

The reason behind the selection of specific raga for intervention at the specific time period of a day is that each raga is closely related to the specific part of the day according to changes in nature and development of a particular emotion, mood or sentiment in the human mind.

Since higher frequency is beneficial rather than harmful (unlike higher doses of drugs which exhibit side-effects), the patients in the intervention group were subjected to each of the aforementioned ragas for a duration of 20 minutes everyday within the above mentioned time period of day as per their convenience for a duration of 6 months.

3.3 Procedure

The patients in the intervention group were subjected to both medicine and music therapy (ragas) while the patients in the control group were given medicine only. A prerecorded cassette and a cassette player alongwith a headset were used for administration of raga. All cassettes, cassette players and headsets used for the patients in the intervention group were identical and of the same company. They were subjected to each of the above-mentioned ragas for duration of 20 minutes everyday (total of 3 hours 20 minutes each day for the all 10 ragas) within the above mentioned time period of day as per their convenience.

Simple steps involved, while listening to the raga, were closing the eyes, focusing on the breathing process by placing the hands on the abdomen and listening to the raga. For the patients who were unfamiliar with ragas, some songs based on a particular raga (even songs from movies) were played first before playing the raga itself.

While undergoing music therapy, empty stomach was avoided. The patients were given liberty to adjust the music sound (volume etc.) as per their liking. They were also encouraged to use their vocal cords through gentle murmurs. This creates a musical and emotional environment that accepts everything the patient tries to formulate.

The patients in both the intervention as well as the control group were monitored and patients in the intervention group were helped listening the ragas directly while their stay in the hospital. Before discharge, the patients were again trained regarding the specific time period of day for listening the specific raga, duration of listening each raga and proper way of listening raga as mentioned earlier so that they could listen to the ragas in a planned manner at home as well.

The patients in both the intervention as well as control group were assessed using the following tools:

- The Memory scale of PGI BBD (Post Graduate Institute Battery of Brain Dysfunction)
- MMSE (Mini Mental Status Examination).

Mini Mental State Examination (MMSE)

The MMSE is a screening tool that provides a brief, objective measure of cognitive function. MMSE scores are useful in quantitatively estimating the severity of cognitive impairment and in serially documenting cognitive change. It tests the individual's orientation, registration of three words, attention, calculation, recall, language and copying skills, each carrying certain points. Maximum score of MMSE is 30 points. A score more than 25 points is taken as normal, 22-25 as borderline and less than 22 as definite impairment.

Post Graduate Institute Battery of Brain Dysfunction (PGI BBD)

These instruments have five components as follows:

  i.   Memory Scale
 ii.   Battery for Performance test of Intelligence
iii.   Verbal Adult Intelligence Scale (VAIS)
 iv.   Nahor-Benson Test (N.B Test)
  v.   Bender Visual –Motor Gestalt Test (BvMGT)

i)   PGI Memory Scale

This scale provides the comprehensive and simple scale to measure verbal and non-verbal memories on the basis of neurological theory; very short term, short term and long term memories on the basis of experimental evidences and remote, recent and immediate memories on the basis of clinical practice of evaluation of memory.

ii)   Battery for Performance Test of Intelligence

It consists of (a) Kohs' Block Design Test and (b) Pass a long test.

> **(a) Kohs Block Design Test** uses 10 cards of design and 16 cubes (6 sides of the cube colored as Blue, White, Red, Green, Half red -half white)
>
> **(b) Pass a long Test as** uses 8 cards of design , 4 boxes and rectangular Blocks (6 blue small ,2 blue long, 1 blue big and 2 red small ,1 red big, 1 red long).

The patients are encouraged to do the design as shown in the cards. The time taken is noted in completion of each item with the help of a stopwatch.

iii)   Verbal Adult Intelligence Scale (VAIS)

It consists of four subtests i.e. Information, Digit span, Arithmetic and comprehension. It gives Test Quotients separately for four subtests and V.Q (Verbal Quotient) that is mean of T.Qs (Test Quotients), separately for male and female of different age and education levels.

iv)   Nahor - Benson Test (N.B Test)

It consists of 8 cards. Out of these five cards contain a design each and three cards contain the instructions to be followed. Patients are asked for copy the 1-5 cards' design one by one. 6-8 cards have some instructions and asked to patients to do the same. Scoring is given on the basis of 'all or none' i.e., either a design is correct or it is incorrect.

v)   Bender Visual - Motor Gestalt Test (BvMGT)

It consists of nine figures characterized by their gestalt. Patients are asked to copy the design as shown in the cards. This is simple and largely a quantitative procedure. In this method, protocol is searched for 15 signs. The signs are Perseveration(Intra/Inter), Rotation or Reversal, Concretism, Added Angles, Separation of lines, Overlap, Distortion, Embellishments, Partial Rotation, Omission, Abbreviation, Separation, Absence or Erasure, Closure and Point of contact. Each sign is scored on the basis of all or none.

It is not a test of visual memory of imagery; rather it is one of perception and visual functioning. It measures visual acuity and motor functioning. The performance is distorted by brain injury, chemical imbalance, toxicity, and degenerative process of the brain cells and nervous system.

Using the aforementioned tools the patients in both the intervention and control groups were assessed as shown in the flowchart (fig 1):

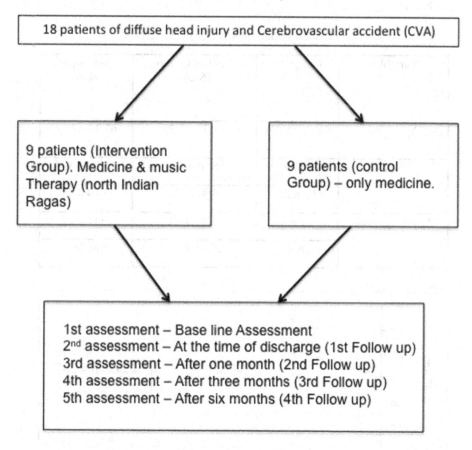

Fig. 1. Flow Chart

Plan for Statistical Analysis (Data Entry and Data Analysis)

Proper template was generated for data entry and 10% data were randomly checked to assure the quality of the data. Test of significance was used to compare rate of recovery between the control group and intervention group. Both parametric tests (such as

Z tests for proportion and mean, t-tests for mean and correlation coefficient, F tests for equality of two variances) and nonparametric tests (such as Chi-Square tests for independence of attributes and goodness of fit, sign and median tests etc.) were used. SPSS package was used for data analysis. Statistical analysis was necessary to confirm that there is **significant** improvement after raga therapy among patients receiving the therapy compared to the patients not receiving the same with respect to the neuropsychological parameters measured. We refer to table 1, where SD stands for standard deviation, for a summary of the results.

4   Results (Interim Analysis)-Based on MMSE and PGIBBD-MS Score

Table 1. Socio-demographic Profile of the Patients

Variables	Category	Control Group (N=9)	Case Group (N=9)
Age (Yrs)	(mean ±SD)	61.33± 7.59	62.22 ±7.57
Sex	Male	5(55.6%)	5(55.6%)
	Female	4(44.4%)	4(44.4%)
Any drug abuse	Yes	1(11.1%)	1(11.1%)
	No	8(88.9%)	8(88.9%)

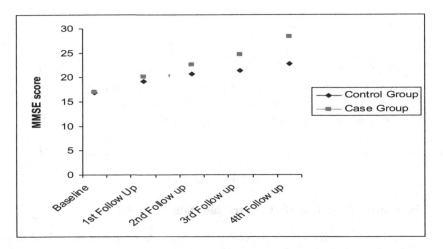

Fig. 2. Mean score of MMSE of the patients at different time interval

- Mini Mental State Examination (MMSE) scores were steadily increasing and higher among patients in intervention (Case) group in comparison to patients in control group indicating a higher degree of improvement in individual's cognitive function i.e., orientation, registration of three words, attention, calculation, recall, language and copying skills among patients in the intervention group compared to the patients in control group.

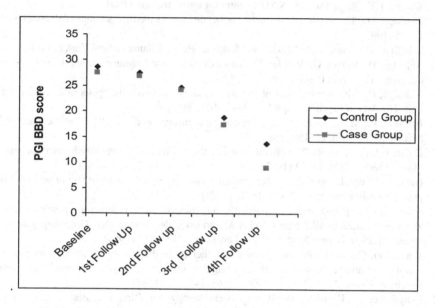

Fig. 3. Mean score of PGI BBD MS of the patients at different time interval

- Post Graduate Institute Battery of Brain Dysfunction Memory Scale (PGI BBD MS) scores were found to be steadily decreasing and lower among patients in the intervention (Case) group in comparison to the patients in control group suggesting a higher degree of recovery in verbal and non-verbal memories; very short term, short term and long term memories; and remote, recent and immediate memories among patients in the intervention group compared to the patients in control group.

5   Conclusion

I.   Overall, trend of recovery of the patients of case group (Music Therapy) is better than the patients of control Group.

II.   Average of Mini-mental State Examination score of the case group's patients have shown increasing trend compared with control group's patients in the different prescribed time interval.

III.   Brain dysfunction score examined by PGI BBD-MS of the case group's patients has shown a decreasing trend compared with the control group.

IV.   Tertiary Care Hospitals should plan to establish a Music Lab in the Medicine & Neurosurgery Department.

Acknowledgement. We thank two anonymous referees for several suggestions.

References

1. Aldridge, D.: An Overview of Music Therapy Research. Complementary Therapies in Medicine 2, 204–216 (1994)
2. Sairam, T.V.: Raga Therapy, NADA centre for music therapy (2004)
3. Aldridge, D.: The music of the body: music therapy in medical settings. Advances 9(1), 17–35 (1993)
4. Schullian, D., Schoen, M.: Music and Medicine. Henry Schuman, New York (1948)
5. Aldridge, D., Brandt, G., Wohler, D.: Towards a common language among the creative art therapies. The Art in Psychotherapy 17, 189–195 (1989)
6. Aldridge, D.: The development of research strategy for music therapists in a hospital setting. The Arts in Psychotherapy 17, 231–237 (1990)
7. Brasseur, F.: Musicotherapies, psychotherapie et institution d'aide: l'impossible marriage? Soins-Psychiatr. 66, 11–15 (1986)
8. Gross, J.-L., Swartz, R.: The effects of music therapy on anxiety in chronically ill patients. Music Therapy 2(1), 43–52 (1982)
9. Heyde, W., von Langsdorff, P.: Rehabilitation of cancer patients including creative therapies. Rehabilitation Stuttg. 22(1), 25–27 (1983)
10. Kaufmann, G.: [Combination of music therapy methods in dynamic group psychotherapy] Zur Kombination musiktherapeutischer Methoden in der dynamischen Gruppenpsychotherapie. Psychiatr. Neurol Med. Psychol. Leipz 35(3), 148–153 (1983)
11. Kaufmann, G.: [Receptive individual music therapy in the concept of ambulatory psycho therapy] Rezeptive Einzelmusiktherapie in der ambulanten Psychotherapie-Konzeption. Psychiatr. Neurol Med. Psychol. Leipz 37(6), 347–352 (1985)
12. Lengdobler, H., Kiessling, W.: [Group music therapy in multiple sclerosis: initial report of experience] Gruppenmusiktherapie bei multipler Sklerose: Ein erster Erfahrungsbericht. Psychother. Psychosom. Med. Psychol. 39(9-10), 369–373 (1989)
13. Moreno, J.J.: The music therapist: Creative arts therapist and contemporary shaman. The Arts in Psychotherapy 15, 271–280 (1988)
14. Pfeiffer, H., Wunderlich, S., Bender, W., Elz, U.: [Music improvisation with schizophrensic patients- a controlled study in the assessment of therapeutic effects] Freie Musikimprovisation mit schizophrenen Patienten – Kontrollierte Studie zur Untersuchung der therapeutischen Wirkung. Rehabilitation stuttg. 26(4), 184–192 (1987)
15. Reinardt, A.,, Rohrborn, H., Scwabe, C.: [Regulative music therapy (RMT) in depressive diseases- a contribution to the development of psychotherapy in Psychiatry] Regulative musiktherapie (RMT) bei depressiven Erkrankhugen-Ein Beitrag zur Psychotherapieentwicklung in der Psychiatrie. Psychiatr. Neurol Med. Psycho. Leipz 38(9), 547–553 (1986)
16. Jochims, S.: [Coping with illness in the early phase of severe neurologic diseases. A contribution of music therapy to psychological management in selected neurological disease pictures] Krankheitsverarbeitung in der Frühphase schwerer neurologischer Erkrankungen. Ein Beitrag der Musiktherapie zur psychischen Betreung bei ausgewählten neurologischen Krankheitsbildern. Psychother. Psychosom. Med. Psychol. 40(3-4), 115–122 (1990)
17. Aldridge, D.: Creativity and consciousness. Art in Psychotherapy 18, 359–362 (1991)
18. Jones, C.: Spark of life. Geriatr. Nurs. 11(4), 194–196 (1990)
19. Sacks, O.: The man who mistook his wife for a hat. Pan, London (1986)
20. Lucia, C.M.: Toward developing a model of music therapy intervention in rehabilitation of head trauma patients. Music Therapy Perspectives 4, 34–39 (1987)

On Tanpura Drone
and Brain Electrical Correlates

Matthias Braeunig[1,*], Ranjan Sengupta[2], and Anirban Patranabis[2]

[1] Institute for Environmental Health Sciences
University Medical Center Freiburg, Germany
matthias.braeunig@uniklinik-freiburg.de
[2] Sir CV Raman Centre for Physics and Music
Jadavpur University, Kolkata, India

Abstract. We describe a new conceptual framework of using tanpura drone for auditory stimulation in EEG. The question of reference for baseline EEG in the resting condition where the subject has no task to perform is addressed. In a laboratory setting we observed spontaneous brain electrical activity during Tanpura drone stimulation and periods of silence. The sound stimulus was given by an electronic substitute Tanpura (EST) that allows to closely control its parameters. The timbral characteristics of the drone samples are given. The brain-electrical response of the subject is analyzed with global descriptors, a way to monitor the course of activation in the time domain in a three-dimensional state space, revealing patterns of global dynamical states of the brain. Preliminary results are presented that serve as a stepping stone for a larger longitudinal study.

Keywords: EEG, global descriptors, Tanpura, drone, timbre, correlates.

1 Introduction

"It's all-important! With the sounding of Tanpura, naturally, you will start to sing." (Ustad Sayeeduddin Dagar at Dhrupad Mela, Varanasi 2011, when asked about the rôle of Tanpura in Indian classical music.)

The *Tanpura* (sometimes also spelled Tampura or Tambura) is a fretless musical instrument that is played traditionally for accompaniment in Hindustani music. As resonance bodies it has a large gourd and a long voluminous neck with four or five metal strings supported at the lower end by a meticulously curved bridge made of bone or ivory. The strings are plucked one after the other in slow cycles of several seconds generating a buzzing drone sound. The peculiar sounding of Tanpura arises from the strings' grazing touch of the bridge in vertical direction, so they are clamped at different lengths, as has been observerd and first described in the 1920s by the famous Indian physicist CV Raman [12]. This phenomenon

---

* Corresponding author.

S. Ystad et al. (Eds.): CMMR/FRSM 2011, LNCS 7172, pp. 53–65, 2012.
© Springer-Verlag Berlin Heidelberg 2012

is called *jvari* (pronounced jovari) in musical terms, which means "life giving". It is evoked by fine cotton threads that are carefully adjusted between the bridge and the strings during instrument tuning. The periodic change of length in the plucked string creates amplitude fluctuations in the higher harmonics so that the mechanical energy is spread out to very high frequencies [1–3, 6]. The listener of Tanpura drone is captivated by its extremely rich harmonic structure. Because there is a felt resonance in perception, psycho-acoustics of Tanpura drone may provide a unique window into the human psyche and cognition.

Tanpura drones can be approximated by technical means – although they compare poorly to a live performance with its presumably important subtle imperfections. Common substitutes for drone instruments are electronic śruti boxes, which are nowadays superseded by software generators and sampled sound. The latter are good for experimentation because the Electronic Substitute Tanpura (EST) allows to control its parameters in a reproducible manner.

Background and Conceptions

The Tanpura is a remarkable drone instrument whose sounding acts as a canvas in Indian Raga Music and provides contrast to the tune and melody without introducing rhythmic content of its own. The jvari phenomenon in Tanpura drones has been found empirically by musicians and instrument makers in careful contemplation of the nature of sound, and in classical North Indian Music there is practically no performance without drone accompaniment. Drones and jvari became closely related. A drone without jvari may be as boring as the buzz of a running motor. With jvari the drone is brought to life and enhances the aesthetic experience of music [4]. What are the psycho-acoustically effective ingredients in Tanpura drone that make it almost ubiquitous in accompaniment for Indian music?

As a working hypothesis we put forward the idea that a psycho-physiological transport process may be responsible for the efficacy of drone. The buzzing of drone sound is physically felt and may be perceived by different centers of the body. It is a common observation that high pitch sounds are felt in the upper parts and bass type sounds are felt in the lower parts of the body. Singers, for example, distinguish physical sensations corresponding to their voice, leading to the (historic) notion of head, throat and chest voice registers [16]. These vibrotactile sensations provide feedback for control of phonation [15, 17]. It can be assumed that a strongly vibrating instrument creates similar resonances with a stimulating effect in the perceiver.

In the listener of music, and even more in the performer, drone can provide a canvas on which the full picture of the composition unfolds. In analogy the situation may be likened to a loom, whose vertical warp threads represent the drone, whereas the weft threads correspond to the melody. The warp has to be held under tension in order to weave the pattern of the carpet. Similarly, drone builds up *neuro-muscular tension* [4], which is then periodically released in the twists and turns of a musical pattern. It is this image and the hypothetical correlates of drones that shall be highlighted in this study.

Furthermore, we hypothesize that drone sounds are sufficiently neutral to the subject in that they are not popping into the fore of cognition, evoking reactions to the stimulus. This assumption is needed in order to define the resting condition where the subject has no task to perform (no-task resting frame). Drone can provide contrast but is not prompting a response. The drone environment is free of semantic content, such as melody or rhythm, similar to an acoustical *Ganzfeld* [9], where no delimitable (sound) objects can be grasped or (re-)cognized. In the Ganzfeld, cognitions arise spontaneously out of intrinsic activity [11]. Conceived as a contrasting condition, however, drone may reveal the relative difference in resting between periods of silence and stimulation.

In order to investigate physiological changes involved with the sensation of drones we are looking at spontaneous brain-electrical activity, breathing and skin conductance. These three parameters appear on different phenomenological levels: (1) brain patterns are the subtle expression of mental activity and cognition; (2) respiration represents our exchange with the outer world and reflects our moods; (3) skin conductance is a general measure of arousal and is closely related to physical tension and emotions. While our main focus is on brain-activity measured through electroencephalography (EEG), with electrodes attached to the head of the proband, the other two parameters may give additional information that helps the interpretation of the patterns observed with EEG.

In a conceptual shift from customary EEG analysis we investigate brain-activity in the time domain to depict the dynamical behavior of global functional states. This can be done through creating snapshots of activation by suitably averaging over epochs of the EEG. We employ the method of Global Descriptors (GD) to transform the multi-channel data to a three dimensional time series [18]. The first two descriptors are time averages of activity (strength) and mobility (change) [5], while the third, Omega-complexity, measures the number of oscillatory modules giving rise to the globally observed activity of the brain [19].

2   Method

The participant (male, age 52, right-handed) was prepared with an EEG recording cap (type EasyCap® EC20) with 19 electrodes (Ag/AgCl sintered ring electrodes) placed in the international 10/20 system, plus one EOG electrode to detect eye movement. Impedances were checked below 4 kOhms. Additionally we recorded skin conductance (GSR) at the inside of the right hand. Breathing was tracked with a tube belt around the abdomen. The recording system was a Brain Products QuickAmp amplifier operated at 1000 samples/s, recording on BrainVision® Recorder (1.20b) software. Seated comfortably in a chair within a shielded measurement cabin, the subject received no instruction as to what to do or how to react during the period of measurement (no-task scheme). The subject decided to keep his eyes closed during the recording. A sound system (Logitech® Z-4 speakers) with very low S/N ratio was set up in the measurement room that received input from outside the cabin. The drone sound stimulation was generated from software (BZHtec Tanpura Generator Light, version 2.2.2) on Windows XP. After initialization, a 15 minutes recording period was started, devoting equal times (5 minutes) to the three periods of silence, drone and no-drone conditions. Silence and no-drone are distinguished here, because the latter is a relaxation from the preceding drone period. Markers were set at start, drone onset/offset, and at the end of the recording.

2.1   Global Descriptors

For off-line analysis the samples were centered to common average reference (zero mean), and a filter set (cut-off below 1 Hz and above 40 Hz) was applied to the individual channels. From the multi-channel EEG thus obtained, we calculated the three global descriptor variables: (1) the *integral field strength* Σ, (2) the *generalized frequency* Φ, and (3) the measure of *spatial complexity* Ω. By taking epochs of 1 second width with 50% overlap this procedure results in a massive reduction of the amount of data, leaving us with a three-dimensional time series that is descriptive of the global dynamic of the brain. EEG artifacts resulting mainly from eye movement and residual muscle contraction, such as frowning, show as outliers in the global descriptors. They are conveniently removed at this stage of analysis and replaced by their following data point to allow for an unbroken time series.

Integral Field Strength and Generalized Frequency

Following procedures in [18] the first two descriptors are calculated from the squares of the centered sample values at time step n, denoted by u_n and their change value $\dot{u}_n$, as central moments M over the epoch for all m channels in the multi-channel EEG:

$$M_0 = \langle \|u_n\|^2 \rangle \text{ and } M_1 = \langle \|\dot{u}_n\|^2 \rangle \ . \tag{1}$$

The integral field strength and the generalized frequency are then given by the formulas

$$\Sigma = \sqrt{\frac{M_0}{m}} \text{ and } \Phi = \frac{1}{2\pi}\sqrt{\frac{M_1}{M_0}} \ . \tag{2}$$

The integral field strength is the average activity of the brain during the epoch and measures in micro-volts ($[\mu V]$). In fact, Σ^2 is the mean squared Global Field Power (GFP). The generalized frequency is the average change of that activity and measures in Hertz ($[Hz]$). It may be construed as the rotational frequency of the main modes of the EEG.

By comparison it can be seen that the integral field strength is actually the effective voltage, V_{eff}, across all electrodes, which can be expressed as the Root Mean Squared (RMS) value in the epoch:

$$\Sigma \sim V_{\text{eff}} = RMS(u) \ . \tag{3}$$

Similarly, the generalized frequency is the RMS of voltage change relative to the effective voltage:

$$\Phi \sim \frac{RMS(\dot{u})}{RMS(u)} \ . \tag{4}$$

Spatial Complexity

The third descriptor, the so-called Omega-complexity (Ω), is of the nature of entropy. By conceiving the total activity of the brain resulting from an inter-play of oscillatory modules, the Omega-complexity measures how many of these modules are active at a time. Clearly, its resolution is limited by the number of electrodes. The quantity Ω is calculated by suitably adding the normalized *eigenvalues* (spectrum denoted *spec*) of the covariance matrix of the sample values for all channels (denoted *cov*) in the epoch.

By normalizing

$$\lambda'_j \equiv \lambda_j / \sum_{i=1}^{m} \lambda_i, \text{ where } \{\lambda_1, \ldots, \lambda_m\} = spec\,(cov\,\{u_n\})_{\text{epoch}} \tag{5}$$

Omega is defined as the Shannon-entropy H for the covariance-spectrum $\{\lambda_j\}$,

$$\log \Omega \overset{\text{def}}{=} H(\{\lambda'_1, \ldots, \lambda'_m\}) = - \sum_{i=1}^{m} \lambda'_i \cdot \log \lambda'_i \ . \tag{6}$$

Derived Quantities

Since Σ and Φ turn out to be roughly inverse of each other, that is $\Sigma\Phi \approx k$ with constant k, two new quantities can be defined, resulting from a rotation of points in the combined $(\log \Sigma, \log \Phi)$-space

$$\begin{aligned} \log E &\overset{\text{def}}{=} \log \Sigma + \log \Phi \\ \log I &\overset{\text{def}}{=} \log \Sigma - \log \Phi \ . \end{aligned} \tag{7}$$

These two dimensions may serve as drop-in variables for characterizing the be-havior of the EEG. It has been shown in application to sleep EEG that the "extrinsic" variable $\log E$ is sensitive to the transition between wakefulness and sleep, while the "intrinsic" measure I reflects the course of the sleep stages. Thus the deviation of $\log E$ from the constant level $\log k$ may serve as an individual measure of vigilance [18]. In our context these derived variables are used for separating the common factor underlying both Σ and Φ.

3 Results

This chapter summarizes the findings in an objective analysis of the drone signal, the time series obtained for EEG global descriptors, and the peripheral physiology signals. These results are providing the basis for the next stage of investigations.

3.1 Acoustical Analysis of EST Drones

The digitization of the sound signal was done at the rate of 22050 samples/s (16 bits/sample). Using the open source software WaveSurfer (v1.8.5) on Windows XP, pitch periods were analyzed at 10 milliseconds interval using a window length of 30 milliseconds. Since the sound of a musical instrument can be qualified by its timbre [8], defining identity and expression of the instrument. From a simplified timbre model perspective we chose only a few among the many timbre parameters that appeared descriptive and readily available. Timbral characteristics such as tristimulus T1, T2, and T3, and the odd and even parameters have been chosen in view of the energy distribution in partials, whereas spectral brightness, irregularity and inharmonicity are descriptive of the harmonic content.

Brightness measures the center of gravity in the partial domain and corresponds to the subjective perception of brightness of a sound. A high value of brightness shows much weight in the higher partials. In harmonic sound the partials are integral multiples of the fundamental frequency. The deviation from harmonic sound can be expressed with a non-zero "inharmonicity" coefficient β [7]. The tristimulus parameters T1–3 are defined in analogy to the trichromatic system of color measurement [10], providing a profile of the tunings of the strings. They are a measure of the spectral energy distribution in the fundamental (T1), the next three partials (T2) and all higher partials (T3). The odd and even parameters measure the energy in odd and even partials, where the odd series starts at the third partial to avoid correlation with T1. As odd, even, and T1 are summing up to unity, they complement the description of energy distribution from a partials perspective. Spectral irregularity is a measure of the "smoothness" of a sound, where the sum of squares of the differences between adjacent partial amplitudes is compared to the total sum of squared partial amplitudes. A value near zero would indicate smooth behavior of partials. Smoothness of a spectrum means that partials belong to the same sound source or process, whereas prominent partials would increase irregularity and be perceived as different sources. This particular parameter reveals the complex resonance structure in string instruments.

Because our software generator is fixed by the internal string samples, assessing the quality of jvari in the combined strings is of prime concern. The table lists the timbre parameters for single and combined strings, recorded directly from Tanpura generator (Tab. 1).

Compared to the other strings, Karaj, the first, thick, string is lacking in brightness and tristimulus T3, while T1 is relatively high, which may have been

Table 1. Timbral and spectral characteristics of Tanpura drone (EST). The combined signal is from parallel tracks of the single strings.

String	Brightness	T1	T2	T3	Odd	Even	Irregularity	Inharmonicity
1 (Karaj)	8.4	0.080	0.161	0.760	0.460	0.460	0.109	0.200
2	10.5	0.053	0.141	0.806	0.484	0.463	0.099	0.118
3	13.2	0.054	0.108	0.838	0.441	0.505	0.114	0.016
4	13.5	0.035	0.072	0.893	0.444	0.521	0.081	0.728
Combined	15.5	0.048	0.078	0.874	0.466	0.486	0.099	0.135

caused by a poor adjustment of the jvari thread. But generally T3 is high which means that much energy goes to the higher partials. With a value about 0.1 irregularity is moderately small, but inharmonicity is high especially in the 4th string. The combined signal, made up of all four strings superposed, profits from contributions of the 3rd and 4th string, where the energy is slightly shifted to the even partials, so that the overall timbre quality of the drone is better than the poorest string.

The amplitude profile of the combined signal (Fig. 1) shows fluctuations of power in time. Its waxing and waning stems from multiple decay of the higher harmonics and is typical for non-Helmholtz'ian excitation of resonances. This property is precisely responsible for the jvari in Tanpuras [13,14]. The impulses arising from the grazing touch of the strings with the bridge are constantly pumping energy to the higher harmonics, leading to a resonant structure that is very different from classical string instruments.

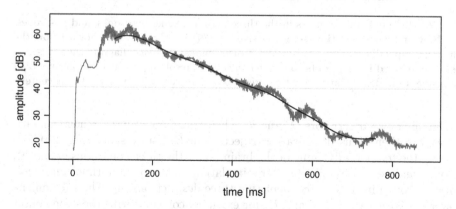

Fig. 1. Amplitude profile for the combined sound signal. The fluctuations are an indication of multiple decay of the higher harmonics.

3.2 EEG Correlates

The EEG signals from 19 electrodes have been averaged in windows of 1 s width. With overlap of 50% the time resolution is 0.5 seconds. After removal of outliers the time series for the three global descriptors are displayed including the derived dimensions E and I (Fig. 2a). The first eye-catching features are the undulations during drone that show 3–4 drops of field strength (activity), which correlate with an increase in frequency and complexity. These undulations have a width of roughly 30 s (which is very slow). The simultaneous increase in Omega complexity can be interpreted as emergence of new cognitive modules (either by insertion or decay). Reduced activity is an indication that available energy is shared by more processes.

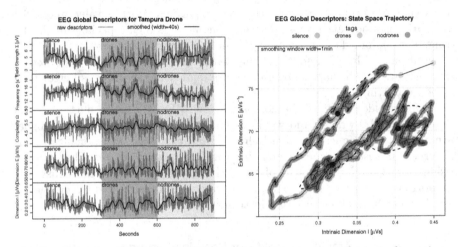

(a) Descriptors and derived quantities.   (b) Extrinsic versus intrinsic dimension.

Fig. 2. EEG Global descriptors in the three periods of silence, drones, and no-drones. (a) Raw and smoothed time series. Derived quantities E and I are shown below the three principal descriptors. (b) In a two-dimensional state space diagram these descriptors are followed in time (dots connected with line), resolving distinct regions of global dynamic. Confidence ellipses for these regions are marked with a black dot at center.

The first two descriptors, Σ and Φ, when transformed into orthogonal variables, can then be used to draw a trajectory in E/I-state space (Fig. 2b), unfolding the temporal dynamic of the brain under the three conditions of silence, drones, and no-drones (silence after stimulation). The points in time can be followed through in state space, depicting three destinct regions. The turn on the lower left corner (lowest E and I), for example, coincides with the drone onset whereas later E reaches almost the same levels as before the drone stimulation, but now at a higher value of the intrinsic dimension I. The two-dimensional time series is a way to separate "attractor spaces" of the global dynamic. Indeed, the three conditions show non-overlapping confidence intervals.

3.3   Peripheral Physiology

Besides the main observation of EEG activity, we monitored respiration and skin conductance (GSR) as indicators of psycho-physical tension. Monitoring of respiration and skin conductance was thought to provide clues on the state of wakefulness and emotional arousal, which may also be reflected in and correlate with patterns in the EEG global descriptors. However, since there are no "events" in the drone itself, we are not expecting any conditioned responses, but are simply observing the natural flow as it unfolds in time.

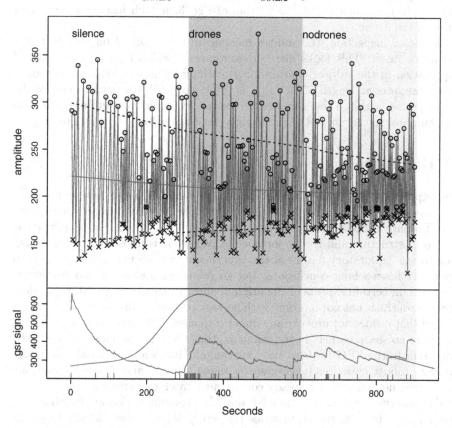

Fig. 3. Respiration and GSR signal before, during and after Tanpura drone. The top panel shows in- and exhalation peaks as well as the overall trend. The span, or tidal volume, decreases with time and respiration becomes increasingly shallow. GSR is shown in the panel below. After smooth decline during the silent phase, a sign of relaxation, the frequency of spikes is again increased at drone onset and offset, continuing with irregularities until the end of the measurement. Spikes are marked at bottom and spike density is shown next to the GSR signal.

The respiration signal has two extremal points at the lower and upper end. The overall tidal volume decreases with time and a second upper turning points emerges several minutes into the experiment. As the second turning point becomes more and more dominant, respiration becomes increasingly shallow and respiration frequency doubles at times. Although modification of the breathing rhythm coincides with the stimulation phase, no immediate reaction to the drone can be seen and the decrease may rather be due to other factors (like fatigue).

The GSR signal falls steadily at first, in the silent period, indicative of a smooth relaxation phase. After several vigorous spikes around drone onset the signal grows sharply and then dies down again, remaining at active levels until the end of the post-stimulation period. The bursts are probably caused by the abrupt changes during drone onset and offset. Consequently, the density of spikes, which are marked at the bottom of Fig. 3, is high just after onset and offset of the drone.

On closer inspection, the sudden increase in GSR turned on shortly *before* the drone onset. This looks like "pre-sentiment", which may be the result of expectation in the subject waiting for something to happen (the subject knew about the interval length). The burst is coinciding with the actual onset of the drone period within a few seconds. Otherwise we could not find any errors in the temporal resolution of the signal that can be attributed to this time lag.

4   Discussion

The experiment has yielded interesting data and enabled us to develop the tools for measurement and analysis of physiological response to drone stimulation. The Tanpura drone remains at the center of inquiry, because of its particular harmonic structure and the importance of jvari that is unlike any other drone. Due to the exploratory nature of the experiment, we are not in the position to draw any far-reaching conclusions, but to refine our questions and to narrow the focus on certain aspects of the original aims. Remembering that drone shall provide contrast, but not interfere with no-task resting condition, it can certainly be said that it does not provoke any direct responses. Besides the onset and offset there are no sharp corners in the stimulus, thus there are no identifiable evoked potentials in the EEG (at least not long range). However, the global descriptors are very robust measures (averages over many samples and channels), and any signal that deviates from a steady course must catch our attention.

The observed undulations that fall into the stimulus period are by no means insignificant. In fact, the state space trajectory shows three distinct locations corresponding to the experimental conditions of silence, drones and no-drones. Even the Omega-complexity, that counts the number of active neural modules, jumps by one at the most prominent peak. The question, indeed, is how the EEG traces are related to the drone stimulation, and if they would have not occured the same when no stimulus had been applied.

From our analysis of the peripheral measures we can say that the participant was sliding into a state where the respiration became shallower and faster, while his emotional arousal was getting increasingly irregular with lots of bursts in the GSR response. Is that a reaction to the drone, or could it rather be a signature of a general transition into a sleepy state?

The state space diagram can be interpreted as follows: A decrease in extrinsic dimension E is a clear sign of loss of vigilance that corresponds with the relaxation seen in GSR and the emergence of a second, shallower, upper turning point in inhalation (less tidal volume). Then the drone stimulus sets in as a gentle wake-up call, with an evoked emotional response (GSR) at onset, and an increase in vigilance in the extrinsic dimension for the first part of the stimulation. As five minutes of drones can be quite long, vigilance begins to drop until the offset again brings the vigilance up to higher levels. In the course of time the intrinsic dimension I underwent a similar scenario, where it remained at higher levels after the application of the drones, and it may be argued, that drone provided for the shift in I.

As we venture out into interpretations, current evidence is necessarily weak, while we did not repeat the session nor allowed for a longer recording. For a definite signature to be clearly established, the design should be repetitive, with randomized inter-stimulus intervals in order to break expectation effects. A more specific timbre model has to reveal the changes in the slow cycles of Tampura drone. It will require a more detailed analysis of the higher harmonic structure. With a higher time resolution (i.e. shorter frames) it should be possible to investigate the auditory driving character of the drone. Furthermore it is not enough to combine the strings into a compound signal. The actual stimulus (as it was played to the subject) has to be considered.

It seems that the measurement of peripheral physiological is a good way to obtain behavioral information that would otherwise be difficult to draw from the EEG data alone. The focus on respiration and skin conductance is simple and effective, and we do not want to make the affairs more complicated. However, the richness of the respiratory signal can be further quantified by suitably transforming the tidal volume and respiration frequency. In particular, because breathing and phonation are so closely related, there may be indications of how the Tanpura drone influences neuro-muscular tension in order to stimulate phonation. The conditions for such expression need to be optimized experimentally (e.g. posture), hinting also at muscle tonus and emotional response.

5   Concluding Remarks

We started out with the idea that drones can provide for an augmented baseline condition, that can be exploited to advantage as a intra-subject reference. The reason for wanting such reference is that many EEG experiments require a specification of the "ground state" of an individual to which an intervention can be compared. Simple baseline measurements are often not enough, as they are contaminated by residual activity that is difficult to assess. Especially in a no-task resting frame, baseline is no different from resting. Therefore we needed a contrasting condition, that does not interfere with the resting state (in a trivial sense). Drones with their smooth ambient character may provide such condition.

In Indian musical tradition drones are an inherent part of every performance. The specific character of the drone instrument Tanpura is its jvari, an essential ingredient that enhances the aesthetic experience of the listener. With the loom image we have formulated an alalogy that describes the interplay between neuro-muscular tension (in the listener/player) and the perception of drone sound, suggesting a framework for auditory driving on several phenomenological levels: mentally (or brain response), physically, and emotionally.

As preliminary evidence we presented time series of global descriptors of the brain, and peripheral measures of behavioral parameters from a single subject. The tools and insights developed through this work serve as a stepping stone for a more in-depth longitudinal study. Our goal will be met, if we could reproduce a paradigmatic trajectory over a series of measurements within the same subject.

Acknowledgments. Special thanks to J. Wackermann for support in the topic of global descriptors. So far this work has been carried out without external funding but has been generously supported with equipment and facilities by the Institute of Environmental Health Sciences at University Medical Center Freiburg.

References

1. Bhattacharyya, K.L., Ghosh, B.K., Chatterjee, S.K.: Observations on the vibration of the indian plucked stringed instrument, tanpura. Naturwissenschaften 43, 103–104 (1956), 10.1007/BF00600870
2. Carterette, E.C., Jairazbhoy, N., Vaughn, K.: The role of tambura spectra in drone tunings of north indian ragas. The Journal of the Acoustical Society of America 83(S1), S121 (1988)
3. Carterette, E.C., Vaughn, K., Jairazbhoy, N.A.: Perceptual, acoustical, and musical aspects of the tambura drone. Music Perception: An Interdisciplinary Journal 7(2), 75–108 (1989)
4. Deva, B.C.: The music of India. Munshiram Manoharial Publishers Private, Limited (December 1995)
5. Hjorth, B.: EEG analysis based on time domain properties. Electroencephalography and Clinical Neurophysiology 29(3), 306–310 (1970)
6. Houtsma, A.J.M., Burns, E.M.: Temporal and spectral characteristics of tambura tones. The Journal of the Acoustical Society of America 71(S1), S83 (1982)
7. Jensen, K., Marentakis, G.: Hybrid perception. Papers from the 1st Seminar on Auditory Models, Lyngby, Denmark (2001)
8. Jensen, K.: Perceptual and physical aspects of musical sounds. Journal of Sangeet Research Academy (2002)
9. Metzger, W.: Optische Untersuchungen am Ganzfeld. Psychological Research 13, 6–29 (1930), 10.1007/BF00406757
10. Pollard, H.F., Jansson, E.V.: A tristimulus method for the specificaton of musical timbre. Acoustica 51, 162–171 (1982)

11. Pütz, P., Braeunig, M., Wackermann, J.: EEG correlates of multimodal Ganzfeld induced hallucinatory imagery. International Journal of Psychophysiology 61(2), 167–178 (2006)
12. Raman, C.V.: On some indian stringed instruments. Proc. Indian Assoc. Cultiv. Sci. 7, 29–33 (1921)
13. Sengupta, R., Dey, N., Datta, A.K., Ghosh, D.: Assessment of musical quality of tanpura by fractal-dimensional analysis. Fractals 13(3), 245–252 (2005)
14. Sengupta, R., Dey, N., Nag, D., Datta, A.K., Parui, S.K.: Objective evaluation of tanpura from the sound signals using spectral features. Journal of ITC Sangeet Research Academy 18 (2004)
15. Sundberg, J.: Phonatory vibrations in singers: A critical review. Music Perception: An Interdisciplinary Journal 9(3), 361–381 (1992)
16. Thurman, L., Welch, G., Theimer, A., Klitzk, C.: Addressing vocal register discrepancies: An alternative, science-based theory of register phenomena. In: Second International Conference, The Physiology and Acoustics of Singing, pp. 4–6. National Center for Voice and Speech (2004)
17. Verrillo, R.T.: Vibration sensation in humans. Music Perception. An Interdisciplinary Journal 9(3), 281–302 (1992)
18. Wackermann, J., Allefeld, C.: State space representation and global descriptors of brain electrical activity. In: Electrical Neuroimaging, pp. 191–214. Cambridge University Press (2009)
19. Wackermann, J., Allefeld, C.: On the meaning and interpretation of global descriptors of brain electrical activity. Including a reply to X. Pei et al. Int. J. Psychophysiol. 64(2), 199–210 (2007)

Musical Instrument Identification Based on New Boosting Algorithm with Probabilistic Decisions

Jun Wu and Shigeki Sagayama

The University of Tokyo, Tokyo 113–8656, Japan
{wu,sagayama}@hil.t.u-tokyo.ac.jp

Abstract. Musical Instrument Identification research is an important problem in Music Information Retrieval (MIR) in which most of the research going on now is using signal processing method. In this paper, at first a model that uses harmonic structured Gaussian mixture for modeling instrument is described and EM algorithm is used to estimate parameters in the model. Therefore features such as Harmonic Temporal Timbre Energy Ratio (HTTER) and Harmonic Temporal Timbre Envelope Similarity (HTTES) are generated from the model. To utilize the features efficiently, a new boosting algorithm based on Probabilistic Decisions is proposed for musical instrument identification. In contrast to the conventional boosting algorithm, which uses a deterministic decision method during the iterations and which does not consider the noise in the data set sufficiently, the new boosting algorithm is proposed to use probabilistic decisions for every hypothesis at the iterations of the boosting scheme, selecting the data events from a dataset, and then combines them. It improves the musical instrument classifier without using boosting approach and the conventional boosting algorithm significantly, which was proved by the experimental.

Keywords: Music Information Retrieval, Musical instrument identification, boosting algorithm, classifier.

1   Introduction

The Music Instrument Identification research is an important problem in MIR. It has both scientific and practical applications. Although it has been considered as difficult problem, some approaches dealing with single instrument identification have recently been developed such as using Cepstral coefficient [1], Temporal features [2], Spectral features [3]. For more difficult problem which is to identify the multi-instrumental polyphonic music, some previous research has been done such as using frequency component adaptation with given correct F0s [4], using Missing feature theory with given correct F0s [5] and using feature weighting to minimize influence of sound overlaps with given correct F0s [6]. However, all of these researches need to have given correct F0 as the basic condition while in real application the correct F0 is not given actually.

We have developed a method for multipitch analysis called Harmonic-Temporal Clustering (HTC) [7] to decompose the spectral energy of the signal in the time-frequency

S. Ystad et al. (Eds.): CMMR/FRSM 2011, LNCS 7172, pp. 66–78, 2012.

domain into acoustic events, which are modeled using acoustic object models with a harmonic and temporal 2-dimensional structure. Unlike conventional frame-wise approaches such as [8,9], HTC deals with the harmonic and temporal structures in both time and frequency directions simultaneously and shows high performance. Then a model named Harmonic-Temporal-Timbral Clustering (HTTC) for the analysis of single channel audio signal of multi-instrument polyphonic music to estimate the pitch, onset timing, power and duration of all the acoustic events was proposed [10]. However, this unsupervised classification approach did not promise high accuracy for identification of musical instruments. For using supervised approach, AdaBoost algorithm is often used by researchers for Music Information Retrieval because it is the most famous boosting algorithm [11,12,13,14,15,16].

However, in the case of musical instrument identification, AdaBoost may not be the most suitable approach because it uses a deterministic decision method during the iterations. But actually the decision for musical instrument in the model is probabilistic. Therefore, a new boosting algorithm is proposed in this paper. The new boosting algorithm uses probabilistic decisions for every hypothesis at the iterations of the boosting scheme, selecting the data events from a dataset, and then combines them. It considers more about the noise in the data set and deals with it efficiently.

At first a model that uses harmonic structured Gaussian mixture for modeling instrument is described in section 2. The model begins with a formulation based on the clustering principle using a harmonic structured Gaussian mixture cluster model in order to try to directly estimate each mean parameter, the pitch to model an observed short-time power spectrum. The Harmonic Temporal Timbre Energy Ratio (HTTER) and Harmonic Temporal Timbre Envelope Similarity (HTTES) features are defined to identify the musical instruments within the music. In section 3, the new boosting algorithm is introduced. In section 4, the experimental results are demonstrated. The proposed algorithm was intuitive and efficient for solving the musical instrument identification problem. At last, the conclusion is made in section 5.

2   Feature Extraction

The observed power spectrogram time series $W(x;t)$ of a music acoustic signal is assumed to be generated as the sum of the spectral energy corresponding to acoustic source events performed with different onset times, pitches, powers and durations and which belong to an unknown timbre category, where x is log-frequency and t is time. The model tries to approximate the power spectrogram as well as possible as the sum of K parametric source models $q_k(x, t; \theta)$ modeling the power spectrogram of K "objects" each with its own contour and harmonic-temporal structure (see Fig 1).

To be more intuitive, we may think each source model $q_k(x, t; \theta)$ to be the model for a single note in the music. So it is composed of the fundamental partial and frequency partials. To approximate the source model $q_k(x, t; \theta)$ as close as possible to the spectrogram in the real music by a meaningful parameter characterized model is important. Given the pitch contour $\mu_k(t)$ in kth HTC source model, the contour of the nth partial is $\mu_k(t) + \log(n)$ (see Fig 2).

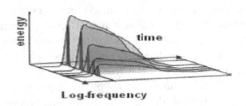

Fig. 1. Profile of the kth HTC source model $q_k(x, t; \theta)$

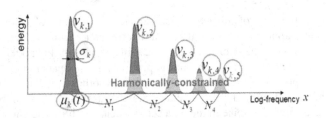

Fig. 2. Cutting plane of $q_k(x, t; \theta)$ at time t

The harmonic component number or the most suitable partial number is different according to different instruments.

The normalized energy density of the nth partial in the kth HTC source model can be assumed to be a multiplication of the power envelope of the nth partial $U_{k,n}(t)$ and the Gaussian distribution centered at $\mu_k(t) + \log(n)$:

$$U_{k,n}(t) \times \frac{v_{k,n}}{\sqrt{2\pi}\sigma_k} e^{-(x-\mu_k(t)-\log(n))^2/2\sigma_k^2} \quad n = 1, ..., N \tag{1}$$

Satisfying $\forall k, \sum_n v_{k,n} = 1$.

Since we do not know in advance what the sources are, it is important to introduce as generic a model as possible for modeling the power envelope function. Therefore we should choose a function that is temporally continuous, nonnegative, having a time spread from minus to plus infinity (assuming the Gabor-wavelet basis as the mother wavelet) and adaptable to various curves. To come up with a function satisfying all these requirements, we let the frequency spread of each harmonic component be approximated by a Gaussian distribution function when the spectra are obtained by the wavelet transform (constant Q transform) using Gabor wavelet basis function. Denote $U_{k,n}(t)$ as the power envelope of the nth partial:

$$U_{k,n}(t) = \sum_{\forall y} \frac{u_{k,n,y}}{\sqrt{2\pi\phi_{k,n}^2}} exp\left\{-\frac{(t-\tau_k-y\phi_{k,n,y})^2}{2\phi_{k,n}^2}\right\} \tag{2}$$

τ_k is the center of the forefront Gaussian, which is considered as an onset time estimate, $u_{k,n,y}$ is the weight parameter for each kernel, which allows the function to have variable shapes for each frequency partial (see Fig 3).

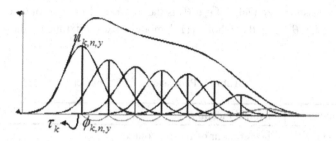

Fig. 3. Power envelope function $U_{k,n}(t)$ at frequency x

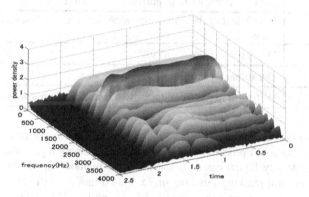

Fig. 4. Power spectrogram of oboe sound

$u_{k,n,y}$ should be normalized to satisfy $\forall k, \forall y: \sum_y u_{k,n,y}(x,t) = 1$. Fig 4 shows the power spectrogram of oboe sound. The three axes are frequency, time and power density respectively. From the figure we can see that the envelope of each partial is different and has different information although there is also relationship between the partials. To approximate the envelope of each specific partial, the proposed model is actually estimating the parameters for each partial even in the same source model $q_k(x,t;\theta)$.

The source models $q_k(x,t;\theta)$ are expressed as a mixture of Gaussian mixture model (GMM) with constraints on the kernel distributions: supposing that there is harmonicity with N partials modeled in the frequency direction, and the power envelope is described using Y kernel distribution in the time direction, which is shown in Fig 2 and Fig 3. The source model can be written in the form:

$$q_k(x,t;\theta) \sum_n \sum_y S_{k,n,y}(x,t;\theta) \tag{3}$$

And the Kernel distribution can be written in the form:

$$S_{k,n,y}(x,t;\theta) = \frac{w_k v_{k,n} u_{k,n,y}}{2\pi \delta_k \emptyset_k} e^{-\frac{(x-\mu_k(t)-\log(n))^2}{2\sigma_k^2} - \frac{(t-\tau_k-y\emptyset_{k,n})^2}{2\phi_{k,n,y}^2}} \tag{4}$$

Therefore the source model $q_k(x,t;\theta)$ is the mixture of mixture of Gaussian distribution $S_{k,n,y}(x,t;\theta)$ and the whole HTC model is the mixture of the source model $q_k(x,t;\theta)$.

Table 1. Parameters of HTC model

Parameter	Physical meaning
$\mu_k(t)$	Pitch contour of the kth source
w_k	Energy of the kth source
$v_{k,n}$	Relative energy of nth partial in kth source
$u_{k,n,y}$	Coefficient of the power envelope function of kth source, nth partial, yth kernel
τ_k	Onset time
$Y\phi_k$	Duration (Y is constant)
σ_k	Diffusion in the frequency direction of the harmonics

The problem becomes how to estimate the parameters of the source model. The proposed algorithm uses EM procedure for the parameter estimation procedure. We assume that the energy density $W(x;t)$ has an unknown fuzzy membership to the kth source, introduced as a spectral masking function $m_k(x,t)$. To minimize the difference between the observed power spectrogram time series $W(x;t)$ and the HTC model $\sum_k q_k(x,t;\theta)$, we use the Kullback–Leibler (KL) divergence as the global cost function.

$$J \sum_k \iint_D m_k(x,t)W(x;t)\log\frac{m_k(x,t)W(x;t)}{q_k(x,t;\theta)} \tag{5}$$

Satisfying with:

$$\forall x, \forall t, \sum_k m_k(x,t) = 1, 0 < m_k(x,t) < 1.$$

Then the problem is regarded as the minimization of (5).

The membership degree $m_k(x,t)$ (spectral masking function) of kth source/stream can be considered to be the weight of the kth source model in the whole spectrogram model. It is unknown at the beginning and need to be estimated. On the other hand, the spectrogram of the kth source can be modeled by a function $q_k(x,t;\theta)$, where θ is the set of model parameters. They are also unknown variables. The proposed model works by using EM algorithm for iteratively updating of: E-step: $m_k(x,t)$ with θ fixed and M-step: θ with $m_k(x,t)$ fixed.

The kth source is composed of fundamental partial and frequency partials. We use another masking function $m_{k,n,y}(x,t)$ that decomposes the kth partitioned cluster $m_k(x,t)W(x;t)$ into the {n,y}th subcluster. Therefore $m_{k,n,y}(x,t)$ can be considered to be the weight of each Gaussian distribution of the kth source model. We use the Jensen's inequality for the cost function and derive the following function:

$$J_k \triangleq \iint_D m_k(x,t)W(x,t)\log\frac{m_k(x,t)W(x,t)}{\sum_{n,y} S_{k,n,y}(x,t;\theta)}\,dxdt \leq J_k^+ \triangleq$$
$$\sum_{n,y}\iint_D m_k(x,t)m_{k,n,y}(x,t)W(x,t)\log\frac{m_k(x,t)m_{k,n,y}(x,t)W(x,t)}{S_{k,n,y}(x,t;\theta)}\,dxdt \qquad (6)$$

The equality holds when

$$m_{k,n,y}(x,t) = \frac{S_{k,n,y}(x,t;\theta)}{\sum_n \sum_y S_{k,n,y}(x,t;\theta)} \qquad (7)$$

Satisfying with:

$$\forall k, \sum_n \sum_y m_{k,n,y}(x,t) = 1.$$
$$\forall n, \forall y, 0 < m_{k,n,y}(x,t) < 1.$$

The E-step is realized by the following equation.

$$m_k(x,t)m_{k,n,y}(x,t) = \frac{S_{k,n,y}(x,t;\theta)}{\sum_k \sum_n \sum_y S_{k,n,y}(x,t;\theta)} \qquad (8)$$

The M-step can be realized by the iteration of the update the parameters depending on each acoustic object (represented in Table 1).

$$\begin{cases} a = \sum_n \sum_y \iint_D y(t-\tau_k)l_{k,n,y}(x,t)dxdt \\ b = \sum_n \sum_y \iint_D (t-\tau_k)^2 l_{k,n,y}(x,t)dxdt \end{cases} \qquad (9)$$

$$\phi_k^{(i)} = \frac{-a+\left(a^2+4b\omega_k^{(i)}\right)^{1/2}}{2\omega_k^{(i)}} \qquad (10)$$

$$u_{k,n,y}^{(i)} = \frac{1}{d_u+w_k^{(i)}}\left(d_u\bar{u}_{k,y} + \iint_D l_{k,n,y}(x,t)dxdt\right) \qquad (11)$$

$$\sigma_k^{(i)} = \frac{1}{w_k^{(i)}}\sum_{n,y}\iint_D \left(x-\mu_{k0}^{(i)}-\log(n)\right)^2 m_{k,n,y}^{(i)}(x,t)W(x,t) \qquad (12)$$

$$\tau_k^{(i)} = \frac{1}{w_k^{(i)}}\sum_{n,y}\iint_D \left(t-y\phi_k^{(i-1)}\right)l_{k,n,y}^{(i)}(x,t)dxdt \qquad (13)$$

$$v_{k,n}^{(i)} = \frac{1}{d_v+w_k^{(i)}}\left(d_v\bar{v}_n + \sum_y \iint_D l_{k,n,y}^{(i)}(x,t)dxdt\right) \qquad (14)$$

$$w_k^{(i)} = \sum_{n,y}\iint_D l_{k,n,y}^{(i)}(x,t)dxdt \qquad (15)$$

$$l_{k,n,y}^{(i)}(x,t) = m_k^{(i)}(x,t)m_{k,n,y}^{(i)}(x,t)W(x,t) \qquad (16)$$

Since each step of this update rule can reduce the objective function (6) successfully, the iteration of these update steps can yield to locally optimal parameters. For length purposes, we skip here the details of the derivation of update equations for each parameter, which can be obtained analytically by the combination of an undetermined multipliers Lagrange's method.

The most difficult problem of identifying the musical instruments is that some parts of different signals are overlapped. For solving this problem, we need to find the different instruments' patterns and identify them based on the multi-instrument identification information. Therefore we can consider that the difference in timbre is derived from the harmonic temporal timbre energy ratio and harmonic temporal timbre envelope similarity, and that the shapes of acoustic events classified into the same timbre category should look alike regardless of the pitch, power, onset timing and duration. We define the Harmonic Temporal Timbre Energy Ratio (HTTER) and Harmonic Temporal Timbre Envelope Similarity (HTTES). HTTER defines the features of the energy ratio of the harmonic temporal timbres. HTTES defines the difference between the envelope shapes of the harmonic temporal timbres.

$$HTTER_{k,n,n'} = \frac{\sum_y S_{k,n,y}(x,t;\theta)}{\sum_y S_{k,n',y}(x,t;\theta)} \tag{17}$$

$$HTTES_{k,n,n'} = \int \left(U_{k,n}(t) log \frac{U_{k,n}(t)}{U_{k,n'}(t)} \right) dt + \int \left(U_{k,n'}(t) log \frac{U_{k,n'}(t)}{U_{k,n}(t)} \right) dt \tag{18}$$

3   New Boosting Algorithm for Instrument Identification

The boosting algorithms use multiple classifiers to improve classification performance. Each classifier provides a solution for the testing data. The combination of these classifiers may provide a superior solution than the one provided by any single classifier.

The primary benefit of using boosting systems is the reduction of variance and increase in confidence of the decision because there are many random variations in a given classifier model such as different training data or different initializations. The decision obtained by any given classifier may be different from each other even if the model structure is kept constant. Therefore, combining the outputs of several such classifiers by some kind of means may reduce the risk of selecting a poorly performing classifier. As the most popular Boosting method, AdaBoost uses distribution of weights over the training events and, at successive iterations, the weight of misclassified events is changed according to the accuracy of the classifier, forcing the weak learner to focus on the hard events in the training set. However, several problems are also discovered such as problems that training event has contained many noise data, event number is not enough to learn, etc which actually exist in musical instrument identification task. In these cases AdaBoost does not produce sufficiently stable results.

To cope with these problems, the new boosting algorithm based on probabilistic decisions is proposed instead of the original AdaBoost which uses a deterministic decision method during the iterations. In the original algorithm, the decision for every classifier is just one class. For example, if the classification result can be guitar, piano and oboe, then the decision for every classifier is just guitar or piano or oboe. However, actually, there can be probability for the classifier. For example, the predicted class of instrument can be guitar (50%), piano (30%) and oboe (20%). For one single classifier the improvement may be small but it may make larger improvement for ensemble algorithm because there are many classifiers to combine in this kind of algorithm. In this way, after classifier ensemble the result could be more precise. We use the classification algorithm as a weak learner in the new boosting algorithm. The update rule reduces the probability assigned to those events on which the hypothesis makes good predictions and increases the probability of the events on which the prediction is poor.

New Boosting Algorithm:

   Step 1.   Initially assign weights $w = \{w_j = 1/N \mid j=1, 2, ...,N\}$ to be the distribution of weights over the N training events.

   Step 2.   Choose k to be the number of the boosting rounds.

   For i=1 to T do:

   Step 3.   Generate the new classifier using data sets. Get back a sis $h_t: X \rightarrow Y$, we set M_{ty} to be the probability of h_t for every $y \in Y$, Y is the output space.

   Step 4.   Compute the error rate ε_t as

   For $j=1$ to N do

   If $y_i \neq h_t$

   $E_j = w(x_j) \cdot M_{ty}(x_j)$

   If $y_i = h_t$

   $E_j = w(x_j) \cdot (1 - M_{ty}(x_j))$

   End for

   $\varepsilon_i = \frac{1}{N}\sum_{j=1}^{N} E_j$

   Step 5.   If $\varepsilon_i > \frac{1}{2}$,

   then set $w = \{w_j = \frac{1}{N} \mid j = 1, 2, ..., N\}$ and go back to step 3.

   Step 6. $\alpha_i = \frac{1}{2}log((1 - \varepsilon_i)/\varepsilon_i)$

   Step 7.   For each x_j

   If $y_i \neq f_i(x_j)$

   Then $w_{i+1}(x_j) = w_i(x_j)/Z_j \cdot exp(\alpha_i)$

   If $y_i = f_i(x_j)$

   Then $w_{i+1}(x_j) = w_i(x_j)/Z_j \cdot exp(-\alpha_i)$

   End for

   End for

   Step 8. $f_{FINAL}(x) = argmax_{y \in Y} \sum_{j=1}^{T} \alpha_i(x)M_{jy}(x)$

Let $\{(x_j, y_j)| j=1,2,...,N\}$ denote a set of N training examples. New AdaBoost calls a given weak classifier repeatedly in a series of Rounds $t=1, 2,...,$T. The main idea of the algorithm is to maintain a distribution or set of weights over the training set. The weight of this distribution on training example j on round I is denoted as $w_i(x_j)$. Initially, all weights are set equally, but after each round, the weights of incorrectly classified examples are increased so that the weak learner is forced to focus on the examples which are more difficult to classify in the training set. The weak learner's job is to find a weak hypothesis f_i appropriate for the distribution w_i. The distribution is obtained by normalizing a set of weights assigned to each event based on the classification performance of the classifiers on that event (Step 1).

Step 2 chose the number of the boosting rounds. The larger number of iteration may give higher accuracy but cost more time.

In this paper the decision tree classifier capable of giving probabilistic decision for every hypothesis is used. We see M_{ty} to be the probability of h_t for every $y \in Y$ while Y is the output space. Then generate the new classifier using data selected form the data set and get back a hypothesis h_t (Step 3).

The goodness of a weak hypothesis is measured by its error rate. The importance of a base classifier f_i depends on its error rate, which is defined as in Step 4:

$$\text{If} \quad y_i \neq h_t$$
$$E_j = w(x_j) \cdot M_{ty}(x_j)$$
$$\text{If} \quad y_i = h_t$$
$$E_j = w(x_j) \cdot (1 - M_{ty}(x_j))$$

For example, if it is guitar, means $y_i=$ guitar. For hypothesis h_t, the probabilistic decision is guitar (50%), piano (30%) and oboe (20%). Then, h_t=guitar, and $M_{t(guitar)}$=0.5, $M_{t(piano)}$=0.3, $M_{t(oboe)}$=0.2. After calculating all of the training data, the error rate ε_i is computed by using $\varepsilon_i = \frac{1}{N}\sum_{j=1}^{N} E_j$

If $\varepsilon_i > 1/2$, current f_i is discarded, a new training subset is selected and a new f_i is generated (Step 5).

The importance of a classifier f_i is given by the following parameter (Step 6)

$$\alpha_i = \frac{1}{2}\log\left(\frac{1 - \varepsilon_i}{\varepsilon_i}\right)$$

The α_i parameter is also used to update the weight of the training samples. To illustrate, let $w_i(x_j)$ denote the weight assigned to example (x_j, y_j) during the ith boosting round. The weight update mechanism is given by the following equations (Step 7):

$$\text{If} \quad y_i \neq f_i(x_j)$$
$$\text{Then} \quad w_{i+1}(x_j) = w_i(x_j)/Z_j \cdot \exp(\alpha_i)$$
$$\text{If} \quad y_i = f_i(x_j)$$
$$\text{Then} \quad w_{i+1}(x_j) = w_i(x_j)/Z_j \cdot \exp(-\alpha_i)$$

Where Z_j is the normalization factor which is used to ensure that $\sum_j w_{i+1}(x_j) = 1$. The weight update mechanism increases the weights of incorrectly classified examples and decreases the weights of those correctly classified examples. The final hypothesis $f_{FINAL}(x)$ is a weighted majority vote of the T weak hypotheses where $\alpha_i(x)$ is the weight assigned to hypothesis h_t and $M_{jy}(x)$ is the probability of h_t for every y ∈ Y (Step 8).

4   Experiments

To evaluate the proposed algorithm, we did the experiments with the real performed music signals chosen from the RWC music database [17]. Since the RWC database also includes the MIDI files associated with each real-performed music signal data, we will evaluate the accuracy by comparing the estimated fundamental frequency and the MIDI files.

To show it more intuitively, we chose a piece of music file played by piano music named RM-J012 in RWC database as the input data. The spectrogram of the input data was shown in Fig 5. Fig 6 showed the result of proposed algorithm for recognizing it. The result was compared with the MIDI data which was in the left part of Fig 6. In MIDI figure, the piano part is represented by deep grey lines while the flute part is represented by light grey lines. In the estimated F0 which was in the right part of Fig 6, the piano part is represented by deep grey lines while the flute part is represented by light grey lines. From the result we can prove that the proposed algorithm is quite promising and feasible.

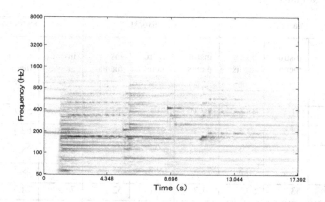

Fig. 5. Spectrogram of the input music file RM-J002

We tested the proposed musical instrument identification algorithm with 271 music instrument pieces (including 6 instruments: 32 altosax pieces, 36 guitar pieces, 88 piano pieces, 45 violin pieces, 36 flute pieces and 34 oboe pieces).

Fig. 6. Testing result for RM-J012 (piano+flute)

Ten cross validation is used for training and testing. First we chose the music instrument pieces for training randomly, the rest of the music instrument pieces are combined randomly for testing. We used the model discussed in this paper to generate the HTTER and HTTES as the temporal timbre features for training classifier. In this paper the decision tree classifier designed by Jun Wu, etc [18] is used. This new decision tree classifier derives from the famous C4.5 and develops it to be more powerful in solving some problems. Then we used boosting algorithms for combing the classifiers.

Table 2 shows the accuracies of musical instrument identification by using classifier, AdaBoost, and new boosting algorithm. Accuracy of using just classifier for musical instrument identification is 71.8%, 57.4% and 49.0% respectively for 2 instruments, 3 instruments and 4 instruments. Therefore we used AdaBoost for the same task and got the accuracy of 76.9%, 63.7% and 52.3% while the accuracy of using the new boosting is 79.0%, 71.7% and 54.9% respectively.

Table 2. Accuracies of musical instrument identification by using classifier, AdaBoost, and new boosting algorithm

Instru-ments	classifier			AdaBoost			new boosting algorithm		
	2 instru-ments (%)	3 instru-ments (%)	4 instru-ments (%)	2 instru-ments (%)	3 instru-ments (%)	4 instru-ments (%)	2 instru-ments (%)	3 instru-ments (%)	4 instru-ments (%)
altosax	75.4	51.4	45.6	79.3	53.2	49.7	81.5	55.7	52.4
guitar	71.3	54.5	43.8	75.5	59.4	48.7	78.4	62.4	50.7
piano	82.5	71.8	61.2	88.2	75.9	65.2	89.3	88.7	68.6
violin	72.6	62.4	50.5	78.5	69.2	55.4	79.3	79.5	56.8
flute	64.8	53.8	50.7	71.7	57.1	52.1	74.5	74.3	54.3
oboe	64.3	50.6	42.6	68.2	67.3	42.8	70.8	69.5	46.7
Total accu-racy	71.8	57.4	49.0	76.9	63.7	52.3	79.0	71.7	54.9

5   Conclusion

The proposed model begins with a formulation based on the clustering principle using a harmonic structured Gaussian mixture cluster model in order to try to directly estimate each mean parameter, the pitch to model an observed short-time power spectrum. New features such as Harmonic Temporal Timbre Energy Ratio (HTTER) and Harmonic Temporal Timbre Envelope Similarity (HTTES) are proposed to generate classifier for instrument identification. Then we proposed a new boosting algorithm based on probabilistic decision for solving the instrument identification problem. The proposed new boosting algorithm gave probabilistic decisions for every hypothesis at the iterations of the boosting scheme and then combined them. It uses distribution of weights over the training events and, at successive iterations, the weight of misclassified events is changed according to the accuracy of the classifier, forcing the weak learner to focus on the hard events in the training set. The proposed algorithm was intuitive and efficient for solving the musical instrument identification problem, which was proved by the experiments.

References

1. Brown, R.J.C.: Computer identification of musical instruments using pattern recognition with cepstral coefficients as features. Journal of the Acoustical Society of America 105(3), 1933–1941 (1999)
2. Eronen, A., Klapuri, A.: Musical instrument recognition using cepstral coefficients and temporal features. In: Proceedings of IEEE International Conference on Acoustics, Speech and Signal Processing (ICASSP 2000), Istanbul, Turkey, vol. 2, pp. 753–756 (2000)
3. Agostini, G., Longari, M., Pollastri, E.: Musical instrument timbres classification with spectral features. EURASIP Journal on Applied Signal Processing 2003(1), 5–14 (2003)
4. Kinoshita, T., Sakai, S., Tanaka, H.: Musical sound source identification based on frequency component adaptation. In: Proceedings of IJCAI Workshop on Computational Auditory Scene Analysis (IJCAI-CASA 1999), Stockholm, Sweden, pp. 18–24 (1999)
5. Eggink, J., Brown, G.J.: Application of missing feature theory to the recognition of musical instruments in polyphonic audio. In: Proceedings of International Symposium on Music Information Retrieval (ISMIR 2003), Baltimore, Md, USA (2003)
6. Kitahara, T., Goto, M., Komatani, K., Ogata, T., Okuno, H.G.: Instrument Identification in Polyphonic Music: Feature Weighting to Minimize Influence of Sound Overlaps. EURASIP Journal on Advances in Signal Processing 2007, Article ID 51979, 15 pages (2007)
7. Kameoka, H., Nishimoto, T., Sagayama, S.: A Multipitch Analyzer Based on Harmonic Temporal Structured Clustering. IEEE Trans. on Audio, Speech and Language Processing 15(3), 982–994 (2007)
8. Klapuri, A.: Multiple fundamental frequency estimation based on harmonicity and spectral smoothness. IEEE Trans. Speech and Audio Processing 11(6), 804–816 (2003)
9. Goto, M.: A real-time music-scene-description system: Predominant-F0 estimation for detecting melody and bass lines in real-world audio signals. ISCA J. 43(4), 311–329 (2004)

10. Miyamoto, K., Kameoka, H., Nishimoto, T., Ono, N., Sagayama, S.: Harmonic-Temporal-Timbral Clustering (HTTC) For the Analysis of Multi-instrument Polyphonic Music Signals. In: Proc. of ICASSP, pp. 113–116 (2008)
11. Healy, M., Sourabh, R., Anderson, D.: Effects of Varying Parameters in Asymmetric AdaBoost on the Accuracy of a Cascade Audio Classifier. In: Proceedings of the Southeastern Conference of the Institute of Electrical and Electronics Engineers, pp. 169–172 (2004)
12. Dixon, S., Gouyon, F., Widmer, G.: Towards characterization of music via rhythmic patterns. In: Proceedings of the 5th International Conference on Music Information Retrieval (ISMIR), pp. 509–516 (2004)
13. McKay, C., Fiebrink, R., McEnnis, D., Li, B., Fujinaga, I.: A framework for optimizing music classification. In: Proceedings of the 5th International Conference on Music Information Retrieval (ISMIR), pp. 42–49 (2005)
14. Bergstra, J., Casagrande, N., Erhan, D., Eck, D., Kégl, B.: Aggregate features and AdaBoost for music classification. Machine Learning 65(2-3), 473–484 (2006)
15. Turnbull, D., Lanckriet, G., Pampalk, E., Goto, M.: A Supervised Approach for Detecting Boundaries in Music Using Difference Features and Boosting. In: Proceedings of the 5th International Conference on Music Information Retrieval (ISMIR), pp. 42–49 (2007)
16. Yang, Y., Lin, Y., Su, Y., Chen, H.: Music Emotion Classification: A Regression Approach. In: Proceedings IEEE Int. Conf. Multimedia and Expo. (ICME 2007), pp. 208–211 (2007)
17. Goto, M., Hashiguchi, H., Nishimura, T., Oka, R.: RWC music database: Popular, classical, and jazz music database. In: Proceedings. ISMIR, pp. 287–288 (2002)
18. Wu, J., Kim, Y., Song, C., Lee, W.: A New Classifier to Deal with Incomplete Data. In: The Ninth ACIS International Conference on Software Engineering, Artificial Intelligence, Networking, and Parallel/Distributed Computing (SNPD 2008), Thailand, pp. 105–110 (2008)

Music Genre Classification
Using an Auditory Memory Model

Kristoffer Jensen

ad:mt. Aalborg University Esbjerg, Niels Bohr Vej 8,
6700 Esbjerg, Denmark
krist@create.aau.dk

Abstract. Audio feature estimation is potentially improved by including the auditory short-term memory (STM) model. A new paradigm of audio feature estimation is obtained by adding the influence of notes in the STM. These notes are identified using the directional spectral flux, and the spectral content that is increased by the new note is added to the STM. The STM is exponentially fading with time span and number of elements, and each note only belongs to the STM for a limited time. Initial investigations regarding the behavior of the STM shows promising results, and an initial experiment with sensory dissonance has been undertaken with good results. The parameters obtained from the auditory memory model, along with the dissonance measure, are shown here to be of interest in music genre classification.

Keywords: dissonance, note detection, memory model, music classification.

1   Introduction

Audio feature extraction is useful in many situations, from digital musical instruments to music playback systems, from speech recognition to music information retrieval. This paper proposes to incorporate a high-level memory model in the feature extraction, in order to improve the estimation of the feature.

Psychologists consider memory to be the process by which we encode, store, and retrieve information. The understanding of the memory model was improved due to the modal model [1]. In this model, the stimuli first enter the sensory system, and then the short-term memory (STM), which has a limited time-span and through rehearsal, it can then enter the long-term memory (LTM). According to [2], stimuli reach STM and LTM simultaneously, while according to [3], stimuli go through LTM to reach STM. As only the STM is modeled here, it is not essential how stimuli reach the STM.

The STM paradigm was later replaced by the working memory [4] to put more emphasis on the active behavior of the STM. This working memory model consists of a central executive and three slave systems: the phonological loop, the visuo/spatial sketchpad, and the episodic buffer [5]. The capacity of the working memory was determined to be 7±2 [6]. Most indicators show the major form of encoding in the STM is acoustic ([7], p289), although this may be more a result of the process

S. Ystad et al. (Eds.): CMMR/FRSM 2011, LNCS 7172, pp. 79–88, 2012.
© Springer-Verlag Berlin Heidelberg 2012

encountered than of the property of the STM. The working memory model puts emphasis on several independent modules, and that the STM is associated with the attention processes.

The sensory store is approximately 250-ms long [8]. During the sensory store, the sound is subject to perceptual processing. It does not seem to be overwhelming evidence for the sensory store to be available for cognitive processing and it is not modeled further here. It seems to be a reason for filtering, i.e., short sounds are not propagated into the STM.

With the increasing amount of music files on personal computers, the necessity of assisting users choosing among the songs has arisen. Such a choice can be random (Shuffle play), using automatic playlist generation, or based on a degree of similarity between songs. Playlist generation can be done based on audio features [9], for instance based on one song, or audio input, as in the query-by-humming systems [10,11,12]. Playlist generation can also be based on meta-data [13] and collaborative filtering.

This paper presents the auditory memory model in Sec. 2. The identification of auditory chunks and the details of the calculation of the auditory memory model content, along with the improved calculation of the sensory dissonance, are presented in Sec. 3. Sec. 4 focuses on how the auditory memory model parameters and the improved sensory dissonance may improve music genre classification.

2 Memory Models

Humans use memory to encode, store and retrieve information. Auditory information enters the brain through the auditory system and reaches the sensory store first. If the information is not reinforced, it is fading. [7] gives an overview of the mechanisms of fading in the STM that include decay (the mental representation breaks down over time), displacement (STM has limited capacity, thus old stimuli are replaced by new stimuli), and interference (learning is affected by context). Apparently, for practical reasons, the limited capacity (7 ± 2 [6]) is the main cause of memory purging in the STM. However, if no new stimulus is entered, the STM is here modeled to have a limited time span (the stimuli is decaying) [1]. This is modeled according to the activation model [14], in which the decay is modeled as,

$$A_{decay} = 1 - d \ln(t+1),\tag{1}$$

where A_{decay} is the activation decay and $d=0.5$, and the time $t>0$ is measured in seconds.

In order to ensure a homogenous model, the limited capacity of the STM is modeled in a similar way,

$$A_{displacement} = 1 - d \ln(N_c).\tag{2}$$

N_c is the number of chunks currently active in the STM. The total activation strength of an acoustic chunk is then,

$$A = A_{decay} + A_{displacement},\tag{3}$$

and the chunk is propagated to the auditory processing if $A>0$ or otherwise purged from the STM.

3   Encoding in Memory Models

The feature extraction is typically done using overlapping frames and extracting the relevant audio features in each frame, as detailed for the sensory dissonance below. In addition to this, it is shown how the sensory dissonance estimation can be improved by the inclusion of the information in the auditory memory.

3.1   Chunks in the Auditory Memory

In order to encore the auditory chunks in the memory model and propagate them to the subsequent processing, a method for separating auditory streams is required. [15] gives a review of features useful for separating auditory streams that include fundamental frequency, onset times, contrast to previous sounds, correlated changes in amplitude or frequency, and sound location. A useful algorithm for simulating most of these features is the directional perceptual spectral flux [16],

$$psf_+^t = \sum_{\left(a_k^t - a_k^{t-1}\right)>0} w_k \left(a_k^t - a_k^{t-1}\right), \tag{4}$$

where a_k is the magnitude spectrum (N point FFT) and w_k is the frequency weight according to the ISO 226 standard, in order to simulate the outer and middle ear filtering. t is the current time frame, and $t-1$ is the previous time frame. If k is the subset of all FFT bins that satisfy either $a^t-a^{t-1}>0$ or $a^t-a^{t-1}<0$, the directional spectral flux is obtained. The positive spectral flux (psf_+) is a measure of auditory onset, while the negative spectral flux, psf_-, is a measure of auditory offset. The chunk is activated when a significant level is found in psf_+. This allows the identification of the content of the auditory chunk within the sensory store time limit. By calculating the directional spectral flux, auditory events that are surrounded by concurrent auditory events can be encoded, assuming they do not start and end at the same time as the current auditory event. In order to identify the spectrum of a new note, this is calculated as the difference between the spectrums just after and just before the onset time t_0,

$$a_n = a^{t_0+T} - a^{t_0-T}. \tag{5}$$

T is set to 0.2 seconds. The peaks of the perceptual spectral flux are found by identifying peaks that are higher than the mean and the max of the psf_+ in the surrounding time. The mean weight $W_{mean}=0.1$, and the mean is taken in the range $R_{mean}=1.5$ seconds, while $W_{max}=0.9$, and $R_{max}=0.9$ seconds. The psf_+ for Stan Getz – First Song (for Ruth) is shown together with the spectrogram in figure 1.

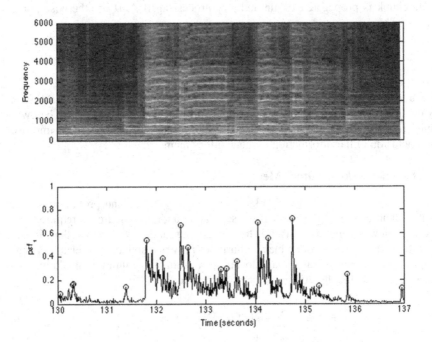

Fig. 1. Spectrogram (top) and positive perceptual spectral flux (bottom) for Stan Getz - First song (for Ruth) (excerpt). Identified psf_+ peaks are indicated with empty circles.

As can be seen, the psf_+ peak detector captures many of the onsets, and it is therefore used as a note detector in this work. Each time the peak detector indicates a peak a new note is inserted into the memory model. When the note has a weight (activation strength), (3) below zero, it is purged from the STM.

3.2 Auditory Memory Content

In order to test the validity of the STM memory model and the note detection, a simulation was made on the Stan Getz – First Song (for Ruth) song. Note onsets were obtained according to (5) and new spectral content according to (4) is inserted into the STM for each new note. The note activation strength is calculated according to (3) and notes are purged when $A<0$. Two measures were obtained; the number of elements in the STM and the time span of the STM, taken as the time the first element have been in the STM. These measures are calculated for each (quantized) time step. The results are shown in figure 2. The song gives 11.43 elements on average (standard deviation 1.60) and an average duration of 3.02 seconds (standard deviation 0.50). The number of elements is above the 7±2 rule of Miller [6]. However, the elements (notes) that have been in the STM model for some time would have a low weight and very little influence. The time span of 3 seconds is a reasonable number, given that the STM has a span of 3-5 seconds according to Snyder [3].

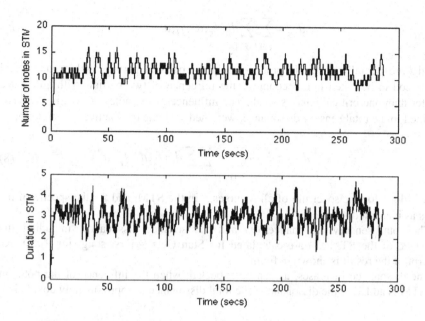

Fig. 2. Number of elements in the STM (top) and duration of STM (bottom) for Stan Getz - First song (for Ruth)

3.3   Sensory Dissonance

The sensory dissonance is here measured as the sum of the beatings over different auditory filters. It is created when two pure tones are creating beatings in the auditory system. If the beating is lower than one critical band, it adds to the total sensory dissonance, otherwise the beating disappears, and two individual tones appear instead. The sensory dissonance is additive [17], meaning that if different partials are causing beating in different critical bands, then each beating is added to the total sensory dissonance. The sensory dissonance is calculated as [18],

$$d_0 = a_1 a_2 \left(e^{\frac{f_1-f_2}{0.0245 f_1 + 22.57}} - e^{\frac{f_1-f_2}{0.015 f_1 + 13.74}} \right), \tag{6}$$

for two pure tones (partials) with frequencies f_1 and f_2 and amplitudes a_1 and a_2, and where $f_1 < f_2$.

The partials to take into account in (6) are the partials in the current frame, and those of the auditory chunks in the STM. Thus, in order to calculate the total STM dissonance, first the total dissonance of the current frame is calculated for all N_p partials as,

$$d_{tot} = \sum_{k=1}^{N_p} \sum_{l>k+1}^{N_p} d_0(f_k, a_k, f_l, a_l). \tag{7}$$

k and l are partial indexes. In practice, only the pairs of partials within one critical band need to be taken into account, as the influence of two partials with a distance greater than one critical band is weak. The influence of the notes present in the STM is added to the total sensory dissonance, weighted with the total activation strength,

$$d_{stm} = d_{tot} + \sum_{n=1}^{N_n} A^n \sum_k \sum_l d_0(f_k, a_k, f_l^n, a_l^n). \tag{8}$$

This is done for the spectrum of all N_n notes n in the STM, and for the spectra of the notes as identified in (5).

The total sensory dissonance (7) and the sensory dissonance, including the influence of the STM (8) are calculated for Stan Getz – First song (for Ruth). An excerpt of the result is shown in figure 3.

The dissonance increases, as can be expected, when the influence of the notes in the STM is added to the dissonance. The total dissonance is approximately doubled.

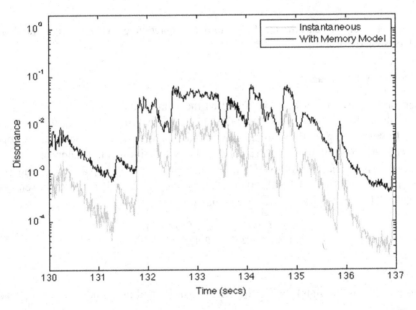

Fig. 3. Instantaneous (eq. 7) and total (eq. 8) sensory dissonance for Stan Getz - First song (for Ruth) (excerpt)

4   Experiment

Music genre classification is an important area of research today. Much research is done in this field using audio features [9], meta-data [13], or collaborative filtering.

The general idea is that automatic genre classification may assist users in selecting the music. While music audio information (timbre, rhythm, melody/chords, etc) may be of interest in the automatic genre classification, often genres are defined by other information such as meta-data, etc. Nonetheless, audio features may still be of assistance in this field.

This work presents initial findings in the use of the features of the auditory memory model (number of elements, duration, dissonance) on a medium size music database. This database, which consists of 1320 songs in 11 different genres, was first used in [19]. The auditory memory model features have been calculated for all songs, and the resulting values are shown in figure 4.

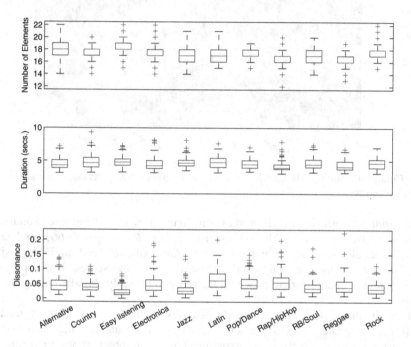

Fig. 4. Boxplot of number of element, duration and dissonance of 11 genres of music

It is clear that there are variations in these features between the different genres. For instance, *easy listening* have relatively many events, while *rap/hiphop* and *reggae* have fewer. *Country, easy listening* and *latin* have longer durations in the auditory memory. *Easy listening* and *jazz* have low dissonance while *latin* and *rap/hiphop* have high dissonance.

An initial experiment has been performed to evaluate the capacity of these features to classify the music into these 11 genres. The classification is done on the mean, max and standard deviation of the number of elements, duration, and dissonance. It is done using discriminant analysis assuming normal data by fitting multivariate densities with covariance estimates.

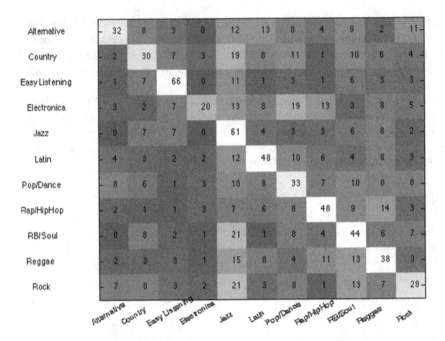

Fig. 5. Confusion matrix of the classification of the 11 genres. The percentages are shown in each classification.

The resulting confusion matrix is shown in figure 5. Some genres give promising results, in particular genres with low dissonance; *easy listening* with 66% and *jazz* with 61%, but also genres with high dissonance; *latin* with 48% and *rap/hiphop* with 48%. *Electronica*, *rock*, *country*, and *pop/dance* have low scores. Perhaps these genres contain too many variations within the genre to be easily classified using audio features.

All in all, the classification using the features of the auditory memory model classifies approximately 40% of the songs correctly. [12] found that humans classify approximately 57% correctly in an experiment using a subset of the same music collection. It is therefore seen as a very promising result to obtain 40% correct song identification using only the auditory memory model features.

5   Conclusion

Audio features are difficult to evaluate objectively in that the comparison with human perception is rendered more difficult by the necessary interpretation of the sensory perception by human subjects. One possible solution to this mismatch is to improve the audio feature estimation in a way so that it is closer to human auditory perception. This is attempted in this work by the inclusion of an auditory short-term memory module. New notes are identified using the perceptual spectral flux and inserted in the STM, and assigned with an activation strength that is exponentially decreasing with time and the number of elements in the STM. When it is below zero, the note is purged from the STM.

An initial experiment shows that the STM behaves in a plausible way, i.e. it has an appropriate number of notes and time span, as compared to the literature.

The STM model has been used in the calculation of the sensory dissonance. When comparing the instantaneous dissonance with the total dissonance obtained by adding the dissonance between the current frame and the notes in the STM, the total dissonance has a higher mean (approximately the double) as could be expected.

The inclusion of a memory model in the estimation of audio features certainly makes sense from a theoretical point of view and it also gave plausible values in an initial experiment.

An experiment using the auditory memory model (number of elements, duration in memory, and dissonance) shows promising results, and it is believed to be a useful inclusion in music information retrieval systems based on auditory features.

References

1. Atkinson, R.C., Shiffrin, R.M.: Human memory: A proposed system and its control processes. In: Spence, K.W., Spence, J.T. (eds.) The Psychology of Learning and Motivation, vol. 2, pp. 89–195. Academic Press, New York (1968)
2. Pashler, H., Carrier, M.: Structures, Processes, and the Flow of Information. In: Bjork, Bjork (eds.) Memory: Handbook of Perception and Cognition, pp. 3–29. Academic Press (1996)
3. Snyder, B.: Music and Memory. An Introduction. The MIT Press, Cambridge (2000)
4. Baddeley, A.D., Hitch, G.: Working memory. In: Bower, G.H. (ed.) The Psychology of Learning and Motivation: Advances in Research and Theory, vol. 8, pp. 47–89. Academic Press, New York (1974)
5. Baddeley, A.D.: The episodic buffer: a new component of working memory? Trends in Cognitive Science 4, 417–423 (2000)
6. Miller, G.A.: The magical number seven plus or minus two: some limits on our capacity for processing information. Psychological Review 63(2), 81–97 (1956)
7. Gross, R.: Psychology: The Science of Mind and Behaviour. Hodder Arnold Publication (2005)
8. Massaro, D., Loftus, G.R.: Sensory and Perceptual Storage. In: Bjork, E.L., Bjork, R.A. (eds.) Memory, pp. 86–99. Academic Press, San Diego (1996)
9. Foote, J.: A similarity measure for automatic audio classification. In: Proceedings AAAI 1997 Spring Symposium on Intelligent Integration and Use of Text, Image, Video, and Audio Corpora, Stanford, Palo Alto, California, USA (1997)
10. McNab, R.J., Smith, L.A., Witten, I.H., Henderson, C.L., Cunningham, S.J.: Towards the digital music library: Tune retrieval from acoustic input. In: Proceedings DL 1996, pp. 11–18 (1996)
11. Rolland, P.Y., Raskinis, G., Ganascia, J.G.: Musical content-based retrieval: an overview of the Melodiscov approach and system. ACM Multimedia 1, 81–84 (1999)
12. Ghias, A., Logan, J., Chamberlin, D., Smith, B.C.: Query by humming - musical information retrieval in an audio database. In: Proceedings Multimedia, pp. 231–236 (2001)
13. Pauws, S., Eggen, B.: PATS: Realization and user evaluation of an automatic playlist generator. In: Proceedings of the 3rd ISMIR, Ircam, France, pp. 222–230 (2002)
14. Anderson, J.R., Lebiere, C.: Atomic components of thought, Hillsdale, NJ (1998)
15. Moore, B.C.J.: Psychology of Hearing. Academy Press (1997)

16. Jensen, K.: Multiple scale music segmentation using rhythm, timbre and harmony. EURASIP Journal on Applied Signal Processing, Special issue on Music Information Retrieval Based on Signal Processing (2007)
17. Plomp, R., Levelt, W.J.M.: Tonal Consonance and Critical Bandwidth. J. Acoust. Soc. Am. 38(4), 548–560 (1965)
18. Sethares, W.: Local consonance and the relationship between timbre and scale. J. Acoust. Soc. Am. 94(3), 1218–1228 (1993)
19. Meng, A.: Temporal feature integration for music organization. Ph.D. dissertation, IMM, Denmark Technical University (2006)

Interactive Music 3.0: Empowering People
to Participate Musically Inside Nightclubs

Yago de Quay

Laboratório Multimédia, FEUP, Universidade do Porto,
Rua Dr. Roberto Frias, s/n 4200-465 Porto, Portugal
yagodequay@gmail.com

Abstract. Nightclubs are powerhouses in western culture for social listening and dancing to music. Here, mostly digital, pre-composed tunes are selected, mixed and played by a person called Disc Jockey. In another digital arena, the internet, a revolution is changing how people connect to each other and making every one a potential vocal agent of an invisible network that is slowly extending beyond their homes. This change is helping improve accessibility, learning, democracy and science, but music—protected by culture of broadcast not participation—remains untouched. This paper explains a project called Interactive Music 3.0 that is revisiting the role of the DJ and experimenting with a multi-disciplinary approach to foster participative musical expression inside nightclubs.

Keywords: Interactive nightclubs, music, dance, motion capture, music information retrieval, mapping.

1 Introduction

We live in a world of user-generated content. Media shared by users from various social media platforms such as Flickr, Facebook, Twitter, and YouTube has become mainstream. Users themselves can create and share plenty of knowledge that is interesting and accurate to a broader audience. In the music industry, more artists are becoming aware of the value of social media with musicians such as Imogen Heap collaborating with her fans on lyrics, remixes, and artwork [1]. All of this is part of the rise of co-creation in innovation; also a product of social interaction whereby users reinterpret and reinvent the meaning of emerging technologies.

Far from being limited to software, data is moving away from centralized computers towards a model of ubiquitous computing. Rich information can be collected from social interaction, but we now see the potential of harnessing the interactions of humans with everyday objects. In this paradigm is a system of standalone microcomputers distributed at all scales throughout daily life that network with each other to accommodate humans to an environment.

Interactive Music 3.0 is a term defined here as a system that generates music using the Web 3.0 approach to making use of, through ubiquitous technology, user activity and algorithmic data management to reach out to an entire network [2]. Previous interactive music works framed the system as the platform in terms of the old centralized, software

S. Ystad et al. (Eds.): CMMR/FRSM 2011, LNCS 7172, pp. 89–97, 2012.

paradigm. Interactive Music 3.0 in contrast, is an online, out-of-the-box software that never sells a package but delivers as a service. There are no scheduled software releases, licensing or sale, just continuous improvement and usage.

Interactive Music 3.0 proposes extending the computer to computer network to human and machine activity to pave the way for exploitation of data capture and communication capabilities to our physical world. If we broaden this network possibilities to disguised, embedded, unsupervised machines we can look forward to a musical system that not only deduces body-sound mappings from interaction but most importantly can connect users across the world to create, share, and combine music and dance in real-time. From this continuous interaction with other people and devices will emerge complex musical systems that can have a profound effect on art as a whole.

This paper will reveal a method for, and the first steps towards, a collaborative method of improvising electronic music through embedded, smart devices by illustrating with two interactive music systems that I developed during my Master's Degree, *Interactive Nightclub* and *Dance Jockey*. The goal of the works presented here was to implement a complete and working system within the context of a nightclub.

2   Background

This section will provide an overview of the domains of knowledge that contributed to the development of Interactive Music 3.0, namely, interactive nightclub, motion capture (MoCap), music information retrieval (MIR) and body-sound mapping. A brief description of each domain will be followed by a discussion of issues that are preventing its artistic development. A more thorough state of the art can be found in my Master's thesis at www.yagodequay.com.

2.1   Interactive Nightclub

Since Interactive Music 3.0 hopes to better understand the sociotechnical aspects of dance and music, nightclubs—western centers for social consumption of music and dance—provide fertile ground for research. Nightclubs are excellent places for multimedia interaction as pointed out by [3]. [4] classified the interaction inside nightclubs as: *Audience-Centered*, audience-to-audience playful interaction; *DJ-Centered*, assisting the DJ with media management, and; *DJ-Audience*, exchanging information like music and MoCap data between the DJ and the audience. My review of this field has identified a number of projects, most of them audience-centered, that work to encourage patrons in nightclubs to use interactive systems. [5-7] suggest that further work can be done on implementing computer-mediated, group music expression tools in public venues. [8] state that most of technologies for DJ-centered and DJ-audience interaction try to circumvent the important role of the DJ.

DJs play a crucial role as gatekeepers and trendsetters in the nightclub environment. The limited bibliography of DJ-audience interaction, like the work done by [9] deliberately side step the current role of the DJ. The pervasive practice among developers in tinkering the DJ's set and using idiosyncratic controllers contributes to the hesitation of DJs in adopting interactive music systems. As long as developers ignore the needs of DJs, implementations will not achieve a lasting foothold inside clubs.

2.2   Motion Capture

[10] examine the history of MoCap and define it as the process of recording motions of humans, animals and objects in a digital format. MoCap technologies are either *optical*, relying on computer vision techniques, or *non-optical*, based on sensors. Applications are mostly limited to the film industry, army and medicine [10-12].

The list of hardware used for manipulating sound is extensive, ranging from off-the-shelve products like Nintendo's Wii remotes, to state of the art MoCap systems like Qualisys, to homebrewed controllers like the one used by the artist Pamela Z [13]. Crowd MoCap is still based on simple sensors due to physical, network and algorithmic limitations. Microsoft's Kinect 3D camera has opened a Pandora box of experiments using full body manipulation of media and standardized, open code libraries for interaction. There are three documented examples that use Dance Jockey's Xsens MVN MoCap suit: The musician Praga Khan used it to control visuals [14]. Ghent and McGill Universities set out to test mapping strategies and gait recognition, using only a few sensors not the full MVN system [15,16].

Most sensors setups used for music interaction cannot provide a holistic interpretation of the body, for example, they capture only one limb. Optical systems that capture all limbs are not mobile; they can only be used as an installation. These two issues, first the alienation of the limb from the body and second the lack of an intimate, personal device produces an out of context, meaningless MoCap data stream. This separation between the individual, his/her body and sound forces us to interpret the aesthetic qualities of the captured features and prohibits user-specific long-term data collection.

2.3   Music Information Retrieval

In their brief overview of MIR, [17] define it as the method of intelligently and efficiently analyzing, recognizing, retrieving and organizing music. Digital audio libraries and collections need efficient methods of organization. Searching through text meta-data such as author, song title and album is cumbersome in large repositories because they might include meta-data errors and require the users to read long lists. MIR techniques can directly analyze the content inside a song and extract features that describe the item. These features, or descriptors, can be for example, melody, harmonics, pitch, timbre, rhythm, beat, tempo or loudness.

To provide a context-driven music interaction a system needs to have as a reference musical elements such as key and tempo. The majority of examples of interactive music systems relied exclusively on preselected tracks or composed pieces with all the musical information provided beforehand, like score following systems. In his study of computer accompaniment for music, [18] claims that research on interactive music systems that can respond appropriately to popular music has been ignored. [19] state that "sensations of body movement are one of the most salient features of musical style and genre" and that more work needs to be done on methods for extracting movement-inducing cues from audio and vice versa. These gaps endure because MIR has prioritized research on automatic search and retrieval of music collections for ever-growing online databases, instead of addressing issues in particular user communities [20-22]. This lack of user-driven models renders MIR systems incapable of harvesting the plethora of knowledge and inputs that other users can provide through social or machine interaction.

2.4   Body-Music Mapping

Sensors convert environmental data into information that can be used to manipulate sound. Within this context, mapping aims to provide a musical role to what is otherwise a non-sonic input. Mapping strategies can be divided into three categories: *Fast mapping* techniques that quickly match input to output; *multi-layered mapping* platforms that add one or more layers of abstraction between input and input, or; *smart mappings* that involve some amount of machine learning to induce mappings from interactions. [23] goes further by dividing input-to-output connections into four types: One-to-one, one-to-many, many-to-one; and many-to-many.

Framing a musical system as an extension of a physical instrument will invariably lead to a more rigid mapping framework. In these situations, some developers may consider mapping as part of the composition. Interaction models based around machine learning and artificial intelligence offer a bottom-up method of interaction with potentially higher levels of participation and possibilities. However, much of the software technology that can enable this level of intelligence is still in its early stages. Although there is ample research in fast, multi-layered and smart mapping techniques, there are no methods for evaluating their implementation.

Top-down approaches to mapping where all possible interactions are designed lead to predictable results. Many art works need this type of control over the music so that the artists can express a desired sound or provoke a specific behavior. This system however, cannot handle unpredictable elements like the number of participants and the type of control devices. Machine learning and artificial intelligence can find patters in the interactions between people and devices and enable the emergence of musical ideas that can become cultural tokens, passed from one individual to another by imitation.

3   Works

Between 2010 and 2011, during my Master's degree, more than a dozen events were held at nightclubs and concert halls in Angola, Portugal and Norway to test and finally to perform the two interactive music systems described below. The first of these systems entitled Interactive Nightclub provides control over music to patrons through various MoCap devices and online services. The second system called Dance Jockey is the first wearable system to provide full body control over music.

3.1   Interactive Nightclub

Interactive Nightclub is a series of installations that aggregate patrons' social behaviors and individual attitudes towards dancing in nightclubs enabling users to create, modify, reconfigure and share media in real time through live motion sensing technologies and online services. It combines the domains of MIR, MoCap and Body-music Mapping to suggest a practical systemic approach for stimulating user's musical expression.

Harmonic content is extracted from the DJ's songs in real time to provide a list of suitable notes for the synths, which are played on top of the music. Three Max/MSP pitch trackers are used to extract these notes: *segment~*, *analyzer~* [24] and *zsa.freqpeak~* [25]. Whenever a specific note coincides in all three trackers it gets selected and sent to a probability table. Movements can have a discrete or a continuous effect on the music. As an example of discrete interaction, a camera allows users to toggle effects by simply placing their hand in a region on the wall. For continuous, periodic movements like the accelerometer data of a Wii remote being swung up and down, a period detection algorithm extracts the slope, frequency, apex and trough, and calculates future apexes and troughs. Using this algorithm, patrons can trigger random notes from the probability table through Wii remotes and cameras as well as apply continuous effects like the frequency of a filter. This method uses one-to-one, fast mappings. Before and during the event people can suggest songs on an online playlist hosted at Grooveshark.com.

Although Interactive Nightclub is based on user-driven models, it still envisions users working in a centralized system through terminals, interfaces, and installations. The next project called Dance Jockey presents preliminary work towards ubiquitous computing in music through sensor suits that can comprehend relationships between music and dance.

3.2 Dance Jockey

Dance Jockey is a performance where the movement of one dancer controls the music. A commercial MoCap suit called Xsens MVN creates a detailed 3D representation of the dancer's body, limbs and gestures that are then are assigned to different sound effect and instruments. The sensors are concealed under clothes, the laptop is placed in a backpack and the sound is played through two small speakers held by the dancer. Ståle Skogstad, a PhD candidate at Oslo University is responsible for the choreography and MoCap, I am the dancer and composer. A typical piece has ordered sections but the dance and music are mostly improvised. The choreography is limited to the limbs since the Xsens MVN only captures relative limb movements, not absolute coordinates on stage. The mapping is multi-layered and the relationships between movements and sounds change throughout the performance.

The suit is composed of 17 inertial sensors, each with a gyroscope, magnetometer and accelerometer. Motion data is transformed to control data using the Standalone Datagram Unpacker and Cooker developed in C++ by Ståle Skogstad [26]. The resulting data is then sent by Open Sound Control through UDP to a control unit developed in Max/MSP that gives a meaningful descriptor to the incoming data. This information is then sent again through UDP to Max for Live devices inside Ableton Live, a digital audio workstation that can host virtual instruments and sound effects. Fig. 1 illustrates the path of the MoCap and audio data. All this can be achieved with a latency as low as 28 milliseconds [26]. In their report on human latency tolerance for gestural sound, [27] conclude that the "just noticeable difference" between delayed and not delayed continuous instruments without tactile feedback is 30ms. However this perception depends on various factors like tempo, reverberation and instrumentation.

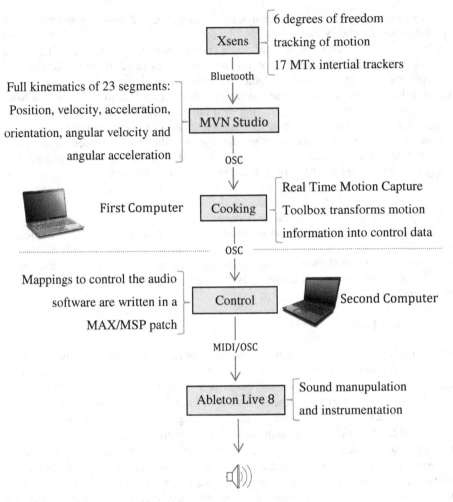

Fig. 1. Dance Jockey data flow

4   Conclusions

An overall look at the fields of MoCap, Interactive Nightclub, MIR and Body-music Mapping discussed in the Background section, will make evident that these terms outline existing technologies that are not necessarily concerned with self-expression. As [28] put it: "A technology is not merely a system of machines with certain functions; rather, it is an expression of a social world"—the above technologies stand a chance of being re-shaped if developed in a different social context. Furthermore, these fields are treated as separate silos with only a few anecdotal juxtapositions. Looking at closing this gap I developed two interactive music systems called Interactive Nightclub and Dance Jockey that integrate these four domains into a holistic approach to fostering music expression inside nightclubs.

Interactive Nightclub's goal was to leverage patrons' and DJs' musical habits (i.e. dance and tracks) and algorithmic data management to reach out to the entire nightclub. The services offered were not in the form of an installation—though they were delivered by a collection of motion capture devices. Nor does its interactive system even produce the content that it enables patrons to interact. Interactive Nightclub exists in the space between hardware and software and content server, as an intermediary between the patron and his or her interactive music experience.

The most challenging part consisted in developing tools that could be flexible to each nightclub's environment and stimulate user participation. The music played by the DJ is unpredictable so MIR was used to analyze it in real-time. Much like the "horseless carriage" framed the automobile as an extension of the familiar, off-the-shelve controllers like Wii remotes and cameras promoted virtual instruments to replace physical instruments. In the end, Interactive Nightclub was able to efficiently harvest harmonic content from the DJ and serve it to patrons so they could collaborate and improvise musically without the danger of ever sounding *bad*. However, it became apparent that interaction should reach beyond terminals to wearable agents in order to secure "the long tail", that is, the collective, pervasive power of the small interactions that make up the bulk of the system's content. This is where Dance Jockey stepped in.

Dance Jockey collects kinetic information from the wearer and diffuses it through a network so other people and device can make music with it. This interactive music system is not separate, but an extension of the previous one, in which movement is given meaningful descriptors better enabling people and computers to cooperate musically. The unique power behind Dance Jockey lays in its ability to offer full body, localized sound manipulation and the possibility of sharing movement data over a network, serving as the basis for a complex musical system that emerges from the continuous interaction with other people and objects.

Although a commercial MoCap suit was used, various network streaming optimizations had to be done before we could focus on artistic expression. Traditionally dance follows music and only now with the advent of user innovation do we see reinterpretation of emerging technologies that are challenging these established practices and blurring the division between music and dance. The works presented here have been limited to the development and implementation of interactive systems and no formal data was collected from participants.

5   Discussion

The real power behind the semantic relationships between music and movement will be realized when people wear sensors, or agents, that collect information, process it and share the results with other people or other things. A typical agent can run without human supervision and uses data (environmental, biological, kinetic, etc.), with the help of other agents, to better its chances of accomplishing a goal set by the user. One can expect the effectiveness of agents to increase exponentially as more people (or things) use them and intelligent environments become available. Instead of having harmonic rules like in Interactive Nightclub that do not necessarily generate anything new but merely point out consistencies in the current composition paradigm, networked, embedded agents will be the foundation for an organized, purposeful activity that encourages moment-by-moment improvisation among a large number of options.

I see a future where people co-create music in real-time regardless of physical and geographical constrains. The growing role of the user in innovation will foster intelligent agents that mediate people's needs, and social machines that improve the diffusion of personal ideas to a wider audience. Amplified by synchronous actions of other people, this spontaneous ripple effect will produce unimaginable cultural trends. Ultimately, learning, creating, and sharing music and dance, will become indistinguishable.

6   Future Work

Future experiments will measure dancers' satisfaction of interactive music/dance systems in comparison with the non-interactive, traditional, music/dance experience. Results will help guide future research and develop sustainable interactive music models for nightclubs as well as other entertainment technologies.

References

1. McCarthy, M.: Imogen Heap: Queen of the digital age. The Independent (2009)
2. Berners-Lee, T.: Long Live the Web. Scientific America (2010)
3. Bayliss, A., Lock, S., Sheridan, J.G.: Augmenting expectation in playful arena performances with ubiquitous intimate technologies. In: PixelRaiders 2, Sheffield (2005)
4. Gates, C., Subramanian, S., Gutwin, C.: DJs' perspectives on interaction and awareness in nightclubs. In: Proceedings of the 6th Conference on Designing Interactive Systems, pp. 70–79. ACM, University Park (2006)
5. Blaine, T., Perkis, T.: The Jam-O-Drum interactive music system: a study in interaction design. In: Proceedings of the 3rd Conference on Designing Interactive Systems: Processes, Practices, Methods, and Techniques, pp. 165–173. ACM, New York City (2000)
6. Tahiroglu, K., Erkut, C.: ClaPD: A testbed for control of multiple sound sources in interactive and participatory contexts. In: The PureData Convention, Montreal, Canada (2007)
7. Feldmeier, M., Paradiso, J.A.: An Interactive Music Environment for Large Groups with Giveaway Wireless Motion Sensors. Computer Music Journal 31(1), 50–67 (2007)
8. Gates, C., Subramanian, S.: A Lens on Technology's Potential Roles for Facilitating Interactivity and Awareness in Nightclub, University of Saskatchewan: Saskatoon, Canada (2006)
9. Ulyate, R., Bianciardi, D.: The interactive dance club: avoiding chaos in a multi participant environment. In: Proceedings of the 2001 Conference on New Interfaces for Musical Expression (NIME 2001), National University of Singapor (2001)
10. Kitagawa, M., Windsor, B.: MoCap for Artists: Workflow and Techniques for Motion Capture. In: Temme, P. (ed.) Focal Press, Burlington (2008)
11. Furniss, M.: Motion Capture (2004), http://web.mit.edu/comm-forum/papers/furniss.html
12. van Dorp Skogstad, S.A., Jensenius, A.R., Nymoen, K.: Using IR Optical Marker Based Motion Capture for Exploring Musical Interaction. The University of Oslo, Oslo (2010)
13. Zone, S.: BodySynth, http://www.synthzone.com/bsynth.html (cited April 2011)
14. Collins, N., Kiefer, C., Patoli, M.Z., White, M.: Musical Exoskeletons: Experiments with a Motion Capture Suit. In: Proceedings of New Interfaces for Musical Expression (NIME), Sydney, Australia (2010)

15. Maes, P.-J., Leman, M., Lesaffre, M., Demey, M., Moelants, D.: From expressive gesture to sound: The development of an embodied mapping trajectory inside a musical interface. Journal on Multimodal User Interfaces 3(1-2), 67–78 (2010)
16. Malozemoff, A.J., Depalle, P.: MUMT 502 Project Report: Gait Recognition Using Accelerometers and Sound. McGill University, Montreal (2009)
17. Lidy, T., Rauber, A.: Music Information Retrieval. In: Theng, Y.-L., et al. (eds.) Handbook of Research on Digital Libraries: Design, Development and Impact, pp. 448–456. IGI Global, New York (2009)
18. Dannenberg, R.B.: Computer Coordination With Popular Music: A New Research Agend. Computer Science Department, Paper 51 (2008)
19. Godøy, R.I., Jensenius, A.R.: Body Movement in Music Information Retrieval. The University of Oslo, Oslo (2009)
20. Futrelle, J., Downie, S.: Interdisciplinary Research Issues in Music Information Retrieval: ISMIR 2002. Journal of New Music Research 32(2), 121–131 (2003)
21. Lesaffre, M., De Voogdt, L., Leman, M., De Baets, B., De Meyer, H., Martens, J.P.: How potential users of music search and retrieval systems describe the semantic quality of music. Journal of the American Society for Information Science and Technology 59(5), 695–707 (2008)
22. Casey, M., Veltkamp, R., Goto, M., Leman, M., Rhodes, C., Slaney, M.: Content-Based Music Information Retrieval: Current Directions and Future Challenges. Proceedings of the IEEE 96(4), 668–696 (2008)
23. Hunt, A., Wanderley, M.M., Kirk, R.: Towards a Model for Instrumental Mapping in Expert Musical Interaction. In: International Computer Music Conference. International Computer Music Association, San Francisco (2000)
24. Jehan, T., Schoner, B.: An Audio-Driven, Spectral Analysis-Based, Perceptual Synthesis Engine. In: Audio Engineering Society, Amsterdam, The Netherlands (2001)
25. Malt, M., Jourdan, E.: Zsa. Descriptors: a library for real-time descriptors analysis. In: Sound and Music Computing, Berlin, Germany (2008)
26. Skogstad, S., Nymoen, K., De Quay, Y., Jensenius, A.: OSC Implementation and Evaluation of the Xsens MVN suit. In: Proceedings of New Interfaces for Music Expression, Oslo, Norway (2011)
27. Mäki-patola, T., Hämäläinen, P.: Latency Tolerance for Gesture Controlled Continuous Sound Instrument Without Tactile Feedback. In: Proceedings of International Computer Music Conference (ICMC), Miami, USA (2004)
28. Nye, D.E.: Technology Matters: Questions to Live With. The MIT Press, Cambridge (2006)

Hierarchical Clustering of Music Database Based on HMM and Markov Chain for Search Efficiency

Joe Cheri Ross and John Samuel

Indian Institute of Technology Bombay
Mumbai, India
joe@cse.iitb.ac.in,
johnsamuel84@gmail.com

Abstract. Music search unlike the regular text search works on huge databases and traditional pattern matching approaches are not feasible. The efficiency of a music search engine solely depends on the data categorization scheme employed. The proposed idea aims to reduce search complexity using tree based organization of music database and also considering scale, chord and note transition of the input query. Probabilistic modeling of chord transition by Hidden Markov model and notes transition through Markov chain improvise on clustering enormous music data, eventually resulting in search complexity reduction. The method inherently supports minor deviations in the input query which may prevent meeting user expectations despite the availability of data.

Keywords: Music, information retrieval, Hidden Markov Model, Markov Chain, Scale based search, music search, content based information retrieval.

1 Introduction

The notion of music search has significantly changed from the traditional approach of search by tags or associated meta data to content based music information retrieval. The music search by content takes as input any part of music and searches in the available music database. Efficiency of a content-based music information retrieval system depends on the accuracy of the resultant music piece, irrespective of the discrepancies in the query provided by the user.

The indexing approach used by the text search engines cannot be used for the musical search. In case of indexing approach used by the text search engines, there are certain fixed set of commonly used words found in the dictionary, colloquially used words and abbreviations which can be found in various web pages or documents in different order. In case of music, there is no concept of fixed set or group of notes that can be called as a word. Considering the western music, there are twelve notes, the various combinations of which give a musical piece. There can be various combinations of a set of notes and only certain combination can be called as invalid (if, at all). The combination is often called

S. Ystad et al. (Eds.): CMMR/FRSM 2011, LNCS 7172, pp. 98–103, 2012.
© Springer-Verlag Berlin Heidelberg 2012

invalid based on the hearing of human. Considering all these facts, one thing is clear, there is nothing like a fixed dictionary of words for music. So a different approach must be used to store and index the musical database. An efficient organization must support fast retrieval and faster search.

A musical piece can be stored in the database in various formats including the commonly used .wav format. It normally requires megabytes of space for even a single piece when compared to the textual web pages which usually consume kilobytes of space. For lesser storage, the method proposed here uses the symbolic notation. Usage of symbolic notation has two major benefits: lesser storage and easier processing. A tree-based organization using the symbolic notation is used for the storage. The categorization used in the tree is based on the scale, chord and note transition of a musical piece. This helps to narrow down the number of files to be searched. But this categorization also has certain challenges: especially when the input query is not same as that of the scale as of the musical piece.

An input query with exact pattern matching cannot be used to retrieve the musical piece searched for. It cannot be guaranteed to have the same scale as that of the music stored in the database. Also there is high possibility that some additional notes may have crept into the query that can lead to totally different results if exact pattern matching is used. The presence of these spurious notes can occur in cases of query by humming and even some minute errors while entering the input query in symbolic notation. In order to deal with these discrepancies in the input query, the information retrieval mechanism must deal with certain allowed deviations. For this purpose, we suggest a three level check to the input query. In the first level, we convert the set of notes into the corresponding chords. This is to deal with the spurious notes that crept in. Then we apply HMM on these chords, which help us to narrow down our search to a certain number of musical pieces. Now in the second level, we utilize the Markov chain on the exact note transition sequence. Finally in the third level, we apply the approximation pattern matching techniques to retrieve the music piece.

2   Data Organization and Clustering

Content based music information retrieval aims at retrieving music through intelligent and automated processing of music [1]. Content based music search takes query from the user in the form of score or audio. This input has to be processed intelligently to extract required parameters for the search. A tree based organization of the content in central database enables hierarchical clustering of the available music. Scale of the input music and chords sequence are taken into consideration for hierarchical clustering. The first level classification of the whole music data set present in the repository is done on the basis of the scale/key of the music. On processing the query at the client side scale of the input is analyzed with Krumhansl method [6].

At the central music repository search is routed to appropriate node pointing to the dataset having the same scale as that of the input query [5].

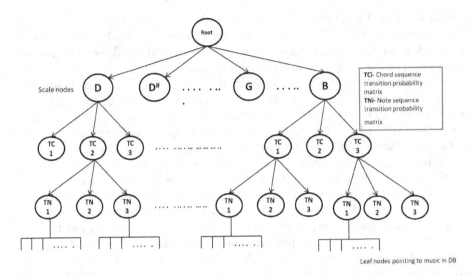

Fig. 1. Tree Organization

2.1 Chord Transition Modeling with HMM

Chords transition sequence of the input query is the determinant at the next level of the tree. Stochastic modeling at this level is done by Hidden Markov Model (HMM) [4]. Goal of this modeling is to probabilistically find the appropriate node where the actual sequence of expected notes can be found. This is found considering the chord transition sequence deduced from the input query. The chords of a music is an abstract representation of a input music piece, which prevents the search from deviating due to unwanted notes that might have crept in to the user input query. The chords inferred are taken as the observed states and the actual notes which the user expects are the hidden states. Even though sequence of notes is readily available in the input query, the notes sequence is considered to be hidden states. The reason is that there may be major discrepancies in notes sequence in the input query when compared to the music piece user intended, whereas the chords sequence remains the same in spite of minor deviations. This approach assures better probability of meeting user expectations.

Each subnode is associated with state transition probability matrix(A) and observation probability matrix(B). If there are N hidden states and M observed states, $A = \{a_{ij}\}$ is an NxN matrix and $B = \{b_j(k)\}$ is an NxM matrix. A denotes transition probabilities between notes and B denotes probabilities for observed chord for each note. A chord corresponds to a set of note transitions, but to align with HMM the chord transition sequence is expanded to form a 1-to-1 correspondence between note transitions and chord transitions. A chord transition C, F, G for note transition $c, e, d, f, a, f, g, b, d$ will be elaborated to $C, C, C, F, F, F, G, G, G$. Considering each nodes model parameters, the node which gives maximum probability value for the observed chord transition is selected for further search traversal. This probability value is obtained by summation of all possible notes sequence. The set of notes consists of only the notes which belong to scale denoted by the parent node.

$$P(C_{Tsn}) = \Sigma \pi_{n0} b_{n0}(C_0) a_{n0,n1} b_{n1}(C_1) a_{n1,n2} b_{n2}(C_2)...a_{nT-2,nT-1} b_{nT-1}(C_{T-1}) \quad (1)$$

where $C_0, C_1, C_2 \cdots \cdots \cdots C_{T-1}$ is the set of chord transition input $n_0, n_1, n_2 \cdot$ $\cdots \cdots \cdots n_{T-1}$ is the set of notes which belong to the scale identified.

2.2   Notes Transition Modeling with Markov Chain

The node identified by the chord transition pattern of the query has narrowed down the search to database containing music pieces which contain similar chord transition pattern. At this level notes in the query is considered to traverse to the next child tree. The child tree which has the highest probability of finding a similar piece to that of input is selected. This selection is done through probabilistic matching using Markov chain model. First order Markov chain models any sequence in which each state changes to its successor state probabilistically [2].

Each node at this level is associated with a transition probability matrix, denoting probability of a note to get transitioned to another note. This 12X12 matrix models transition probabilities of all notes independent of octave. The behavior of music pieces held by each node is modeled by the transition probability matrix associated with it. Given below is an example of transition probability matrix (T_{ab}), which shows only a certain set of notes.

The decision on best node to be selected for the input query is made through the equation (Eqn. 2), by getting the node for which the equation gives the maximum value for the notes transition in the query.

$$P(inputnotesequence) = \Pi_1^n \{t_{ab} | a = n_i, b = n_{i+1}, 1 < i < n\} \quad (2)$$

where t_{ab} is the probability of transition from note a to b w.r.t the transition probability matrix of a node.

	c	d	e	f	g
c	0.15	0.2	0.15	0.2	0.2
d	0.2	0.14	0.3	0.16	0.2
e	0.12	0.18	0.15	0.4	0.15
f	0.2	0.3	0.2	0.1	0.2
g	0.13	0.12	0.14	0.16	0.15

Fig. 2. Transition Matrix

If the query contains the notes sequence c f g e f the probability with which the node with aforementioned T_{ab} selected is 0.2 x 0.2 x 0.14 x 0.4= 0.00224. The distinct patterns determine the number of nodes at this level.

3   Pattern Matching

The selected node at the last level is expected to contain the music piece which matches with the query sequence. An exact pattern matching takes into account even the errors or the onset time differences in the input query. A fuzzy search through an approximate pattern-matching algorithm is used to get rid of these variations. The approximate string matching algorithm by Baeza-Yates is adopted with certain modifications. This algorithm ignores mismatches up to k which is defined. It finds all instances of a pattern $P = p_1 p_2 p_3 p_4 \cdots p_m$ having m characters in a text $T = t_1 t_2 t_3 \cdots t_n$ having n characters [3].

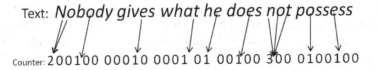

Fig. 3. Approx. Pattern Matching

A counter is associated with each character in the text, which get incremented on finding a character that is present in the pattern while matching. If 2 adjacent characters in pattern are present in the text preserving the order, the counter corresponding to the first character of these is incremented twice. In the given example in Fig.3 if the number of mismatches k=1, substring having counter=3 is accepted as a match. Value of counter is m minus number of mismatches.

This approach with some modifications can serve for pattern matching of query against the pieces in the music database. The pattern matching takes place on the children of selected node at the last level of the search tree. This algorithm has the feature to disregard repeating characters which is critical for musical score pattern matching. Notes getting repeated like in $c, c, f, g, b, c, d, d, e,$ will get ignored while getting compared with a music containing $c, f, g, b, c, d, e.$ The key modification required for better score search is to consider adjacent notes in the octave to the expected notes as error like in notes repetition. An input query containing the sequence c, d, g, a, b, c has to match against $c, d, g, a, b, d.$

4   Scale Shifting and Search Diversion

At the last level of the search tree if the intended music piece cannot be found, the search has to be directed to the node with next higher probability computed by Eqn. 2. The same operation has to be performed at the immediate parent level which considers chord transition, if the result is again negative. Even at the scale nodes level if the search cannot find the desired result, the scale of the query might be different from the actual scale of that music. The search has already taken a path through the scale identified from the input query. To get over this, scale of query music is shifted one above or below and the search process is reinitiated. If the query is deviated from the actual scale of the music, the search process cannot find the intended music from the database.

5   Conclusion

This paper bring forth hierarchical clustering of music database in order to narrow down search procedure especially on an enormous database. HMM models directing search to the right target based on chord transition of the input sequence. This modeling averts search getting biased to a wrong path due to minor variations or unexpected onset time of notes. Markov chain models further classification of music data at the next level. The variations in the input are so critical and usual that when searching at the leaf nodes which point to the music files, approximate pattern matching is used. The scale shifting method to resolve query given in a wrong scale performs well enough. But this counteracts efficiency as in many cases the input is sung in a different scale. A method has to be identified restricting scale shifting grouping together songs in similar scale on the basis of scale changing trends. In spite of the complexity of computation involved for probabilistic selection, the effective categorization contributes significantly to search complexity reduction.

References

1. Casey, M.A., Veltkamp, R., Goto, M., Leman, M., Rhodes, C., Slaney, M.: Content-Based Music Information Retrieval: Current Directions and Future Challenges. Proceedings of the IEEE 96(4), 668–696 (2008)
2. Hoos, H., Renz, K., Gorg., M.: GUIDO/MIR: An Experimental Musical Information Retrieval System Based On Guido Music Notation. In: Proceedings of the 2nd International Symposium on Music Information Retrieval (ISMIR 2001), pp. 41–50. Indiana University, Bloomington (2001)
3. Baeza-Yates, R.A., Perleberg, C.H.: Fast and Practical Approximate String Matching. Inf. Process. Lett. 59(1), 21–27 (1996)
4. Rabiner, L.R.: A Tutorial on Hidden Markov Models and Selected Applications in Speech Recognition. Proceedings of the IEEE 77(2), 257–286 (1989)
5. Ross, J.C., Samuel, J.: Scale-Beat Tree Organization for Efficient MIDI Retrieval Mechanism. In: Proceedings of International conference on Advanced Computation and Communication, Kanjirapally, Kottayam, pp. 112–116 (2010)
6. Krumhansl, C.L.: Cognitive Foundations of Musical Pitch. Oxford University Press, New York (1990)

Fundamental Frequency Modulation in Singing Voice Synthesis

Ryan Stables[1], Cham Athwal[1], and Jamie Bullock[2]

[1] The School of Digital Media Technology, Birmingham City University
Faculty of Technology, Engineering and The Environment
Millennium Point, Curzon St., Birmingham, UK. B47XG
[2] Birmingham Conservatoire, Birmingham City University,
Paradise Place, Birmingham, UK. B3 3HG
{ryan.stables,cham.athwal,Jamie.bullock}@bcu.ac.uk

Abstract. A model is presented for the analysis and synthesis of low frequency human-like pitch deviation, as a replacement for existing modulation techniques in singing voice synthesis systems. Fundamental frequency (f_0) measurements are taken from vocalists producing a selected range of utterances without vibrato and trends in the data are observed. A probabilistic function that provides natural sounding low frequency f_0 modulation to synthesized singing voices is presented and the perceptual relevance is evaluated with subjective listening tests.

Keywords: Singing Voice Synthesis, Drift, Fundamental Frequency, Humanisation.

1   Background

The increasing intelligibility of synthesized voice has contributed to a rise in the amount of studies that attempt to evaluate and improve the perceived naturalness of the vocal. In singing it can be argued that the intelligibility of the voice is often secondary to the quality of phonation. In a considerable section of operatic and classical styles for example, listeners will often listen to the piece with very little understanding of the language, suggesting the focus is primarily on the quality of the singer. Furthermore, the prosodic features that provide us with cues to the emotional state and attitude of the speaker, are often augmented for the purpose of musicality.

Singing voice synthesis systems such as [1] and [4] are being used extensively to generate new expressive musical instruments and have even been used in professional music production [6][5]. In this study we aim to investigate the control of Fundamental frequency (f_0) in sustained vowels, in an attempt to improve the perceived realism of synthesized singing.

In order to do this we first investigate the drift that occurs in human singing voices and compare it to existing models. A dataset of human voices is collected, and selected features are extracted. Observations are then made and a parametric model is developed. Finally, the effectiveness of the model is verified with subjective listening tests.

S. Ystad et al. (Eds.): CMMR/FRSM 2011, LNCS 7172, pp. 104–119, 2012.
© Springer-Verlag Berlin Heidelberg 2012

1.1 f_0 Modulation in Speech and Singing

In both speaking and singing, the f_0 contour of one's voice contains both intentional and unintentional modulation. In speech for example, the contour can be increased towards the end of a statement in order for it to be perceived as a question, this is often referred to as high rising terminal or upspeak. Other studies such as [19] demonstrate that along with linguistic states, various modes of affect can be achieved using f_0 modulation.

Similarly, in singing, mechanisms such as vibrato can be achieved through the intentional application of quasi-sinusoidal modulation to the voice source during phonation. This can often add naturalness and musicality to the voice, and is used across several singing styles. Unintentional modulation in singing can also occur, this deviation can range from variations in glottal pulse length, to low frequency modulation over the period of a musical phrase. Although some professional vocalists will regard these deviations as unwanted additions to the signal, they are difficult to avoid and can contribute to the perceived naturalness of the human voice.

1.2 Terminology

Due to the complex nature of the sound source, inconsistent and often overlapping terminologies have been used when referencing sub-features of the f_0 contour in voice. In order to outline the modulation that is present in singing, we aim to summarise the previous findings and unify some of the labels given to the associated features.

One of the most fundamental differences between speech and singing [12][26] is the addition of *vibrato*. Along with variances in the ranges of f_0 and phonation period, vibrato is a feature that is not commonly found in speech. For the frequently Studied Bel-Canto style of classical singing, vibrato rates have been shown to vary between $5 - 8Hz$ [20] and have an almost sinusoidal modulation.

Although it could be argued that f_0 modulation is the most audible component in vibrato, studies such as [21] and [26] have suggested the fluctuation of sub-glottal pressure also provides a mechanism for production of the technique in popular music. This suggests that there is also a strong perceived vibrato effect in amplitude modulation. In order to demonstrate the concept with reference to other F_0 sub-features, the modulation frequency (mf) of vibrato is illustrated in Figure 1. Both the conscious effort and periodicity of this modulation technique separate it from the the other terms discussed in this section.

Wow is a term given to low frequency f_0 deviations that typically occur below the rate of vibrato. Ternström & Friberg [27] suggest the concept is most prominent at period lengths above 200ms. This form of modulation has been attributed to physiological and psychological events such as perceived differences in the auditory system [3] and the pulsatile blood flow, caused by beating of the heart [14]. As wow is an engineering term that was originally used to describe the undesirable errors in motor-driven tape machines, Cook [3] suggests the use of the term *drift* as a measurement for long term pitch deviation. This naming

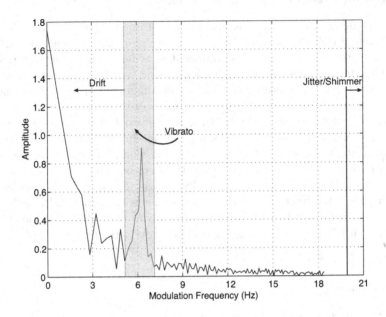

Fig. 1. A spectral analysis of an f_0 contour, illustrating the frequencies at which Drift, Vibrato and Jitter concepts occur

convention is adopted for more recent studies, including ours. Figure 1 illustrates the modulation frequency of drift, when a spectral analysis is performed on an f_0 contour.

Modulation that occurs above $20Hz$ ($< 50ms$) is perceptually related to the roughness of the voiced signal, and is often more prominent in pathological voices [8], this is essentially caused by variations in the cycle lengths of the glottal source signal. The terminology associated with these deviations is quite varied, however some of the more popular terms are *jitter*, *flutter* and *aperiodicity*. The term flutter is also given to low frequency variations by Klatt [7] however, with reference to a control parameter for the singing voice synthesizer KLGLOTT88.

Fluctuation and *fine-fluctuation* are terms suggested by Saitou [17] which encompass all deviations in f_0. Fluctuation refers to low frequency oscillations such as drift and vibrato, whereas fine-fluctuation is associated with higher frequency components such as jitter.

Micro-tremmor is again a concept which covers a wide range of frequencies. The term is semantically linked with emotional states such as fear and anxiety. Several studies approximate the modulation to be most prominent between 7-10hz and it is assumed to be a result of physiological factors linked with the synchronisation of motor-neurons in the brain [18].

Shimmer is the cycle-to-cycle amplitude deviation of the glottal source during phonation. Although this is not strictly a f_0 sub-feature, this modulation is analogous to jitter due to the relationship of the physical components in the production of voiced utterances. As a result of this, it is influential in the perceived naturalness of modified voices. Voices with high levels of shimmer are also linked with pathological disorders [16].

Preparation and *overshoot* are terms given to the modulation that occurs at the onset and offset of an utterance. Preparation is attributed to the movement (usually an increase) in f_0 that occurs when a vocalist is attempting to stabilise the contour, whereas overshoot refers to the modulation that occurs either as a result of an offset, or the glide to a new discrete event.

1.3 Approaches to Synthetic Drift

Drift in singing voice synthesis is acknowledged in numerous papers, however most authors approach this as a minor addition to the synthesis procedure. Studies such as Macon's [13] stress the requirements for human error in the f_0 contour. This is reinforced in the perceptual experiments undertaken by Saitou [17], in which the least natural sounding synthesized singing voices are found to be those with a smoothed f_0 contour. This smoothing removes the majority of involuntary pitch deviation, demonstrating the importance of drift to human perception.

Alternative methods for generating low frequency modulation, used by both Lai [9] and Macon [13] are derived from a function used in Klatt's KLGLOT88 formant synthesizer [7]. The study describes the technique as an aperiodic wavering of f_0. Klatt's original algorithm uses the sum of three sinusoids as a multiplier for f_0 modulation. The three chosen frequencies [12.7, 7.1, 4.7] allow long periods until repetition. The range of perturbation (or the modulation amplitude) of the deviation is influenced by a flutter 'FL' coefficient.

$$\Delta f_0 = (FL/50)(f_0) \begin{bmatrix} sin(2\pi 12.7t) \\ +sin(2\pi 7.1t) \\ +sin(2\pi 4.7t) \end{bmatrix} \tag{1}$$

Klatt states that whilst this approach seems to be sufficient for their singing synthesis engine, it is highly unlikely to accurately represent the human deviations from a fixed frequency. The same function is used by Macon in the concatenative synthesis engine developed in 1997, and later by Lai in 2007. Both of the more recent systems use a range of $0.33 * f_0$.

2 Experimental Measurement of f_0 Drift in Singing

2.1 Compiling a Dataset

In order to gather information regarding the features of our drift model (defined in section 2.4), a dataset of human singers was recorded and the f_0 contours were analysed. Our dataset consisted of 20 vocalists, 15 of whom were labeled as untrained and 5 of whom were labelled as trained. The untrained subjects were those that had previously performed in musical groups, but had no professional training whereas the trained subjects were vocalists from the Birmingham Conservatoire and had at least 3 years classical training. All of the subjects were aged between 18 and 35.

To gather information regarding the state of the f_0 over various conditions in singing, we took several different recordings from each vocalist. Subjects were asked to listen to a range of sine waves between 100Hz and 800Hz at 70dB through headphones and simultaneously produce an /a/ phoneme without vibrato at the same perceived pitch. Between each sound, 5 seconds of silence was played and throughout the recordings subjects were able to monitor their own voice through headphones.

The same process was then repeated for /o/ and /e/ phonemes, in order to measure the variation in drift with different modes of phonation. After these tests had been conducted, the trained subjects were asked to repeat the process with vibrato applied to the phoneme for a single attempted f_0. This allowed us to get recordings of the vocalists producing more natural sounds.

In total, three sustained vowels (/a/, /o/ and /e/) were taken from 20 subjects, over a range of 8 different attempted frequencies, with 5 separate samples containing vibrato. This gave us a corpus of 485 samples. Each of the samples were normalised and periods of silence were removed. Recordings were taken using a MacBook Pro with an external Mackie Onyx sound card and an AKG414 condenser microphone. All recordings were taken in acoustically treated environments. Subjects were able to monitor their recordings with Beyerdynamic DT990 headphones.

2.2   Feature Extraction

Once the data was recorded, it was analysed using a subharmonic-to-harmonic ratio f_0 tracking algorithm [25] with a frame size of 40ms, taken every 10ms. The f_0 tracker was chosen due to its accuracy with voiced signals, parameters were set based on the level of resolution required for our experiment. Observations were then made and features such as the mean, standard deviation, amplitude spectrum and distributions were recorded using standard statistical techniques.

2.3   Findings

A feature that is salient across samples in our dataset, which is not necessarily evident in other models of drift, is the existence of smaller regions of modulation, within a global structure. This essentially means that the signals display some form of pseudorandom modulation, which occurs in smaller, relatively stable segments. When modelled, these regions have independent mean values (μ_n), standard deviations (σ_n) and lengths (l_n). Furthermore, the number of regions would be based on a stochastic component. Our dataset demonstrates that on average, 1.5 to 2 regions are observed per second, taken over the period of 5 seconds for each sustained vowel. This concept is illustrated in Figure 2. Here, the 3 individual regions are denoted with the r_n label.

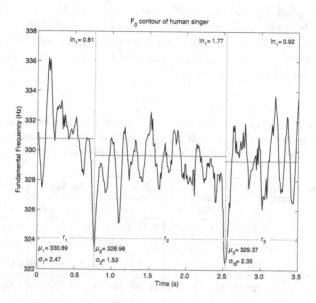

Fig. 2. A sample from the dataset of a sustained vowel exhibiting the regional drift behaviour

The corresponding mean values for each region are given the μ_n label, and Standard deviation for each corresponding region is denoted using the σ_{nn} label. The sample contains 3 regions, over a duration of 3.5 seconds. The lengths of the regions are given using the l_n label and have an average of 1.66 seconds.

Our recordings show that the recorded f_0 contours can be represented by smaller Gaussian-like regions modulated by a low frequency component, this corresponds with the work carried out in [22] and [23] and can be seen in figure 2. Here the signal exhibits clear shifts in μ and σ as time increases.

Each of the 5-second segments in our dataset contained between 2 and 6 regions of drift, with an average of 4 regions, all of which were between 0.5 and 2 seconds in length. The minimum σ was $0.39Hz$, and the Maximum was $15.6hz$. Each μ_n value is considered to be a differential from the global mean μ. Our dataset shows that the smallest recorded μ_n is -0.02Hz and the greatest is -21.35Hz.

To illustrate the typical features in our dataset at selected frequencies, a list of average global feature values are presented in Table 1. Here, three vowels recorded by the trained and untrained vocalists have been separated to highlight the differences between the two groups. Table 2 illustrates the local parameters observed over the same samples in the dataset. Here we give an average of the features associated with the first 3 regions of an attempted f_0. Both global and local features are defined in our modelling stage (Section 3.1).

As the attempted f_0 value increases, the μ and σ of the drift signals were measured in order to observe any trends. The results show that generally, higher σ and Δf_0 values are found at higher attempted f_0's, however there is no clear correlation between the two. The r_n parameter is also relatively inconsistent, with no clear trends in l_n's, μ_n's and σ_n's.

Table 1. Sample of average global feature values across variations in model conditions. Here μ and σ are measured in Hz and R_n indicates the average quantity of discrete regions. Here, μ is recorded as the difference from the attempted f_0.

Vocalist	Phoneme	164Hz			196Hz			261Hz			330Hz		
		μ	σ	R_n	μ	σ	R_n	μ	σ	R_n	μ	σ	R_n
Trained	/a/	0.25	2.16	1.25	3.92	2.01	1.25	-1.80	3.81	2.30	-0.18	5.44	2.00
	/e/	0.96	2.80	2.00	2.82	1.61	2.00	1.10	2.13	2.30	5.69	2.23	2.20
	/o/	2.91	1.67	2.00	1.35	1.32	3.00	-0.19	1.86	2.30	1.64	3.127	1.75
Untrained	/a/	2.28	8.02	3.75	-1.83	13.30	3.00	10.40	3.79	3.30	-1.93	2.52	3.00
	/e/	1.20	2.84	3.00	-1.19	2.47	3.75	-1.39	1.76	3.50	-1.58	2.6	2.25
	/o/	-1.27	2.78	3.50	-4.94	3.76	3.50	1.43	3.06	4.00	-0.58	2.51	3.50

Table 2. Sample of average local feature values across variations in model conditions, with an /a/ phoneme. Here, μ_n and σ_n are measured in Hz, whereas l_n values are measured in seconds.

Vocalist	Region	164Hz			196Hz			261Hz			330Hz		
		μ_n	σ_n	l_n	μ_n	σ_n	l_n	μ_n	σ_n	l_n	μ_n	σ_n	l_n
Trained	r_0	-16.3	3.64	1.01	0.61	0.94	1.30	-1.60	2.01	1.25	-0.49	2.38	1.13
	r_1	-10.93	0.88	1.13	0.02	1.86	1.71	-2.51	1.05	0.76	1.00	3.50	0.88
	r_2	-1.5	0.98	1.05	-0.60	0.68	1.09	-2.81	1.15	1.41	-2.30	1.08	1.75
Untrained	r_0	-21.32	4.75	0.67	-1.47	1.19	1.80	5.86	3.31	1.43	1.76	3.79	1.51
	r_1	-19.61	2.19	1.07	0.96	1.63	1.60	6.88	2.43	1.10	0.74	1.73	1.01
	r_2	-21.20	0.89	1.91	3.99	0.85	1.35	4.98	1.76	0.89	-1.23	1.71	0.57

From Tables 1 and 2, it is clear that the classical training seems to improve the accuracy of the vocalist. Here, the global mean values tend to be closer to the attempted f_0 and the regional mean values show lower levels of deviation than that of the untrained subjects. Figure 3 shows a comparison between typical distributions of the two sources. The samples from subjects with classical training also tend to contain fewer regions. Qualitatively, the distribution for the trained vocalist appears more Gaussian than for the untrained vocalist.

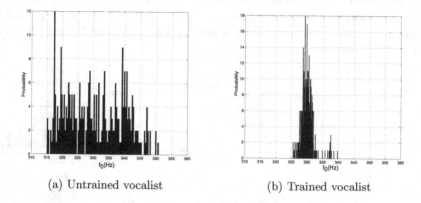

(a) Untrained vocalist   (b) Trained vocalist

Fig. 3. Distributions of (a) an untrained vocalist and (b) a trained vocalist attempting an f_0 of 330 Hz

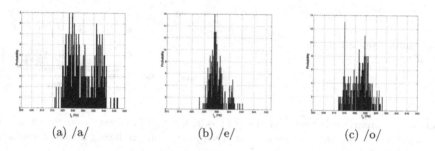

(a) /a/   (b) /e/   (c) /o/

Fig. 4. Example Distributions of the Recorded Phonemes in our dataset, sung by the same vocalist at the same attempted f_0 (330Hz)

Three voiced phonemes were measured over a range of frequencies in order to assess the impact of linguistic content on the parameters of drift. From our recordings, the /o/ phoneme frequently had the lowest σ, however features in the model such as R_n and μ_n had no obvious correlation with linguistic content. Figure 4 demonstrates this across the three sustained phonemes that were recorded.

2.4   Comparison of Models

To illustrate the key differences between stochastic/aperiodic drift models and the drift that exists in real human singing voices, we compare the findings from our dataset of vocalists producing sustained vowels (see Section 2.1) with samples produced using existing drift models.

Figure 5 shows a comparison between two models for f_0 drift and a sample from our dataset. The human sample (Figure 5(c)), is deemed to be a representative example from our data. From these plots, it is evident that the distributions of all models vary greatly.

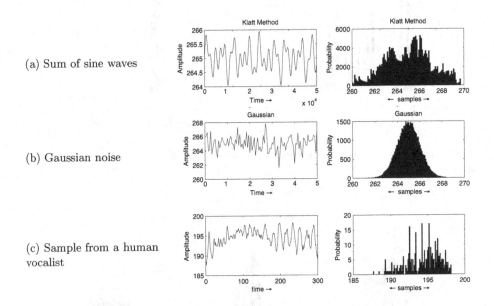

(a) Sum of sine waves

(b) Gaussian noise

(c) Sample from a human vocalist

Fig. 5. A comparison between Klatt's (a) model for drift in singing voice synthesis, A Gaussian model (b) and a trained Human singer (c), all producing a fixed frequency for a period of 3 seconds

As the Gaussian model generates pseudorandom deviates from a probability distribution, shown in Figure 5(b), the samples are unlikely to represent the same values found in the dataset. Essentially, the non-Gaussian nature of the human samples suggest that modelling the articulation with this form of noise will not produce human-like results.

The method used by Klatt in [7] is based on a combination of sinusoidal partials, this indicates that the distribution of samples will remain the same on each instance of a phonation period. Although the signal takes a long time to complete a cycle, this still contains an element that is not visible in the human contours.

In general, the samples that were recorded from human vocalists had no evidence of periodicity in the contour. In Figure 6, the aperiodic nature of the dataset is demonstrated using a spectral analysis of some example f_0 contours. Here it is evident that there are no prominent sinusoidal components. As the signals were already down sampled, a lower samplerate of 39Hz was used (blocksize/originalFs), leaving a Nyquist frequency of 19.5Hz. This was not deemed to be a problem as drift is assumed to occur predominantly wbelow 7Hz.

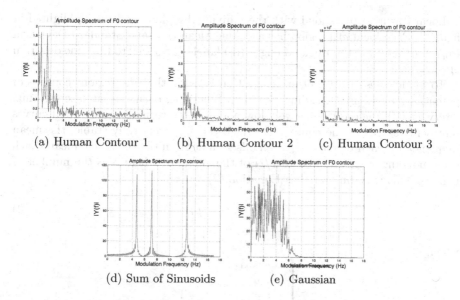

Fig. 6. Spectral analysis of 3 sample f_0 contours (a-c), taken from the dataset. Here, there is no evidence of periodicity. A reference of Klatt's method is shown in (d) and a Gaussian method is shown in (e).

3 Modelling Drift in Singing Voice Synthesis

Previous methods of implementing drift such as [7] and [9] use stochastic or aperiodic variables in an attempt to emulate the seemingly unpredictable nature of frequency modulation in the singing voice. Whilst this adds randomness to the signal, detailed research into the perceptual relevance of these features has yet to be done. In this section, we suggest ways in which the human properties presented in section 2 can be synthesized using a probabilistic model.

3.1 Model Parameters

In order to develop a parametric model for the analysis and resynthesis of Drift in singing, all of the aforementioned parameters need to be quantified and evaluated over a series of possible conditions. Here, we lists these parameters and the conditions that need to be considered in order to produce a comprehensive, realistic model.

The model consists of global parameters (those that affect the whole contour), and local parameters (those that correspond to individual regions of Drift). Global parameters refer to features such as Mean (μ) and Standard Deviation (σ), both of which are directly correlated with the attempted f_0 and the capability of the singer, to produce an accurate note. The total number of regions (r_N) is also a feature that could be assumed to be global. This is discussed in our results (Section 4).

Local features correspond with the individual regions of drift, highlighted in figure 2. Each local nth region has a unique Mean (μ_n) and Standard Deviation (σ_n). Furthermore, the Region Length (l_n) label is attached to the time duration of each local segment.

To model these features,the assumption is made that the regions consists of potentially overlapping, sliding Gaussian functions, occurring at discrete time intervals with regions of relatively low power in between. The individual curves represent regions in the contour at which the f_0 is relatively stable, the mean frequency for each region in x_t is an offset value from the the global mean. Each corresponding $x\sigma_n$ is limited to 1/N of the global σ, where N is the number of regions. This is is illustrated in Equation (2).

$$\Delta f_0 = x_t\sigma_n + \mu_n \tag{2}$$

when:

$$\begin{cases} t < l_1, & n = 0 \\[2ex] t \geq l_1, & n = 1 \\[2ex] t \geq \Sigma_{j=0}^{j=2}l_j, & n = 2 \\[2ex] t \geq \Sigma_{j=0}^{j=N}l_j, & n = r_N \end{cases}$$

Here x_t, l, σ_n and μ_n are independent random variables and t is a vector which is linearly increasing with time, in order to produce a drift contour with N regions. This provides a system for mapping pseudorandom normally distributed values to an empirical distribution, based on the observed trajectory of the f_0 in human contours. The distribution of each region is considered to be Gaussian for synthesis purposes, a result of this function is shown in Figure 7.

3.2 Probabilistic Model

So far, the model suggested in section 3.1 is based on observations made from a recorded dataset. Each of the global and local features are stochastically selected and processed in order to modify a Gaussian distribution. The output of the model is a contour with N discrete states labelled as regions r_n. In order to emulate the temporal patterns observed in the dataset, a probabilistic model is used. This ensures that the parameters attached to each state are reflective of the recorded data. A similar technique is demonstrated in [24], using percussive sequences.

For this study, a Hidden Markov Model is used to dynamically weight the l_i, σ_i and μ_i features in Equation (2). For each of the chosen parameters, a State Transition Matrix (STM) is created and populated with the corresponding feature vectors. This allows us to weight the features with probability coefficients taken empirically from our dataset.

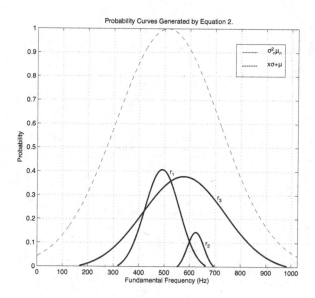

Fig. 7. PDF of Distributions created by the suggested model. Here, the global Gaussian function is decomposed into three Gaussian regions.

In order to generate each state, the l_n, σ_n and μ_n parameters are separated into discrete Markov processes. Each process is given an STM, which is populated with measurements taken from the dataset. Each of the matrices are normalised so that $STM_{ij} \geq 0$ and $\Sigma_{j=1}^{N} STM_{ji} = 1$. Each feature STM contains eight equally-spaced bands, all of which represent a percentile of the enclosing parameter. Outer limits of the matrix are selected empirically and the states are presented as deviations from the corresponding global parameters. This means, for example, that μ_i values are actually calculated as $\mu - \mu_i$ in order to represent a variable relative to it's attempted f_0.

In the model, each time $(t > l_n)$, a new nth region is generated and the next discrete state is selected. If the criteria, $n > 0$ is met, these states contain information regarding the states of previous parameters. Each time this occurs, the STM acts as a probability matrix and current parameters in Equation (2) are weighted accordingly. The result of this process is a Δf_0 that contains human-like variations in l_n, σ_n and μ_n. A comparison between this technique and the previously defined methods is shown in Figure 8.

3.3   Proposed Explanation

Although it requires extensive physiological and psychoacoustic investigation, a proposed explanation for the phenomena described in this study is that as vocalists hear excessive deviation from a desired frequency in the perceived pitch of their voice, an unconscious process alters this pitch in an attempt to become

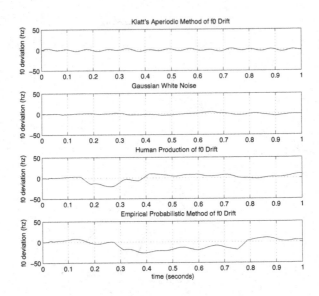

Fig. 8. Comparison between previous and suggested models

closer to the target frequency [11][2][10]. This automatic process produces small jumps in f_0 between relatively stable but slowly deviating regions. When the sample points from a human f_0 contour are mapped to a histogram, smaller clusters of sample points at varying offsets from a mean frequency are evident.

4   Subjective Evaluation of Models

In order to evaluate the perceptual relevance of adding the human character-istics of drift to a synthesized singing voices, listening tests were conducted. A synthesized /a/ phoneme was created using the CHANT formant synthesis tech-nique [15] with a global f_0 of 261Hz (C4). The synthesiser was used due to it's flexibility, availability and quality.

The output of the synthesiser was modulated with three different types of drift. The first type of modulation used the model suggested by Klatt and used in [7], [17] and [13]. The second form used Gaussian noise to modulate the contour and the third was selected empirically, based on previous studies by the author [22][23]. Three categories were chosen with the intention to represent aperiodic, random and human-like features respectively. For reference purposes, subjects were played a voice with no modulation before the test.

Thirty subjects were chosen to participate in AB paired listening tests, all of whom were familiar with singing synthesis. Subjects were aged between 18-55 and all had normal hearing. Each of the subjects were played 12 pairs and asked to choose the sample from each pair that sounded more human. In order to keep the tests fair, all other variables such as formant frequencies and phonemes were kept constant.

In order to evaluate the perceived naturalness of the model, listening tests were conducted. Using a singing synthesiser, the source signal was manipulated using the different models referenced in this study. The first of these models labelled as "Sines" uses the combination of low frequency sinusoidal partials in order to produce modulation. The second, labelled as "Gaussian" uses a stochastic, normally distributed signal and the third labelled as "Empirical" uses the probabilistic method suggested in Section 3.

Results show that for an attempted f_0 of 330Hz, the empirical method was assumed to be the most natural from all of the tested methods. In total, 43% of all subjects selected the Empirical method as most natural. The Method used in [7] was second, with 37%, and the least natural was the Gaussian method, which received 20% of the selections.

5 Conclusion

In order to produce a drift signal, which mirrors that of the human f_0 control system, we have applied a novel probability based function to Gaussian noise. This results in a signal that fluctuates between regions of normally distributed values with local standard deviations and amplitudes. This could be attributed to the influence of the auditory feedback mechanism on f_0 in singing, encountered when a vocalist attempts to match a target frequency. As the subject's phonation frequency drifts further away from the target frequency, larger jumps in f_0 are made in an unconscious attempt to become closer to the target.

As trends in the number of regions and the region lengths were not immediately evident over a series of different fundamental frequencies and phonemes, we use a probabilistic model to produce a statistical representation of our dataset. From preliminary listening tests, we area able to produce f_0 contours which have a more natural, human like deviation in μ and σ when compared to existing systems.

6 Future Work

In future work, extensive listening tests are planned. These will allow us to better asses the perceptual relevance the model. In order to do this, subjects will be asked to give a qualitative evaluation of a dataset created using the previous and current techniques. Each stimulus will be given a rating of naturalness, and compared with a human utterance.

Currently, the model features are estimated over a small range of parameters. In order to create a more robust model, more linguistic components are needed over a much wider range of attempted f_0's. Furthermore, a much wider range of subjects is required, with a variation in singing experience. Other aspects such as vibrato and musical context also need to be included in the study.

References

1. Bonada, J., Serra, X.: Synthesis of the singing voice by performance sampling and spectral models. IEEE Signal Processing Magazine 24(2), 67–79 (2007)
2. Burnett, T., Senner, J., Larson, C.: Voice F0 responses to pitch-shifted auditory feedback: a preliminary study. Journal of Voice 11(2), 202–211 (1997)
3. Cook, P.R.: Identification of control parameters in an articulatory vocal tract model, with applications to the synthesis of singing. Ph.D. thesis, Stanford University, Stanford, CA, USA (1991), uMI Order No. GAX91-15756
4. Fabig, L., Janer, J.: Transforming singing voice expression - the sweetness effect. In: Proc. of the 7th Int. Conference on Digital Audio Effects (DAFX 2004), Naples, Italy (2004)
5. Goto, M., Nakano, T.: Vocalistner: a singing-to-singing synthesis system based on iterative parameter estimation. In: Sound and Music Computing Conference (2010)
6. Kenmochi, H., Ohshita, H.: Vocaloid-commercial singing synthesizer based on sample concatenation. In: Eighth Annual Conference of the International Speech Communication Association (2007)
7. Klatt, D., Klatt, L.: Analysis, synthesis, and perception of voice quality variations among female and male talkers. The Journal of the Acoustical Society of America 87, 820 (1990)
8. Kreiman, J., Gerratt, B.: Perception of aperiodicity in pathological voice. The Journal of the Acoustical Society of America 117, 2201 (2005)
9. Lai, W.: F0 control model for mandarin singing voice synthesis. In: International Conference on Digital Telecommunications, p. 12 (2007)
10. Larson, C., Burnett, T., Bauer, J., Kiran, S., Hain, T.: Comparison of voice f responses to pitch-shift onset and offset conditions. The Journal of the Acoustical Society of America 110, 2845 (2001)
11. Leydon, C., Bauer, J., Larson, C.: The role of auditory feedback in sustaining vocal vibrato. The Journal of the Acoustical Society of America 114, 1575 (2003)
12. Loscos, A.: Spectral Processing of the singing voice. Ph.D. thesis, Universitat Pompeu Fabra, Barcelona (2007)
13. Macon, M., Jensen-Link, L., Oliverio, J., Clements, M., George, E.: Concatenation-based MIDI-to-singing voice synthesis. Audio Engineering Society Journal (1997)
14. Orlikoff, R., Baken, R.: Fundamental frequency modulation of the human voice by the heartbeat: preliminary results and possible mechanisms. The Journal of the Acoustical Society of America 85, 888 (1989)
15. Rodet, X.: Synthesis and Processing of the Singing Voice. Ph.D. thesis, IRCAM, Paris (2002)
16. Ruinskiy, D., Lavner, Y.: Stochastic models of pitch jitter and amplitude shimmer for voice modification. In: IEEE 25th Convention of Electrical and Electronics Engineers in Israel, IEEEI 2008, pp. 489–493. IEEE (2009)
17. Saitou, T., Unoki, M., Akagi, M.: Development of an F0 control model based on F0 dynamic characteristics for singing-voice synthesis. Speech Communication 46(3-4), 405–417 (2005)
18. Schoentgen, J.: Estimation of the modulation frequency and modulation depth of the fundamental frequency owing to vocal micro-tremor of the voice source signal. In: Eurospeech, p. 1499 (2001)
19. Schröder, M.: Emotional speech synthesis: A review. In: Proceedings of EUROSPEECH, vol. 1, pp. 561–564 (2001)

20. Shipp, T., Sundberg, J., Doherty, E.: The effect of delayed auditory feedback on vocal vibrato. Journal of Voice 2(3), 195–199 (1988)
21. Shipp, T., Doherty, E.T., Haglund, S.: Physiologic factors in vocal vibrato production. Journal of Voice 4(4), 300–304 (1990)
22. Stables, R., Bullock, J., Athwal, C.: The humanisation of stochastic processes for the modelling of f_0 drift in singing. In: CMMR-FRSM 2011 Joint International Symposium on Computer Music Modelling and Retrieval with Frontiers of Research on Speech and Music (2011)
23. Stables, R., Bullock, J., Athwal, C.: Towards a model for the humanisation of pitch drift in singing voice synthesis. In: International Computer Music Conference (ICMC 2011), Huddersfield, UK (2011)
24. Stables, R., Bullock, J., Williams, I.: Perceptually relevant models for drum pattern humanisation. In: Proceedings of 131st Audio Engineering Society Convention. AES, New York (2011)
25. Sun, X.: Pitch determination and voice quality analysis using subharmonic-to-harmonic ratio. In: Proceedings of the IEEE International Conference on Acoustics, Speech, and Signal Processing, (ICASSP 2002), vol. 1. IEEE (2005)
26. Sundberg, J.: Science of the Singing Voice. Northern Illinois University Press (1987)
27. Ternström, S., Friberg, A.: Analysis and simulation of small variations in the fundamental frequency of sustained vowels. STL-QPSR 30(3), 1–14 (1989)

A Statistical Approach
to Analyzing Sound Tracings

Kristian Nymoen[1], Jim Torresen[1],
Rolf Inge Godøy[2], and Alexander Refsum Jensenius[2]

[1] University of Oslo, Department of Informatics, Oslo, Norway
{krisny,jimtoer}@ifi.uio.no
[2] University of Oslo, Department of Musicology, Oslo, Norway
{r.i.godoy,a.r.jensenius}@imv.uio.no

Abstract. This paper presents an experiment on *sound tracing*, meaning an experiment on how people relate motion to sound. 38 participants were presented with 18 short sounds, and instructed to move their hands in the air while acting as though the sound was created by their hand motion. The hand motion of the participants was recorded, and has been analyzed using statistical tests, comparing results between different sounds, between different subjects, and between different sound classes. We have identified several relationships between sound and motion which are present in the majority of the subjects. A clear distinction was found in onset acceleration for motion to sounds with an impulsive dynamic envelope compared to non-impulsive sounds. Furthermore, vertical movement has been shown to be related to sound frequency, both in terms of spectral centroid and pitch. Moreover, a significantly higher amount of overall acceleration was observed for non-pitched sounds as compared to pitched sounds.

1 Introduction

Research on music and motion is an interdisciplinary area with links to a number of other fields of research. In addition to traditional research on music and on kinematics, this area relates to neuropsychology, cognition, linguistics, robotics, computer science, and more [20]. To be able to grasp the complexity of the relationship between music and motion, we need knowledge about how different factors influence the motion and how the musical sound is perceived and processed in the brain. In addition, a certain understanding of experimental and mathematical methods is necessary for analyzing this relationship.

In several fields dealing with sound and motion, it is essential to identify how features of sound relate to events in other modalities. This includes disciplines like auditory display, interaction design, and development of multi-modal interfaces [23,27]. Furthermore, it has been suggested that this aspect could be utilized in music information retrieval research, for instance by querying sound data bases with body motion [3,13].

S. Ystad et al. (Eds.): CMMR/FRSM 2011, LNCS 7172, pp. 120–145, 2012.
© Springer-Verlag Berlin Heidelberg 2012

In this paper we present an experiment where motion capture technology was used to measure people's motions to sound. This data has been analyzed in view of perceptual correspondences between lower-level features of sound and motion. The participant's motion was evaluated statistically to find cross-modal relationships that have significance within our data set. There is a need for systematic experiments on sound-action relationships to build a larger corpus of examples on the links between perception of music and motion. The findings in this paper serve as a contribution to this corpus.

We shall begin by introducing the background and motivation for this particular research, including elements from music cognition, accounts of previous experiments on music and motion, as well as our own reflections on the implications of these works. In Section 3 we introduce our experimental setup, followed by a description of the recorded data set, with necessary preprocessing and feature extraction in Section 4. Section 5 presents analysis of the data set, and the results are discussed in Section 6. Conclusions are provided in Section 7.

2   Background

Presently, we have observed an increased popularity of a so-called theory of *embodied cognition*, meaning that bodily sensorimotor processing is understood as an important factor in our cognitive system [28]. Leman [19] put this theory into a musical context in his introduction of *embodied music cognition*. This theory describes how people who interact with music try to understand musical intentions and forms by imitation through corporeal articulations like body motion (e.g. tapping the beat, attuning to a melody or harmony, etc.) and empathy (e.g. attuning to certain feelings or a mood conveyed by the music).

Godøy [9] posits that our understanding of discrete events in music can be explained through *gestural-sonic objects*. These objects are mental constructs that combine the auditory input with gestural parameters, enabling an understanding of the sonic object through its causality (e.g. a perceived sound producing action). The idea of a gestural-sonic object as a discrete perceptual unit, or *chunk*, is based upon Pierre Schaeffer's *sonic object* [26], on Miller's theory of recoding complex sensory information into perceptual chunks [22], and also on the phenomenological understanding of perception as a sequence of now-points introduced by Husserl [14]. According to Godøy, these objects take form at the *meso level* of a musical timescale [10]. In contrast, the *macro level* of a musical timescale could be a whole musical piece, and the *micro level* of the timescale takes place within the sonic object. We believe that *action-sound relationships* [15] are found at all timescale levels, which coexist when a person is involved in a musical experience. Certain musical features like rhythmic complexity or emotional content require a larger timescale perspective than for instance musical features like pitch and timbre which operate in the millisecond range [7].

In a similar manner to the listening experiments Schaeffer performed on sonic objects, we can learn more about gestural-sonic objects by studying lower-level features of sound-related motion. In other words, one can look at the meso level object from a micro-level perspective. Godøy et al. explored gestural-sonic objects in an experiment they referred to as *sound tracing* [12]. Nine subjects were given the task of making gestures they believed corresponded well with the sounds they heard, by using a pen on a digital tablet. By qualitative comparisons of the sound tracings, the authors found a fair amount of consistency between subjects, and argued that this type of experiment should be done in a larger scale, and include more complex sound objects, to learn more about sound-gesture relationships. The same material was later also analyzed quantitatively by extracting features and classifying the sound tracings using a support vector machine classifier [8]. We shall inherit the term *sound tracing* in the experiment presented in this paper. To be more precise, a *sound tracing* in this sense describes a bodily gesture that has been performed in free air to imitate the perceptual features of a sound object.

Other researchers have also studied how lower-level features of sound objects are related to motion or motion descriptors. Merer et al. [21] asked people to put their own motion-labels on sounds with different sound features. This way they determined which sound parameters were most pertinent in describing motion-labels such as "rotate" and "pass by". Eitan et al. found that for sounds with changing pitch, people imagined the movement of an animated character to follow the pitch up or down, however the authors also argued that changing pitch is related to other dimensions than simply vertical position [5,6]. This corresponds well with previous research on metaphors and auditory display where increasing pitch has been related to an increase in other dimensions in other modalities, such as temperature [27]. The relationship between pitch and verticality was also found by Nymoen et al. [25] in a sound tracing experiment where participants used a rod to trace the perceptual features of a selection of sounds. In an experiment on synchronization with music, Kozak et al. [17] observed differences for quantity of motion between different lower-level features of sound like pitch, spectral centroid and loudness. Caramiaux et al. [2] applied Canonical Correlation Analysis to a set of sound and motion features derived from sound tracings.[1] This method gave promising results in identifying correlations between features of sound and of motion, and was later applied by Nymoen et al. [24].

The present paper is intended to follow up on the sound tracing experiments presented above. The main idea in this research was to study sound tracings from a more systematic perspective, in particular by using systematically varied sound parameters. This entailed using a number of short sounds, some where only a single sound parameter was varied, and some where multiple sound parameters were varied. In this manner, it was possible to understand how the different sound parameters influenced the sound tracings. Our analytical approach operates at the meso and micro levels of the musical timescale, combining features that describe chunks of sound and motion with continuously varying sound and motion features.

---

[1] Caramiaux et al. do not refer to them as *sound tracings*, but following the definition presented above, their experiment falls into this category.

3   Experiment

A sound-tracing experiment was designed to be able to systematically distinguish between how people's motion changes and varies in relation to changes in sound features. The data presented in this paper was recorded in Fall 2010.

3.1   Aim

The aim of the experiment was to identify how lower-level features of motion corresponded with features of sound across different participants. By using systematically designed sounds, we can isolate a single sound feature and compare how it relates to motion by itself, or in combination with other sound features.

3.2   Participants

38 people (29 male and 9 female) volunteered to participate in the experiment. They were recruited through mailing lists for students and staff at the University of Oslo and by posting an advertisement on the project website. After participating in the experiment, the participants filled out a questionnaire concerning their level of musical training. 12 people rated their level of musical training as extensive, 11 as medium, and 15 as having little or no musical training. The level of musical training was used in the analysis process to distinguish between experts and non-experts (cf. Section 5). They were also given the opportunity to comment on the experiment. The subjects were not asked for their age, but we estimate the age distribution to be 20–60 years, with most participants aged somewhere between 25 and 35.

3.3   Task

The participants were presented with a selection of short sounds (the sounds will be discussed in Section 3.5). They were instructed to imagine that they could create sound by moving their hands in the air, and move along with the sounds as if their hand motion created the sound. First, each participant was given a pre-listening of all 18 sounds. Following this, the sounds were played one by one in random order. Each sound was played twice: the first time, the participant would only listen, and the second time the participant's hand motion was recorded. A three second countdown was given before each sound, so the participant would know exactly when the sound began.

3.4   Motion Capture

A Qualisys optical infrared marker-based motion capture system was used to record the motion of the people that participated in the experiment. The participants grasped two handles (Figure 1), each one equipped with 5 markers, and the center position of each handle was recorded. There are several advantages to using this technology for recording motion. The system is very accurate, with a high resolution in both time and space. In our recordings, we used a sampling frequency of 100 Hz. Using several markers on each handle made it possible to uniquely identify the left and right handle, respectively, and enabled tracking of the position and the orientation of each handle.

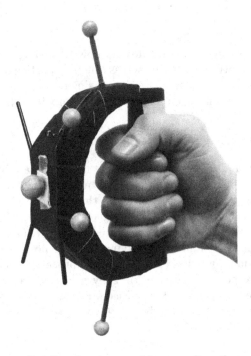

Fig. 1. One of the two handles that was used for recording the participant's motion

The main limitation we have experienced with the technology is so-called *marker-dropouts*. This happens when a marker is occluded (e.g. by the body limbs of the participant) or moved out of the calibrated capture space. Marker-dropouts caused a loss of a number of data-frames in several recordings, and it became necessary to perform so-called gap-filling. We will return to how this was done in Section 4. The marker dropouts made it necessary to disregard the orientation data from the handles, although this was initially recorded. This is because gap-filling of the orientation data was more difficult than gap-filling of the position data (interpolation even over small gaps introduces large errors).

3.5   Sounds

A total of 18 short sound objects, each 3 seconds in length, were designed in Max5 using *frequency modulation* (FM) synthesis and digital filters. The design process was to a large extent based on trial and error, to find sounds where the envelopes of *pitch* (perceived tone height) and *spectral centroid* (here interpreted as perceived brightness) were distinct. *Envelope*, in this sense, is a generic term for a curve describing the development of a sound feature in the time domain. An example of the sound feature envelopes is given in Figure 2. The sound files are available for download at the project website.[2]

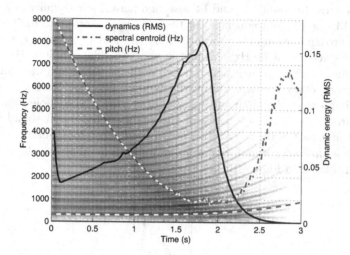

Fig. 2. Spectrogram and corresponding sound features for Sound 15. Pitch and spectral centroid (in Hz) on the left axis. The dynamic envelope scale is on the right axis.

Table 1. Simple description of the sounds used in the experiment. The columns display the pitch envelope, spectral centroid envelope and the dynamic envelope of each sound.

Sound	Pitch	Sp.Centroid	Dyn.Env.	Sound	Pitch	Sp.Centroid	Dyn.Env.
1	Rising	Falling	Bell-shape	10	Noise	Falling	Bell-shape
2	Falling	Rising	Bell-shape	11	Noise	Rising	Increasing
3	Falling	Falling	Bell-shape	12	Noise	Steady	Increasing
4	Rising	Rising	Bell-shape	13	Steady	Rising	Increasing
5	Rising	Steady	Increasing	14	Steady	Falling	Increasing
6	Falling	Steady	Increasing	15	Rising	Falling	Impulsive
7	Steady	Falling	Bell-shape	16	Steady	Steady	Impulsive
8	Steady	Rising	Bell-shape	17	Noise	Steady	Impulsive
9	Steady	Steady	Increasing	18	Noise	Falling	Impulsive

An overview of all of the sounds is presented in Table 1. In the first nine sounds, pitch and spectral centroid were manipulated by controlling the fundamental frequency of the FM sound, and the center frequency of a parametric equalizer which boosted certain parts of the sound spectrum. These sounds were generated by changing the envelopes of pitch between 300 and 1000 Hz (*rising*,

---

[2] http://folk.uio.no/krisny/cmmr2011

falling and *steady*) and equalizer center frequency between 50 and 13000 Hz (*rising* and *falling* as well as filter bypass, here interpreted as *steady* spectral centroid). This allowed for an appropriate discrimination between the individual sound parameter changes taking place within the sound. Sounds 10–12 were based on noise rather than a pitched FM sound, and only the filter was adjusted for these sounds. In Sounds 13 and 14, a second parametric equalizer was added. In Sound 13, the center frequencies of the equalizers started at 1000 and 5000 Hz and approached each other towards 3000 Hz, and in Sound 14, the center frequencies started at 3000 Hz, and moved apart to 1000 and 5000 Hz.

The synthesized sounds mentioned in the previous paragraph were multiplied by a window function to control the overall dynamic envelope. Here, we wanted to keep a main focus on the pitch and spectral properties of the whole sound, while influence from onset characteristics of the sounds (changes in sound features during the first part of the sound) was not desired. Therefore, Sounds 1–14 were made with a slow attack and increasing amplitude by applying the amplitude envelope displayed in Figure 3(a).

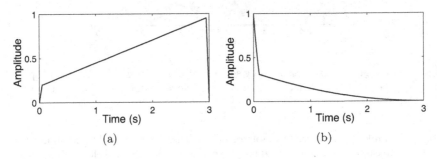

(a)   (b)

Fig. 3. The envelopes that were used for the amplitude control: (a) Non-impulsive sounds, and (b) Impulsive sounds

The characteristics of the pitch envelope and the filter frequency also influenced the final dynamic envelope of the sounds. Some of which had a bell-shaped dynamic envelope, displayed in Figure 4(a), while others had a continuously increasing one, displayed in Figure 4(b).

We also wanted to investigate how the onset characteristics of a sound influenced the sound tracings that were performed to it. Therefore, impulsive versions of four of the sounds were made. Sounds 15–18 were versions of Sounds 1, 9, 10 and 12, the only difference was that instead of the slowly increasing dynamic envelope, we applied the impulsive envelope shown in Figure 3(b). It should be noted that the dynamic envelope of Sound 15 was different compared to the other impulsive sounds, because the varying pitch and filter frequency influenced the dynamics. This resulted in a dynamic envelope which was a combination of the impulsive and bell-shaped envelopes, as shown in Figure 4(c).

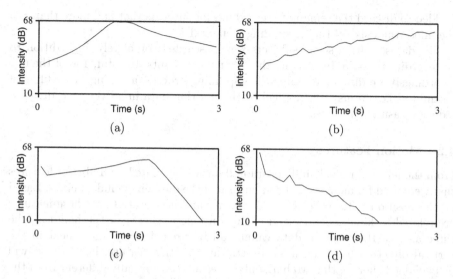

Fig. 4. The figure displays the dynamic envelopes of 4 sounds, analyzed with a perceptual model in the sound analysis software Praat. (a) Bell-shaped envelope (Sound 2), (b) Increasing envelope (Sound 9), (c) Impulsive and Bell-shaped envelope (Sound 15), and (d) Impulsive envelope (Sound 16).

4   Data Processing

In this section, we will describe the processing that was performed on the motion data to prepare it for the analysis process. The position data from the two handles was used, but it was not sufficient for our purpose to use it directly, and hence a number of data processing steps were taken. These steps included gap-filling, smoothing, feature extraction, data reduction and normalization.

4.1   Preprocessing

As mentioned in Section 3.4, some recordings contained missing data frames, and therefore gap-filling was required. We applied gap-filling on small data gaps by interpolating between the first and last missing frame using a piecewise cubic Hermite spline function with the preceding and succeeding frames as reference. A number of gaps were too large for gap-filling to be possible. In these cases, the recordings were discarded.

Certain participants had a large number of discarded recordings, which was due to poor calibration of the system in some sessions, but also because some participants repeatedly occluded the reflective markers or moved the handles out of the capture space. If a single participant had too many discarded recordings, the consequence would be that this person only influenced a small portion of the data set, and we could risk that one participant only influenced one side of the analysis when two subsets of the dataset were compared. For this reason, we decided to discard the remaining recordings for subjects that had more than 1/3 (i.e. more than six) of their recordings removed.

The datasets from seven subjects were discarded completely, in addition to 30 recordings distributed among the other participants. In total, 156 of the 684 recordings were discarded. After the gap-filling process, a sliding mean filter of 5 samples (i.e. 50 ms) was applied to the position data in all the recordings to reduce measurement noise.

4.2   Motion Features

From the left and right handle position data we calculated a number of features that were used for analysis and comparison of the different sound tracings. Based on the position data, we calculated velocity and acceleration, as these features are related to kinetic energy and change in kinetic energy of the handles. The three axes of the position data cannot all be used directly. Movement in the vertical direction has been used directly as a motion feature, however, as will be explained shortly, the two horizontal axes are conceptually different from the vertical one, and have not been used directly.

The position data describes the position of each handle in relation to the room, or more precisely, in relation to the position of the calibration frame that was used when calibrating the motion capture system. This calibration frame determined the origin of the coordinate system and the direction of the axes. The position of the handles in relation to the calibration frame is not really relevant in light of the task that was given to the participants. The participants could not relate to the position of the calibration frame since it was removed after calibration. Furthermore, the participants were not instructed to face in any particular direction during the experiment, or precisely where to stand in the room. For this reason, we find it misleading to base our analysis directly on the horizontal position data. In contrast, the vertical position of the handles is a reference that was the same for all participants. The floor level remained constant, and was independent of where an individual stood, regardless of the direction he or she faced.

The one thing that varied between the subjects was the height range, as one participant could reach his arms to 2.2 m, while another up to 2.5 m. This was adjusted for by normalization as we will return to in Section 4.4. Based on these considerations, and on experiences regarding which features have proven to be most pertinent in previous experiments [2,24,25] the following data series for motion features were calculated:

- Vertical position: The distance to the floor.
- Vertical velocity: The derivative of the vertical position feature.
- Absolute velocity: Euclidean distance between successive position samples.
- Absolute acceleration: Euclidean distance between the successive derivatives of the position data.
- Distance: Euclidean distance between the hands.
- Change in distance: The derivative of the distance feature.

The features mentioned above are all data series, which we shall refer to as *serial features*. From these data series we calculated *single-value features*, meaning features that are given by a single number. These features describe a general tendency for an entire sound tracing. Examples of such features are mean vertical velocity and mean acceleration.

4.3   Data Reduction

To be able to compare the sound tracings, the data representation of each recording should be equal. In our case, this is not the case with the raw data, since some participants varied between using both hands, and only the left or right hand. Out of the 528 recordings, 454 were performed with both hands, 15 with only the left hand, and 59 with only the right hand. The participants were not specifically instructed whether to use one or two hands. In order to achieve equal data representation for all sound tracings, we had to choose between using the separate data streams from both hands in all cases, or reducing the data to fewer data streams keeping only the pertinent information from each sound tracing. Basing the analysis on data from a hand that was clearly not meant to be part of the sound tracing appeared less accurate to us, than to base the analysis on the data streams from only the active hand(s). Therefore, we calculated one serial position feature from each sound tracing, as well as one velocity feature, acceleration feature, and so forth. For the one-handed sound tracings, we used feature vectors of the active hand directly, and for the two-handed sound tracings, we calculated the average of both hands on a sample-by-sample basis. We did not change the distance feature for the single-handed sound tracings.

Admittedly, this difference between single-handed and two-handed performances presents a weakness in our experiment design, and we could have chosen different approaches to dealing with this challenge. We will continue searching for more comprehensive analysis methods which take into account this extra degree of freedom. If new methods for analysis are not found, a solution could be to instruct the participants to always use both hands.

4.4   Normalization

All feature vectors have been normalized for each subject. This means that all the calculated features were scaled to a range between 0 and 1, where the value was determined by the particular subject's maximum value for that feature. For example, if Subject 14 had a maximum vertical position of 2 meters across all of their sound tracings, all of the vertical position data series related to Subject 14 were divided by 2 meters. This type of normalization reduced individual differences that were due to height, arm length, and so forth. This means that the data displayed in the plots in the coming section will all be scaled between 0 and 1. A similar normalization was performed on all of the single-value features.

5   Analysis and Results

The following sections present comparisons between three different aspects of the sounds. We will start in Section 5.1 by introducing our analysis method. In Section 5.2, the effect of the onset properties of the sounds are presented. In Sections 5.3 and 5.4, we present how the envelopes of pitch and spectral centroid tend to influence the sound tracings. Finally, in Section 5.5, differences between pitched and non-pitched sounds are presented.

5.1   Analysis Method

Our analysis is based on statistical comparisons between the individual data series, both sample-by-sample in serial features, and also on a higher level, comparing single-value features for the whole data series. The analyses of serial features are presented in plots where the individual data series are displayed together with the average vector of the data series. To facilitate the reading of these plots, we include a small example plot in Figure 5. This particular plot displays five data series ranging between 0 (white) and 1 (black). The vertical dashed lines show the beginning and end of the sound file, the motion capture recording began 0.5 seconds before the start of the sound file, and also lasted beyond the entire duration of the sound file. The black solid and dashed lines show the mean and standard deviations across the five data series on a sample-by-sample basis. From this figure, it is difficult to get precise readings of the values of the individual sound tracings, but the horizontal grayscale plots still give some impression of the distribution of this data set. The 0–1 scale on the y-axis is for the mean and standard deviation curves.

When certain tendencies are observed for different groups, we evaluate the statistical significance of the tendencies by applying one-tailed t-tests.[3] Results from the tests are presented in tables, where df denotes the degrees of freedom,[4] and t is the t-value from the t-test. p is calculated based on df and t, and denotes the probability that the two data sets are equally distributed, a p-value of less than 0.05 denotes a statistically significant difference between the groups.

Two subgroups were selected from the data set for analyzing the impact of musical training on the results in the experiment. Because of the somewhat imprecise classification of subjects' level of musical training, we chose to look at only the subjects that labeled themselves as having either no musical training or extensive musical training. This was done to ensure that there was indeed a difference in musical experience between the two groups.

---

[3] A t-test is a method to estimate the probability that a difference between two data sets is due to chance. See http://en.wikipedia.org/wiki/T-test for details.

[4] df is a statistical variable related to the t-test, denoting the size of the data material. It is not to be confused with e.g. 6DOF position-and-orientation data.

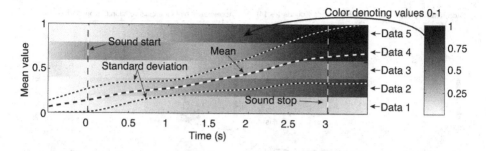

Fig. 5. The figure explains how to read the plots presented below. This is a reduced example with only 5 data series. The data series range between 0 (white) and 1 (black). Please refer to the text for explanation. A single subject is typically associated with multiple data-series, and tick marks on the right Y-axis denote different subjects. The ticks are not equidistant since some recordings were discarded (cf. Section 4.1). Furthermore, some plots display more data series per subject than others, thus the Y-axis resolution differs between plots.

5.2 Onset Acceleration for Impulsive and Non-impulsive Sounds

We evaluated how the onset characteristics of sound influence sound tracings by comparing the acceleration envelopes of impulsive sounds to non-impulsive sounds. We observed a distinct difference in acceleration envelope for sound tracings of the impulsive sounds compared to the rest of the data set, as displayed in Figure 6. To evaluate the significance of this difference, we compared the onset acceleration of the sound tracings. *Onset acceleration* is a single-value feature, which was calculated as the mean acceleration in the beginning of the sound tracing. Figure 6(b) shows that most subjects made an accentuated attack after the start of the sound file. Therefore we used a window from 0.2 seconds (20 samples) before the sound started to 0.5 seconds (50 samples) after the sound started to calculate the onset acceleration. The results of t-tests comparing the onset acceleration for impulsive and non-impulsive sounds are displayed in Table 2. The table shows that onset acceleration values for impulsive sounds are significantly higher than non-impulsive sounds, $t(526) = 13.65$, $p < 0.01$.[5]

Figure 7 displays separate acceleration curves of impulsive sounds for musical experts and non-experts. The figure shows that both groups have similar onset acceleration levels, and a t-test showed no statistical difference between the onset acceleration levels from the two groups, $t(84) = 0.55$, $p = 0.29$. However, the plots do show a difference in timing. By defining time of onset as the time of maximum acceleration within the previously defined onset interval, experts hit on average 163 ms after the start of the sound file, while non-experts hit 238 ms after the start of the sound file, a difference which was statistically significant, $t(63) = 2.51$, $p = 0.007$. This calculation was based only on Sounds 16–18, because several subjects did not perform an accentuated onset for Sound 15.

---

[5] This is the American Psychological Association style for reporting statistical results. Please refer to [1] for details.

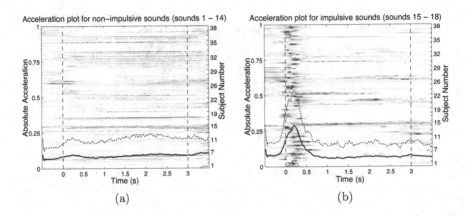

Fig. 6. Acceleration for (a) non-impulsive sounds (406 sound tracings) and (b) impulsive sounds (122 sound tracings). The black solid and dashed lines show the mean value and standard deviation across all sound tracings. Each horizontal line in the image displays the acceleration vector of a single sound tracing ranging between 0 (white) and 1 (black), normalized per subject. See Figure 5 for guidelines on how to read these plots.

Table 2. Results from t-tests comparing onset acceleration for impulsive sounds to non-impulsive sounds. There was a significant difference between the groups for both expert and non-expert subjects. See the text for explanation of the variables.

Onset acceleration, impulsive and non-impulsive sounds

Test description	df	t	p
Impulsive vs non-impulsive, all subjects	526	13.65	< 0.01
Impulsive vs non-impulsive, expert subjects	182	8.65	< 0.01
Impulsive vs non-impulsive, non-expert subjects	183	7.86	< 0.01
Onset acceleration level, experts vs non-experts	84	0.55	0.29
Onset time, expert vs non-expert subjects	63	2.51	< 0.01

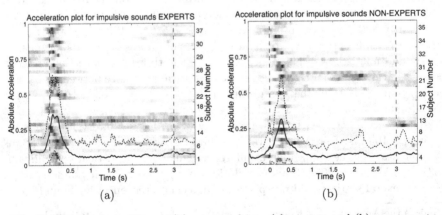

Fig. 7. The plot from Figure 6(b) separated into (a) experts and (b) non-experts

5.3   Vertical Position and Sound Frequency Features

As mentioned in Section 2, other researchers have documented a relationship between vertical position and pitch. Not surprisingly, this relationship was also found in the data set presented in this paper. In addition to pitch, we observed that the frequency of the spectral centroid is relevant to the vertical position.

Sounds 1, 4 and 5 all had rising pitch envelopes, and Sounds 8 and 11 had rising spectral centroids combined with stable pitch and noise respectively. For the sound tracings of these sounds, there was a clear tendency of upward movement. Similarly, for the sounds with falling pitch, or with falling spectral centroid, there was a clear tendency of downward movement. t-tests comparing the average vertical velocity of the "rising" sounds to the "falling" sounds showed highly significant distinctions between the groups, as shown in Table 3. The mean normalized vertical velocity for the first group was 0.74, and for the second group 0.28 (a value of 0.5 indicates no vertical motion). This is shown in Figure 8.

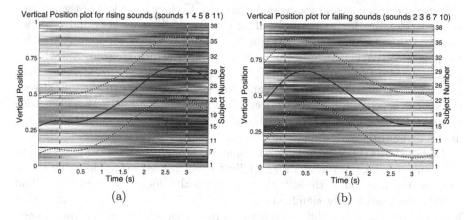

(a)   (b)

Fig. 8. Vertical position for (a) rising sounds (142 sound tracings) and (b) falling sounds (144 sound tracings). The black line shows the mean value across all the data series, each horizontal line in the image displays the vertical position of a single sound tracing normalized per subject between 0 (lower position, white) and 1 (higher position, black).

Table 3. T-tests comparing the average vertical velocity of rising and falling sounds

Average vertical velocity, rising and falling sounds

Test description	df	t	p
Rising vs falling, all subjects	284	18.89	< 0.01
Rising vs falling, non-expert subjects	98	8.86	< 0.01
Rising vs falling, expert subjects	97	11.69	< 0.01
Rising, experts vs non-experts	98	0.58	0.28
Falling, experts vs non-experts	97	1.79	0.04

There was no significant difference between the average vertical velocity for experts and non-experts for the rising sounds, however, for the falling sounds there was some difference between the two groups. Experts had a higher extent of downward motion than non-experts, $t(97) = 1.7982$, $p = 0.04$.

It is worth noting that even though Sounds 1 and 2 had increasing and decreasing pitch envelopes, respectively, they had opposing spectral centroid envelopes. When the spectral centroid envelope and the pitch envelope moved in opposite directions, most subjects in our data set chose to let the vertical motion follow the direction of the pitch envelope. The direction of vertical motion seems to be more strongly related to pitch than to spectral centroid.

The observed difference between sounds with varying pitch and sounds with only varying spectral centroid makes it interesting to take a more in depth look at the individual sounds in the *rising* and *falling* classes. Since subjects tended to follow pitch more than spectral centroid in the sounds where the two feature envelopes moved in opposite directions, it is natural to assume that subjects would move more to sounds where the pitch was varied, than to sounds where only the spectral centroid was varied. Figure 9 displays box plots of the average vertical velocities for rising and falling sounds. In Figures 9(a) and 9(b), we observed that the difference between the sounds is larger for falling than for rising sounds. We can also see that Sounds 7 and 8, which are sounds where the pitch is constant but spectral centroid is moving, show less extreme values than the rest of the sounds. Figures 9(c) and 9(d) suggest that the difference between the sounds is larger for expert subjects than for non-expert subjects. There also seems to be more inter-subjective similarities among experts than non-experts, as the variances among experts are lower.

Table 4 shows the results of one-way analyses of variance (ANOVAs) applied to the sound tracings in the rising and falling class, respectively. The table shows that on the one hand, the difference in vertical velocity between the falling sounds was statistically significant $F(4, 139) = 7.76$, $p < 0.01$. On the other hand, the corresponding difference between the rising sounds was not statistically significant $F(4, 137) = 1.53$, $p = 0.20$. The table also reveals that the significant difference between the groups was only present for expert subjects, $F(4, 44) = 4.92$, $p < 0.01$, and not for non-experts, $F(4, 45) = 1.52$, $p = 0.21$.

Table 4. Results from one-way ANOVAs of the vertical velocity for sound tracings within the *rising* and *falling* classes. There is a significant difference between the five falling sounds for expert subjects. *df* are the degrees of freedom (between groups, within groups), *F* is the F-value with the associated f-test, *p* is the probability that the null-hypothesis is true.

Subjects	Rising sounds			Falling sounds		
	df	*F*	*p*	*df*	*F*	*p*
All subjects	(4, 137)	1.53	0.20	(4, 139)	7.76	< 0.01
Expert subjects	(4, 45)	0.39	0.81	(4, 44)	4.92	< 0.01
Non-expert subjects	(4, 45)	0.25	0.90	(4, 45)	1.52	0.21

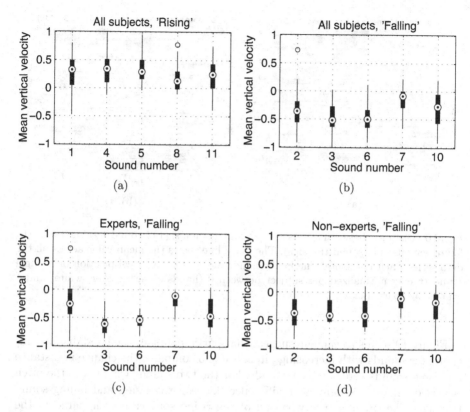

Fig. 9. Box plots of average vertical velocities for (a) rising sounds and (b) falling sounds. The difference between the sounds is greater for falling sounds than for rising sounds, and greater for (c) experts than for (d) non-experts. Note also that the sounds where the pitch is constant and only the spectral centroid is manipulated (Sounds 7 and 8) have the least extreme values in all the plots.

5.4   Pitch and Distance between Hands

Eitan and Timmers pointed out that the relationship between pitch and motion features may be more complex than mapping pitch to vertical position [6]. For this reason, we have also analyzed how the distance between the hands corresponds to pitch frequency.

Figures 10(a) and 10(b) display the distance between the hands for sound tracings to rising and falling sounds, respectively. On the one hand, the black lines displaying the average distance features do not show very clear overall tendencies towards increasing or decreasing distance, but on the other hand, the underlying images, displaying the individual sound tracings, show that there is a substantial amount of change in the distance between the hands, both for the rising and the falling sounds.

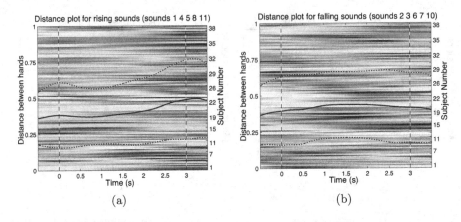

Fig. 10. Distance between hands for (a) rising sounds (142 sound tracings) and (b) falling sounds (144 sound tracings). The black line shows the mean value across all the data series, each horizontal line in the image displays the vertical position of a single sound tracing normalized per subject between 0 (hands close together, white) and 1 (hands far apart, black).

Figure 10 seems to vaguely suggest that participants let the hand distance increase for sounds with increasing pitch. Table 5 compares the change in distance for rising sounds versus falling sounds. For the two sounds where only the pitch is varied, there is a significant difference between the rising and falling sound tracings. The same is true when all of the rising sounds are compared to the falling sounds. On the contrary, we do not observe significant differences in the instances where the spectral centroid is varied.

Table 5. Results from t-tests comparing the average change in distance between hands of rising and falling sounds

Average change in hand distance, rising versus falling sounds

Sounds	Varying features	df	t	p
5 vs. 6	Pitch	52	3.24	< 0.01
4 vs. 3	Pitch and spectral centroid	54	1.50	0.07
1 vs. 2	Pitch, opposing spectral centroid	53	1.09	0.14
8 vs. 7	Spectral centroid, pitched	60	0.48	0.32
11 vs. 10	Spectral centroid, non-pitched	57	-0.44	0.67
All rising sounds vs. all falling sounds		284	2.60	< 0.01

5.5   Acceleration Envelope for Pitched and Non-pitched Sounds

We have evaluated how the presence of a distinct pitch influences the sound tracing by comparing acceleration envelopes of sound tracings performed to pitched sounds and non-pitched sounds.

Three of the sounds used in the experiment were based on noise, and three were based on a stable tone with a fundamental frequency of 342 Hz. Within each of these categories, one sound had a falling spectral centroid, one had a rising spectral centroid and one had a stable spectral centroid.[6] Figure 11 shows the acceleration curves from the sound tracings to non-pitched and pitched sounds respectively. The mean acceleration was significantly higher for non-pitched sounds than pitched sounds, $t(179) = 5.53$, $p < 0.01$. For non-pitched sounds the mean normalized acceleration was 0.52, and for pitched sounds it was 0.28.

This significant distinction between acceleration values for pitched and non-pitched sounds was also found when the data from experts and non-experts was analyzed individually. Furthermore, no significant difference was found between the acceleration levels of experts and non-experts, $p = 0.46$ for both pitched and non-pitched sounds, respectively. See Table 6 for statistical results.

Table 6. Results from t-tests comparing acceleration of pitched to non-pitched sounds

Acceleration, non-pitched and pitched sounds			
Test description	df	t	p
Non-pitched vs pitched, all subjects	179	5.53	< 0.01
Non-pitched vs pitched, expert subjects	62	3.31	< 0.01
Non-pitched vs pitched, non-expert subjects	62	3.68	< 0.01
Noise, experts vs non-experts	61	0.10	0.46
Stable tone, experts vs non-experts	63	0.11	0.46

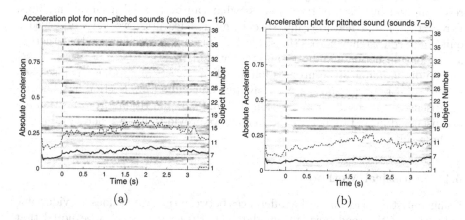

(a)   (b)

Fig. 11. Acceleration for (a) non-pitched sounds and (b) pitched sounds. The black line shows the mean value per sample, each horizontal line displays the acceleration of a single sound tracing ranging from 0 (white) to 1 (black). The mean acceleration levels for the non-pitched sounds are generally higher than for pitched sounds.

---

[6] Sounds based on noise: 10, 11, and 12. Sounds based on a stable tone: 7, 8, and 9.

5.6   Summary of the Results

The results in this section have shown that the participants produced sound tracings with higher onset acceleration for impulsive sounds than for non-impulsive sounds. This was true for experts and non-experts. The onset time of musical experts was on average 75 ms ahead of non-experts. Furthermore, sounds without a distinct pitch seem to induce higher acceleration than pitched sounds.

Vertical displacement of the hands was found to be related to pitch and to spectral centroid. When pitch and spectral centroid moved in opposite directions, most subjects let the vertical position of the hands follow the perceived pitch. When only the spectral centroid was varied, there was less vertical motion than for sounds with varying pitch. This was particularly true for sounds with a stable pitch, as opposed to no perceivable pitch. Overall, falling sounds induced more vertical motion than rising sounds. For the falling sounds, the variance between the vertical velocity of the subjects was low, suggesting that there is more consistency within the expert group than in the non-expert group. Finally, there was significant difference between the change in hand distance for some of the sounds with falling and rising envelopes. We will discuss these findings in the next section.

6   Discussion

The following discussion will address the analysis method, the results from the previous section, as well as how the experiment setup and task may have influenced the results. We will put the results into context in relation to previous research, and in this way try to assess what can be learned from our findings. For certain sound features and specific motion features, we have observed a quite high consistency across the subjects. This supports the claim that there is a relationship between auditory and motor modalities.

The discussion is structured as follows: The statistical approach is discussed in Section 6.1. In Section 6.2, we evaluate the results from Section 5.2. Section 6.3 discusses the results from Sections 5.3 and 5.4, and results from Section 5.5 are discussed in Section 6.4. In Section 6.5, we provide a more general evaluation of the results.

6.1   Statistical Method

Using statistics to evaluate the differences between the groups does provide some indication of the tendencies in our data set. However, it should be noted that the t-test and ANOVA methods assume that the data is normally distributed. The subsets of data in our statistical analyses were tested for normality using a Jaque-Bera test[7] with significance level 0.05. This test revealed that 13 out of the 52 data sets in our experiments do not follow a normal distribution, and thus the statistical results can not alone be used to make strong conclusions.

---

[7] http://en.wikipedia.org/wiki/Jarque-Bera_test

Nevertheless, the results from the statistical tests support the results that are shown in the corresponding feature plots. This gives us reason to believe that the statistical results are trustworthy for our data set.

It should be noted that for the sample-by-sample based plots, the standard deviations are quite high, particularly for the acceleration curves shown in Figure 11. Since these plots were derived on a sample-by sample basis, the high standard deviations are not very surprising. In Figure 11, the high standard deviation reflects that even though several subjects had a high overall acceleration, they vary between high and low acceleration throughout the sound tracing. This demonstrates the importance of looking at the individual sound tracings in the plot, not only the mean and standard deviation curves.

6.2   Impulsive Sound Onset

Let us have a look at the results presented in Section 5.2, where the onset acceleration of sound tracings to impulsive sounds was shown to be much higher than for non-impulsive sounds. In our opinion, these results can best be explained from a *causation* perspective. In other words: people link the impulsive characteristics of the sound to some sort of impulsive action that could have caused the sound. An example of an impulsive action is displayed in Figure 12. The figure shows how the subject performs an accentuated attack, with high acceleration, followed by a slower falling slope down to a resting position. The sound tracing resembles that of crashing two cymbals together.

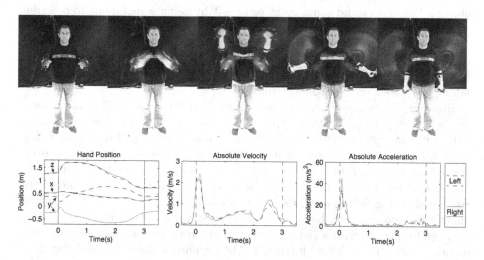

Fig. 12. The figure displays an impulsive action, with motion history images and the calculated motion features for the left (black) and right (red) hand. Motion history images show the current frame and the average frame difference for past video frames [16]. x (back/forth), y (sideways) and z (up/down) are position coordinates from the motion capture system.

Lakoff and Johnson [18] talk about causation as an important element in understanding objects and events in the world. As an example, they mention a paper airplane which we understand primarily as paper, and secondarily as airplane. The making, or cause, of the paper airplane is an essential element in our understanding of this object. It is interesting to compare the *causation* term to Schaeffer's theory of the sonic object [26]. According to Schaeffer, sonic objects are defined by their *causal coherence*, something which Godøy linked to gesture-sensations and chunking in sound [9]. According to Lakoff and Johnson [18], the causation of an object is partly emergent, or something that is present in the object itself, which makes it possible to understand an object as a holistic and metaphorical unit. Again, compared with the sonic object, this emergent property works well with Schaeffer's principle of *stress-articulation*, or natural discontinuities in the continuous sound signal [26].

Following these thoughts, it seems apparent that people link the impulsive onset of sounds to some sort of impulsive or ballistic action or event. Given the constraints of two handles to imitate the sound, some participants imitated the action of crashing two cymbals together, while others imitated a single-handed or two-handed striking action. The discontinuity of stress-articulation in sound has its motor counterpart in the higher derivatives of position data, here shown by a high onset acceleration.

6.3 Sound Frequency Features

In addition to the causation perspective, Lakoff and Johnson also introduced the *metaphor* perspective. Metaphors are crucial to our understanding of events and objects. We understand some event or object by using a metaphor to describe it. According to Eitan and Timmers [6], Cox [4] has linked the metaphor "more is up" to a perceptual relationship between vertical position and pitch. In our experiment, the results show clearly that there is a relationship between these features, and that most subjects follow rising pitch with upward motion, and falling pitch with downward motion.

However, Eitan and Timmers have shown that for pitch, "up" is not always the best metaphor [6]. In their experiments, low pitch has also been associated with with metaphors like "heavy" or "big". Also, Walker [27] described rising pitch to be a good descriptor for increasing temperature. For this exact reason, we also investigated if the motion feature *hand distance* was related to the rising and falling envelopes. Our results show that when all the rising sounds were compared to the falling ones, there was a significant difference in the average change in hand distance. However, a closer look at the results revealed that on average, for sounds with a rising envelope and with a falling envelope alike, the distance between the hands increased. The significant difference was therefore only due to a faster increase in distance for rising sounds than for falling sounds. In addition, a significant difference between rising and falling envelopes occurred when only the parameter *pitch* was varied. In this case, the average hand distance decreased for falling pitch and increased for rising pitch, and thus to some extent, defined a relationship between these features. Nevertheless, even though several subjects did change the distance between their hands for these sounds, there was much less similarity among the subjects compared to the vertical position feature. Some subjects moved their hands apart while other moved them towards each other. So to conclude, the "more-is-up" metaphor for pitch seems to be the best metaphor to describe the results in our data set.

An example of a sound tracing performed to a sound with falling pitch and rising spectral centroid is shown in Figure 13. The motion history images show how the subject prepares for the sound tracing by moving his hands up, then moving them down and out in such a way that the vertical position follows the pitch envelope. At the end of the sound tracing, the subjects increasingly vibrates the right hand, as shown in the acceleration plot. This might be a gesture performed to imitate the increased spectral centroid which is increasingly prominent towards the end of the sound file. As the motion history images show, the hand distance first increases and then decreases in a sound where the pitch is constantly falling and the spectral centroid is constantly rising.

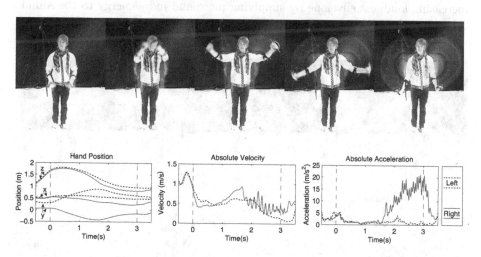

Fig. 13. The figure displays motion history images and feature plots for the left and right hand for a sound tracing performed to a sound with falling pitch, rising spectral centroid, and a bell-shaped dynamic envelope

An interesting feature regarding the rising and falling sounds, and the correlation to vertical position, is that sound seems to be more descriptive than motion. Our results show that even though the sounds were easy to tell apart, the sound tracings that were performed to the different sounds were similar. This implies that although you can describe certain perceptual features of the sound through an action, it is not necessarily clear which perceptual feature(s) the action imitates. Elevating a hand might refer to increasing pitch or to increasing spectral centroid, or to something else.

6.4   Pitched versus Non-pitched Sounds

We observed a significantly higher amount of acceleration in sound tracings performed to non-pitched sounds than to pitched sounds. This may be explained by participant's associations with this sound property. Sounds based on noise have wind-like properties, which might cause people to move a lot, as if they were blowing with the wind or creating the wind themselves. Pitched sounds, on the other hand, seem to provide something stable for the participants to "hold on to", that is not provided by the non-pitched sounds.

For Sounds 9 and 12, which both had stable spectral centroids, we observed that some participants started shaking or rotating their hands, gradually increasing the frequency or amplitude of the shaking. One example of this is shown in Figure 14. As these sounds had no change in pitch or spectral centroid, the loudness envelope of the sounds seem to have been the main influence in these instances. The increased shaking or rotation intensity may be explained by some sort of engine metaphor: we believe participants wanted to follow the gradually increasing loudness envelope by supplying more and more energy to the sound through their motion.

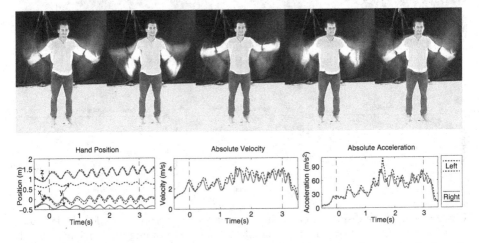

Fig. 14. The figure shows motion history images of a subject moving to a noise-based sound. Plots of xyz-position, velocity, and acceleration are shown below.

6.5   Final Remarks

Admittedly, the results presented in this paper are related to the context of the experiment, and cannot necessarily be claimed to be valid outside this setting. The way in which subjects solved the task may have been influenced by the instructions, which were to imagine that moving the hands in the air created the sound. Even though we did not provide the subjects with a priori metaphors like connecting upward motion to increasing pitch, the options for movement were limited. Godøy has postulated that our musical motions are goal-directed, and that these motions are guided by goal-postures describing the shape and position of our end-effectors [11]. These positional goal-points may have been more consciously exposed than features describing the relationship between the hands or details of the trajectory between, for instance, a high and low goal point. In light of the experiment task, other pitch relationships like the one between low pitch and "heavy" or "big" [6], may have been less accessible than drawing a trajectory between two positional goal points. Some subjects may have consciously or unconsciously used a feature like hand distance to describe pitch, but as our results show, this was more inconsistent between subjects.

Even though the experimental setup may have prevented the subjects from using other descriptors than spatio-temporal ones, we are confident that the results show some indication of how people relate spatio-temporal features of motion to features of sound. The participants were given an imagined instrument, and they made their own mental model of how this instrument worked. Some aspects of these mental models were similar for the majority of the subjects.

7 Conclusions and Future Work

We have presented an experiment on sound tracing, where motions performed to sound have been analyzed from micro and meso timescale perspectives. Plotting of serial motion features at the micro timescale was used to obtain impressions of general tendencies in the data set, and statistical evaluations of single-value features at the meso timescale indicated the significance of these tendencies.

Rising pitch, and rising spectral centroid correlated strongly with upward motion, and similarly, falling pitch and spectral centroid, correlated strongly with downward motion. When pitch and spectral centroid moved in opposite directions, participants followed the pitch feature. Furthermore, sounds based on noise induced higher overall acceleration than sounds based on a steady pitch, and sounds with an impulsive onset caused a high acceleration peak in the beginning of the sound tracing.

To follow up on this experiment, we are currently starting to evaluate advantages and disadvantages of different methods for analyzing sound tracings. We believe that the different approaches that have been taken to analyze such data provide different types of knowledge, and that the choice of analysis method is important. For instance, some methods may be good at revealing action-sound relationships at a low timescale level, while others may work better at chunk-level or higher. We are also moving towards applying the results from our studies in development of new interfaces for musical expression.

Acknowledgements. The research leading to these results has received funding from the European Union Seventh Framework Programme under grant agreement n° 257906, Engineering Proprioception in Computer Systems (EPiCS).

References

1. Publication Manual of the American Psychological Association, 6th edn. American Psychological Association, Washington, DC (2010)
2. Caramiaux, B., Bevilacqua, F., Schnell, N.: Towards a Gesture-Sound Cross-Modal Analysis. In: Kopp, S., Wachsmuth, I. (eds.) GW 2009. LNCS, vol. 5934, pp. 158–170. Springer, Heidelberg (2010)
3. Caramiaux, B., Bevilacqua, F., Schnell, N.: Sound selection by gestures. In: Proceedings of the International Conference on New Interfaces for Musical Expression, Oslo, Norway, pp. 329–330 (2011)
4. Cox, A.W.: The Metaphoric Logic of Musical Motion and Space. Ph.D. thesis, University of Oregon (1999)
5. Eitan, Z., Granot, R.Y.: How music moves: Musical parameters and listeners' images of motion. Music Perception 23(3), 221–248 (2006)
6. Eitan, Z., Timmers, R.: Beethoven's last piano sonata and those who follow crocodiles: Cross-domain mappings of auditory pitch in a musical context. Cognition 114(3), 405–422 (2010)
7. Gjerdingen, R., Perrott, D.: Scanning the dial: The rapid recognition of music genres. Journal of New Music Research 37(2), 93–100 (2008)
8. Glette, K., Jensenius, A.R., Godøy, R.I.: Extracting action-sound features from a sound-tracing study. In: Proceedings of the Second Norwegian Artificial Intelligence Symposium, pp. 63–66 (2010)
9. Godøy, R.I.: Gestural-sonorous objects: Embodied extensions of Schaeffer's conceptual apparatus. Organised Sound 11(2), 149–157 (2006)
10. Godøy, R.I.: Chunking Sound for Musical Analysis. In: Ystad, S., Kronland-Martinet, R., Jensen, K. (eds.) CMMR 2008. LNCS, vol. 5493, pp. 67–80. Springer, Heidelberg (2009)
11. Godøy, R.I.: Gestural affordances of musical sound. In: Godøy, R.I., Leman, M. (eds.) Musical Gestures: Sound, Movement, and Meaning, ch. 5, pp. 103–125. Routledge (2010)
12. Godøy, R.I., Haga, E., Jensenius, A.R.: Exploring music-related gestures by sound-tracing. A preliminary study. In: Ng, K. (ed.) COST287-ConGAS 2nd Int. Symposium on Gesture Interfaces for Multimedia Systems, Leeds, pp. 27–33 (2006)
13. Godøy, R.I., Jensenius, A.R.: Body movement in music information retrieval. In: Proceedings of the 10th International Society for Music Information Retrieval Conference, Kobe, Japan (2009)
14. Husserl, E.: The Phenomenology of Internal Time Consciousness. Indiana University Press, Bloomington (1964, trans. Churchill, J.S.)
15. Jensenius, A.R.: Action–Sound: Developing Methods and Tools for Studying Music-Related Bodily Movement. Ph.D. thesis, University of Oslo (2007)
16. Jensenius, A.R.: Some video abstraction techniques for displaying body movement in analysis and performance. Leonardo Music Journal (forthcoming, 2012)
17. Kozak, M., Nymoen, K., Godøy, R.I.: The Effects of Spectral Features of Sound on Gesture Type and Timing. In: Efthimiou, E., Kouroupetroglou, G., Fotinea, S.-E. (eds.) GW 2011. LNCS(LNAI), vol. 7206, Springer, Heidelberg (to appear, 2012)
18. Lakoff, G., Johnson, M.: Metaphors We Live By. University of Chicago Press, Chicago (1980)
19. Leman, M.: Embodied Music Cognition and Mediation Technology. MIT Press, Cambridge (2007)

20. Leman, M.: Systematic musicology at the crossroads of modern music research. In: Schneider, A. (ed.) Systematic and Comparative Musicology: Concepts, Methods, Findings, Hamburger Jahrbuch für Musikwissenschaft, vol. 24, pp. 89–115. Peter Lang, Frankfurt (2008)
21. Merer, A., Ystad, S., Kronland-Martinet, R., Aramaki, M.: Semiotics of Sounds Evoking Motions: Categorization and Acoustic Features. In: Kronland-Martinet, R., Ystad, S., Jensen, K. (eds.) CMMR 2007. LNCS, vol. 4969, pp. 139–158. Springer, Heidelberg (2008)
22. Miller, G.A.: The magical number seven, plus or minus two: Some limits on our capacity for processing information. Psychological Review 63, 81–97 (1956)
23. van Nort, D.: Instrumental listening: sonic gesture as design principle. Organised Sound 14(02), 177–187 (2009)
24. Nymoen, K., Caramiaux, B., Kozak, M., Torresen, J.: Analyzing sound tracings: a multimodal approach to music information retrieval. In: Proceedings of the 1st International ACM Workshop on Music Information Retrieval with User-Centered and Multimodal Strategies, pp. 39–44. ACM, New York (2011)
25. Nymoen, K., Glette, K., Skogstad, S.A., Torresen, J., Jensenius, A.R.: Searching for cross-individual relationships between sound and movement features using an SVM classifier. In: Proceedings of the International Conference on New Interfaces for Musical Expression, Sydney, pp. 259–262 (2010)
26. Schaeffer, P., Reibel, G.: Solfège de l'objet sonore. ORTF, Paris, France (1967, Reedited by INA-GRM 1998)
27. Walker, B.N., Kramer, G.: Mappings and metaphors in auditory displays: An experimental assessment. ACM Trans. Appl. Percept. 2(4), 407–412 (2005)
28. Wilson, M.: Six views of embodied cognition. Psychonomic Bulletin & Review 9(4), 625–636 (2002)

Auditory Time-Frequency Masking: Psychoacoustical Data and Application to Audio Representations

Thibaud Necciari[1,2], Peter Balazs[1], Richard Kronland-Martinet[2], Sølvi Ystad[2], Bernhard Laback[1], Sophie Savel[2], and Sabine Meunier[2]

[1] Acoustics Research Institute, Austrian Academy of Sciences,
Wohllebengasse 12–14, A-1040 Vienna, Austria
http://www.kfs.oeaw.ac.at
[2] Laboratoire de Mécanique et d'Acoustique, CNRS-UPR 7051,
Aix-Marseille Univ., Centrale Marseille, F-13402 Marseille cedex 20, France
http://www.lma.cnrs-mrs.fr

Abstract. In this paper, the results of psychoacoustical experiments on auditory time-frequency (TF) masking using stimuli (masker and target) with maximal concentration in the TF plane are presented. The target was shifted either along the time axis, the frequency axis, or both relative to the masker. The results show that a simple superposition of spectral and temporal masking functions does not provide an accurate representation of the measured TF masking function. This confirms the inaccuracy of simple models of TF masking currently implemented in some perceptual audio codecs. In the context of audio signal processing, the present results constitute a crucial basis for the prediction of auditory masking in the TF representations of sounds. An algorithm that removes the inaudible components in the wavelet transform of a sound while causing no audible difference to the original sound after re-synthesis is proposed. Preliminary results are promising, although further development is required.

Keywords: auditory masking, time-frequency representation, Gabor, wavelets.

1   Introduction

The main goal of this study was to collect data on time-frequency (TF) auditory masking for stimuli with maximal concentration in the TF plane. The results of such measurements served as a basis to examine the accuracy of simple TF masking models currently implemented in some perceptual audio codecs like MP3 and develop a perceptually relevant *and* perfectly invertible audio signal representation. The latter aspect was achieved by improving an existing algorithm [3] designed to remove the inaudible components in a TF transform while causing no audible difference to the original sound after re-synthesis.

S. Ystad et al. (Eds.): CMMR/FRSM 2011, LNCS 7172, pp. 146–171, 2012.

1.1 Representations of Sound Signals in Audio Signal Processing

In the field of audio signal processing, many applications involving sound analysis-synthesis (*e.g.*, virtual reality, sound design, sonification, perceptual audio coding) require specific tools enabling the analysis, processing, and re-synthesis of non-stationary signals. Most of them are based on linear TF representations such as the Gabor and wavelet transforms. These transforms allow decomposing any natural sound into a set of elementary functions or "atoms" that are well localized in the TF plane (for a review on TF analysis see, *e.g.*, [4,10,35]). For the cited applications, obtaining a perceptually relevant (*i.e.*, providing a good match between signal representation and human auditory perception) and perfectly invertible signal representation would be of great interest. To that end, the long-term goal of the present study is to propose a signal representation being as close as possible to *"what we see is what we hear"*. Because the achievement of such a sparse representation would facilitate the extraction and reconstruction of perceptually relevant sound features, it would also be of great interest for music information retrieval applications.

To date, two approaches exist to obtain a perceptually motivated *time versus frequency* representation of an audio signal. The first approach includes models of auditory processing providing an "internal" representation of sound signals like in [17,26,27]. While this approach is useful to improve our understanding of auditory processing, it does not enable reconstruction of the input signal. Thus, it is not useful as a TF analysis-synthesis tool. The second approach includes TF transforms whose parameters are tuned to mimic the spectro-temporal resolution of the auditory system [1,16,24]. While this approach is useful for audio signal analysis, the cited algorithms feature some limitations. In particular, [1,16] can only approximate the auditory resolution because the temporal and spectral resolutions cannot be set independently. The use of a bilinear transform in [24] overcomes this limitation but, on the other hand, this method does not allow reconstruction of the input signal. More recently, Balazs *et al.* [3] proposed a new approach to obtain a perceptually relevant and perfectly invertible signal representation. They introduced the concept of the "irrelevance filter", which consists in removing the inaudible atoms in a perfectly invertible Gabor transform while causing no audible difference to the original sound after re-synthesis. To identify the *irrelevant* atoms, a simple model of auditory spectral masking was used. A perceptual test performed with 36 normal-hearing listeners in [3] revealed that, on average, 36% of the atoms could be removed without causing any audible difference to the original sound after re-synthesis. The work described in the present paper can be considered as an extension of the irrelevance filter. Mostly, we attempt to improve it in two aspects: (i) overcome the fixed resolution in the Gabor transform by using a wavelet transform and (ii) replace the simple spectral masking model by using psychoacoustical data on auditory TF masking for stimuli with maximal concentration in the TF plane.

1.2 State-of-the-Art on Auditory Masking

Auditory masking occurs when the detection of a sound (referred to as the "target") is degraded by the presence of another sound (the "masker"). This effect is quantified by measuring the degree to which the detection threshold of the target increases in the presence of the masker.[1] In the literature, masking has been extensively investigated with simultaneous and non-simultaneous presentation of masker and target (for a review see, *e.g.*, [20]).

In simultaneous masking, the masker is present throughout the presentation time of the target (*i.e.*, the temporal shift between masker and target, ΔT, equals zero) and the frequency shift (ΔF) between masker and target is varied, resulting in the *spectral masking* function. To vary the ΔF parameter, either the target frequency (F_T) is fixed and the masker frequency (F_M) is varied, or vice versa. When F_T is fixed the masking function measures the response of a single auditory filter (*i.e.*, the filter centered on F_T).[2] As a result, such functions (called "psychoacoustical tuning curves" or "filter functions" depending on whether the masker or the target is fixed in level) are commonly used as estimates of auditory frequency selectivity [20, Chap. 3]. When F_M is fixed it is common to plot the target level at threshold (L_T) or amount of masking (see Footnote 1) as a function of F_T for a fixed-level masker, which is called a "masking pattern". Because a masking pattern measures the responses of different auditory filters (*i.e.*, those centered on the individual F_Ts), it can be interpreted as an indicator of the spectral spread of masking produced by the masker. The physiological mechanisms of simultaneous masking can be of two origins [5]: excitation and suppression. Excitation refers to the spread of excitation produced by the masker to the place responding to the target on the basilar membrane (BM). In other terms, the spread of excitation masks the BM response to the target. Suppression refers to the suppression or "inhibition" of the BM response to the target by the masker, even if the masker does not produce excitation at the place responding to the target (for an illustration of the excitatory and suppressive masking phenomena see [5, Fig. 1]). Excitation and suppression are not mutually exclusive. Their relative contributions depend on the frequency and level relationships between masker and target.

In non-simultaneous masking, ΔF most often equals zero and ΔT is varied, resulting in the *temporal masking* function. Backward masking (the target precedes the masker, $\Delta T < 0$) is weaker than forward masking (the masker

---

[1] The detection threshold of the target measured in presence of the masker represents the masked threshold, whereas the detection threshold of the target measured in quiet represents the absolute threshold. The difference between the masked threshold and the absolute threshold (in dB) represents the "amount of masking".

[2] The spectral resolution in the auditory system can be approximated by a bank of bandpass filters with a constant relative bandwidth. Each of these filters, named *auditory filters*, is characterized by its equivalent rectangular bandwidth (ERB) in Hz. This concept led to the definition of the so-called "ERB scale" that allows to plot signals or psychoacoustical data on a frequency scale related to human auditory perception [20, Chap. 3].

precedes the target, $\Delta T > 0$). The amounts of backward and forward masking depend on masker duration [6, 7, 36]. Although the mechanisms underlying
backward masking remain unclear, the most accepted explanation is that it is
of peripheral origin. Backwards masking would be caused by the temporal overlap of the BM responses to masker and target at the outputs of the auditory
filters [6]. The amount of overlap depends on the "ringing" time of the BM, *i.e.*,
the length of the impulse response of the BM, which itself depends on signal
frequency.[3] Note, however, that backward masking studies often reported large
inter-listener differences (*e.g.*, [7]) and that trained listeners often show little or
no backward masking. Thus, backward masking may also reflect some confusion effects between masker and target [20]. Forward masking can be attributed
to three mechanisms. The first is the temporal overlap of the BM responses to
masker and target at the outputs of the auditory filters as a consequence of the
filters' ringing. This phenomenon is more likely to be involved with small values
of ΔT. The second is short-term adaptation or "fatigue": the exponential decay
of masker-induced excitation over time in the cochlea and in the auditory nerve
can reduce the response to a target presented shortly after the extinction of the
masker [6, 7, 31, 36]. The third is temporal integration or "persistence" of masker
excitation: the neural representation of the masker is smoothed over time by an
integration process so that the representation of the masker overlaps with the
representation of the target at some stage in the auditory system [27, 28]. To
date, however, the distinction between short-term adaptation and temporal integration as the most probable explanation to forward masking is still a matter
of debate [25].

Because of the specific demands in the simultaneous and non-simultaneous
masking experiments reported in the literature, the experimental stimuli were
almost always broad either in the temporal domain (*e.g.*, long-lasting sinusoids),
the frequency domain (*e.g.*, clicks), or both.

A few studies investigated how masking spreads in the TF domain (*i.e.*, by
measuring masking patterns for various ΔTs) [7, 18, 21, 31]. Those studies involved relatively long (duration $\geqslant 100$ ms) sinusoidal maskers, that is, maskers
with good concentration in frequency but not in time. Overall, little is known
about the spread of TF masking for a masker with good concentration both in
time *and* frequency.

1.3   Models of Auditory Masking

The results of the spectral and temporal masking experiments reported in the
literature were used to develop models of either spectral, temporal, or TF masking. Masking models are useful to both the fields of psychoacoustics and sound
signal processing. In psychoacoustics they allow to improve our understanding
of auditory processing. In signal processing they allow to exploit auditory masking in some applications, for instance in perceptual audio coding. To reduce the

---

[3] An estimation of the ringing time at a given frequency can be obtained by considering
the inverse of the ERB (in Hz) of the auditory filter centered on that frequency.

digital size of audio files, audio codecs decompose sounds into TF segments and use masking models to reduce the bit rates in those segments (for a review on audio coding techniques see [32]).

Masking models can be classified into two groups: excitation pattern-based models and auditory processing-based models. Excitation pattern-based models transform the short-term spectrum of the input signal into an excitation pattern reflecting the spread of excitation induced by the signal on the BM. This approach is based on the power-spectrum model of masking in which the auditory periphery is conceived as a bank of bandpass filters (see Footnote 2). Masking is then determined by the target-to-masker ratio at the output of each filter. This group of models mostly includes spectral masking models (*e.g.*, [9, 13]) and is the technique most frequently employed in audio codecs [32].

In contrast, auditory processing-based models attempt to simulate the effective signal processing in the auditory system. Such models consist of a series of processing stages and a decision stage on which the prediction of masking is based [17, 27]. The model described in [27] is able to predict temporal and TF masking data. The model described in [17] is able to predict temporal and spectral masking data but has not been tested on TF conditions. Because auditory models usually have a high computational complexity and are not invertible, they are rarely used in audio processing algorithms.

To obtain a perceptually relevant audio signal representation based on a perfectly invertible transform, we propose to exploit masking in TF representations of sounds, that is, predict the audibility of each TF atom in the signal decompositions. To do so, a model of TF masking is required. There exist some models of TF masking that are currently implemented in audio coding algorithms [11, 12, 14, 34]. In the cited studies, the predictions of TF masking are based on a simple superposition of spectral and temporal masking functions (typically, only forward masking is considered). The decay of forward masking is modeled with a linear function of $\log(\Delta T)$ [11, 12, 34], or with an exponential function of the form $e^{-(\Delta T/\tau)}$ where τ is a time constant depending both on frequency (ΔF) and level [14]. Given the highly nonlinear behavior of cochlear mechanics (*e.g.*, [29]), such a simple combination of spectral and temporal masking functions is unlikely to correctly predict TF masking. Accordingly, the results presented in Sec. 2.3 reveal that such approaches are not adequate for predicting the audibility of TF atoms. To do so, it seems more appropriate to use masking functions that are based on the spread of TF masking produced by a maximally-compact masker. Because previous psychoacoustical studies mostly focused either on temporal or on spectral masking and used stimuli with temporally and/or spectrally broad supports, the spread of TF masking for a signal that is maximally compact in the TF plane cannot easily be derived from available data and therefore has to be measured.

1.4 Outline of the Present Study

The present paper consists of two main parts. In the first part, the results of psychoacoustical experiments on masking using maximally-compact stimuli are presented. To best fulfill the requirement of maximum compactness in the TF plane, we used Gaussian-shaped sinusoids (referred to as Gaussians) as masker and target stimuli. Three experiments were conducted. The spectral and temporal masking functions for Gaussian maskers were measured in Experiments 1 and 2, respectively. In Experiment 3, the TF spread of masking was measured. We then tested with which accuracy the results from Exp. 3 can be predicted based on the results from Exps. 1 and 2 (assuming a simple superposition of spectral and temporal masking effects). This allowed us to examine the accuracy of simple TF masking models currently implemented in some perceptual audio codecs.

In the second part, the "extended" irrelevance filter based on psychoacoustical data on TF masking is described. Then, preliminary results are presented and discussed.

2 Psychoacoustical Measurements of Masking Using Gaussian Stimuli

2.1 General Methods

Stimuli. Masker and target were Gaussian-shaped sinusoids (Gaussians) defined by [23, 30]

$$s(t) = \sqrt{\Gamma} \sin \left(2\pi f_0 t + \frac{\pi}{4} \right) e^{-\pi (\Gamma t)^2} \qquad (1)$$

where f_0 is the carrier frequency, Γ defines the equivalent rectangular bandwidth (ERB), and Γ^{-1} defines the equivalent rectangular duration (ERD) of $s(t)$. In our experiment, Γ was set to 600 Hz, corresponding to $\Gamma^{-1} = 1.7$ ms. The f_0 value varied depending on ΔF. By introducing the $\pi/4$ phase shift, the energy of the signal is independent of f_0. Since a Gaussian window has infinite duration, the signals were windowed in the time domain using a Tukey window. The "effective duration" (defined as the 0-amplitude points duration) of the stimuli was 9.6 ms and the cutoff in the frequency domain was located at the 220-dB down points. The sound pressure level (SPL) of the Gaussian was specified by measuring the SPL of a long-lasting sinusoid having the same frequency (f_0) and maximum amplitude as the carrier tone of the Gaussian.

Procedure. Thresholds were estimated using a three-interval, three-alternative forced-choice procedure with a 3-down-1-up criterion that estimates the 79.4%-correct point on the psychometric function. Each trial consisted of three 200-ms observation intervals visually indicated on the response box, with a between-interval gap of 800 ms. The masker was presented in the three intervals and the target was presented with the masker in one of those intervals, chosen randomly. The listener indicated in which interval he/she heard the target by pressing one of three buttons on the response box. Immediate feedback on the correctness of the response was visually provided to the listener. The target level varied adaptively by initial steps of 5 dB and 2 dB following the second reversal. Twelve reversals were obtained. The threshold estimate was the mean of the target levels at the last 10 reversals. A threshold estimate was discarded when the standard deviation of these 10 reversals exceeded 5 dB. Two threshold estimates were obtained for each condition. If the standard deviation of these two estimates exceeded 3 dB, up to four additional estimates were completed. The final threshold was the average across all estimates (maximum = 6).

Apparatus. A personal computer was used to control the experiments and generate the stimuli. Stimuli were output at a 48-kHz sampling rate and a 24-bit resolution using an external digital-to-analog converter (Tucker-Davis Technologies (TDT) System III), attenuated (TDT PA5) and passed to a headphone buffer (TDT HB7), and to the right ear-pad of a circumaural headphone (Sennheiser HD545).The headphones were calibrated so that levels were considered as SPL close to the eardrum. Listeners were tested individually in a double-walled, sound-attenuated booth.

Listeners. Six normal-hearing listeners participated in Exps. 1 and 2. Four of the listeners (L1–L4) participated in Exp. 3.

Experimental Conditions. Throughout the experiments, the carrier frequency of the masker was fixed to 4 kHz. Its sensation level (*i.e.*, the level above the absolute threshold of the masker for each listener, see Footnote 1) was fixed to 60 dB, which corresponded to SPLs of 81–84 dB across listeners.

Spectral Masking. Masker and target were presented simultaneously ($\Delta T = 0$). Masking patterns were measured for 11 values of ΔF, defined in the ERB scale: -4, -3, -2, -1, 0, +1, +2, +3, +4, +5, and +6 ERB units.[4] To prevent cochlear combination products from being detected and thus from producing irregularities in the masking patterns [20], a continuous background noise was added for all ΔFs > 0 [23]. Each session contained conditions measured either with or without background noise. The order of sessions (with noise; without) was counterbalanced over days. Within a session, ΔF was chosen randomly.

Temporal Masking. Masker and target had the same carrier frequency ($\Delta F = 0$). Because a pilot experiment indicated very little backward masking for such short maskers, we focused on forward masking. ΔT, defined as the time shift between masker onset and target onset, was 0, 5, 10, 20, or 30 ms. Within a session, ΔT was chosen randomly.

---

[4] The target frequencies corresponding to these ΔFs were 2521, 2833, 3181, 3568, 4000, 4480, 5015, 5611, 6274, 7012, and 7835 Hz, respectively.

Time-Frequency Masking. Both ΔT and ΔF were varied. Masked thresholds were measured for 30 out of 40 possible $\Delta T \times \Delta F$ combinations (*i.e.*, 5 ΔTs from Exp. 2 $\times$ 8 ΔFs from Exp. 1). Although the effect of cochlear combination products is usually ignored in forward masking studies, we used a background noise identical to that of Exp. 1 to mask potential cochlear combination products (when $\Delta F > 0$) because of the small ΔT values. The whole set of conditions was split into two groups: frequency separations measured with and without background noise. Then, experimental blocks were formed that contained the ΔT conditions for each ΔF. The order of blocks and groups was randomized across sessions. Within a session, the target frequency was fixed and ΔT was chosen randomly.

2.2   Results

This section presents the data with respect to their applications described in Secs. 2.3 and 3. A more thorough description and interpretation of the data can be found in [23].

Experiment 1: Spectral Masking. Figure 1 presents the individual and mean amounts of masking (in dB) as a function of ΔF (in ERB units). First, in some listeners a dip (L1, L3 and L4) or a plateau (L5) was observed instead of a peak at $\Delta F = 0$.[5] It has to be considered that this represents a special condition, where masker and target were exactly the same stimuli presented at the same time. Thus, the listeners could only use as a cue the intensity increase in the interval containing the target. In other words, the listeners performed an intensity discrimination task in this condition [8, 22, 23].

Second, for all listeners and $|\Delta F| \geqslant 2$ ERB units, the amount of masking decreased as $|\Delta F|$ increased. The decrease was more abrupt for $F_T < F_M$ than for $F_T > F_M$. Regression lines computed for each side of the masking patterns and listener (straight lines in Fig. 1) indeed show that, on average, the slopes for $F_T < F_M$ (mean slope = +60 dB/octave) are 1.6 times those for $F_T > F_M$ (mean slope = -39 dB/octave). This steeper masking decay for $F_T < F_M$ is consistent with that reported in classical spectral masking studies (see, *e.g.*, [20, 22] for a review).

Experiment 2: Temporal Masking. Figure 2 presents the individual and mean amounts of masking as a function of ΔT on a logarithmic scale. On average, masking decreased from 50 dB for $\Delta T = 0$ to about 6 dB for $\Delta T = 30$ ms. The data for $\Delta T > 0$ are well fitted with straight lines, a result consistent with almost all previous forward masking studies using various types of maskers (*e.g.*, [6, 7, 36]). A straightforward description of these data is provided by

$$AM = \alpha \log(\Delta T) + \beta \tag{2}$$

---

[5] In simultaneous masking, the greatest amount of masking, also referred to as the "maximum masking frequency", is classically located at $F_T = F_M$, which results in a peak in the masking pattern at $\Delta F = 0$ [22].

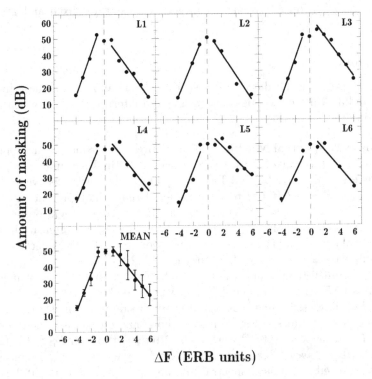

Fig. 1. Results of Experiment 1: amount of masking (in dB) as a function of ΔF (in ERB units). Data were fitted with linear regression lines on each side of the masking patterns (excluding the point at $\Delta F = 0$). The bottom panel shows the mean data with ± 1 standard deviation bars [23].

where AM is the amount of masking, α is the slope of the forward masking decay, and β is the offset of the forward masking decay. Table 1 lists the values of α and β determined by applying a weighted-least-squares fit of (2) to the data for $\Delta T > 0$. To take the variability of each data point into account in the estimation of parameters α and β, the weight of each data point corresponded to the reciprocal of the variance of the measurement.

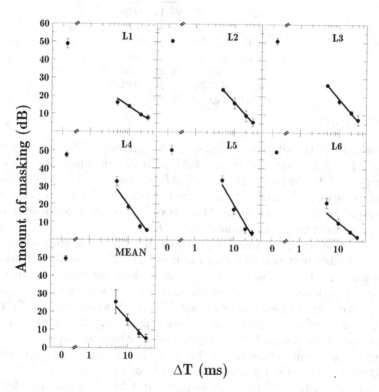

Fig. 2. Results of Experiment 2: amount of masking (in dB) as a function of ΔT (in ms) on a logarithmic scale with straight-line fits to the data for $\Delta T > 0$ according to (2). The fit parameters are listed in Tab. 1. Error bars in the individual panels indicate ± 1 standard deviation across measurements. The bottom panel shows the mean data with ± 1 standard deviation bars [23].

Experiment 3: Time-Frequency Masking. Figure 3 presents the results as simultaneous and forward masking patterns, that is, the amount of masking as a function of ΔF with ΔT as the parameter. For all ΔFs, the largest amount of masking was obtained in the simultaneous condition ($\Delta T = 0$). Masking dropped as ΔT increased to 5 ms. For ΔTs > 10 ms, masking was generally less than 10 dB for all ΔFs. To assess whether the patterns broadened or narrowed with increasing ΔT, we estimated the quality factors at the -3-dB bandwidth (Q_{3dB}) [18]. The mean values of Q_{3dB} are 12, 3, and 2 for $\Delta T = 0$, 5, and 10 ms,

Table 1. Values of parameters α (in dB/log(ΔT)) and β (in dB) determined by fitting (2) to the data for $\Delta T > 0$ in Fig. 2 using a weighted-least-squares criterion. Note that because the ΔT axis is logarithmically scaled in Fig. 2, the values of β correspond to the y-intercepts at $\Delta T = 1$ ms. The last column indicates r^2 values.

Listener	α	β	r^2
L1	−14.39	28.46	0.98
L2	−23.38	39.93	1.00
L3	−25.61	44.28	0.99
L4	−29.37	48.60	0.95
L5	−36.00	56.01	0.96
L6	−17.76	28.26	0.97
MEAN	−23.18	39.12	0.97

respectively, *i.e.*, the patterns flattened as ΔT increased. The mean masking patterns in Fig. 3 are asymmetric for all ΔTs. Finally, the dip/plateau observed in listeners L1, L3, and L4 at $\Delta F = 0$ for $\Delta T = 0$ (see also Fig. 1) disappeared when ΔT increased. For $\Delta T > 0$, listeners L1 and L3 exhibited a peak at $\Delta F = +1$ instead of 0. In other terms, these two listeners revealed a shift in the maximum masking frequency towards $F_{TS} > F_M$.

Our pattern of results is consistent with the few preceding studies that measured TF masking patterns with long maskers [7, 18, 21, 31] in that (i) masking patterns flatten with increasing ΔT, (ii) the masking patterns' asymmetry remains for $\Delta T > 0$, and (iii) a shift in the maximum masking frequency towards $F_{TS} > F_M$ is observed in some listeners for $\Delta T > 0$. However, because TF masking is affected by nonlinear processes in the cochlea [19, 20, 23], the present data could not have been deduced from existing data for long maskers.

Our results are summarized in the three-dimension plot in Fig. 4. To provide a smooth and "complete" representation of TF masking (*i.e.*, one that reaches 0 dB of masking), the ΔT axis was sampled at 1 kHz and the data for ΔFs below -4 and above +6 ERB units were then extrapolated based on a two-dimensional cubic spline fit along the TF plane. Overall, the function shown in Fig. 4 represents the TF spread of masking produced by a Gaussian TF atom.

2.3 Accuracy of Simple Time-Frequency Masking Models Used in Perceptual Audio Codecs

To examine the accuracy of simple TF masking models currently used in some audio codecs, we tested two prediction schemes assuming a linear combination of spectral and temporal masking. Specifically, we tested with which accuracy the results of Exp. 3 can be predicted based on the results of Exps. 1 and 2. The general idea of the prediction is that the spread of TF masking caused by a masker can be described by the spectral masking pattern combined with the decay of forward masking from each point of the masking pattern. In the

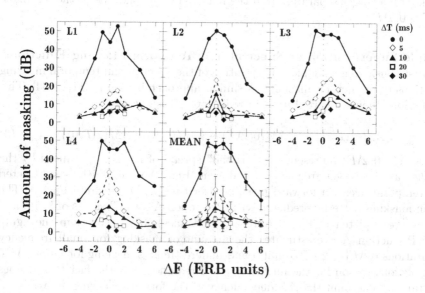

Fig. 3. Results of Experiment 3: amount of masking (in dB) as a function of ΔF (in ERB units) obtained for five ΔTs [23]

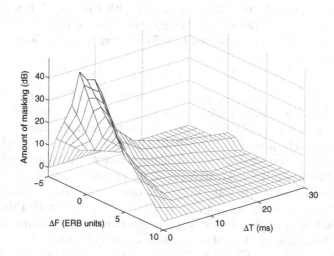

Fig. 4. Mean TF masking data extrapolated and plotted in the TF plane [23]

following, let $AM(\Delta T, \Delta F)$ denote the amount of masking produced by the masker on a target separated from the masker by ΔT and ΔF in the TF plane ($\Delta T > 0, \Delta F \neq 0$).

Simple Superposition of Spectral and Temporal Masking Functions.
We first considered a simple superposition of the spectral and temporal masking functions to predict TF masking. A similar approach is used in [11, 12, 34]. This prediction scheme, referred to as "Prediction A", is given by

$$AM(\Delta T, \Delta F) = AM(0, \Delta F) - \big(AM(0,0) - AM(\Delta T, 0)\big) \qquad (3)$$

where $AM(0, \Delta F)$ represents the "initial" spread of masking produced by the masker at the target frequency (read from Fig. 1) from which is subtracted the temporal decay of forward masking over time ΔT (read from Fig. 2). The mean masking patterns predicted with Prediction A for ΔT values of 5, 10, and 20 ms are depicted in Fig. 5 (crosses, solid lines). It is clear from the figure that Prediction A overestimates the amount of masking for small frequency separations ($|\Delta F| \leqslant 2$ ERB units) and underestimates masking for larger ΔF's. One obvious reason for the inefficiency of Prediction A is the fact that it does not take into account the ΔF dependency of the forward masking decay.

Superposition of Spectral Masking Function and Level-Dependent Temporal Masking Function. An approach which takes into account the ΔF dependency of forward masking is used in [14]. In this approach (referred to as "Prediction B"), each point of the spectral masking pattern with $F_M \neq F_T$ is considered as a hypothetical forward masker with $F_M = F_T$ but with a lower level. This consideration follows from the analogy reported between the ΔF- and level-dependency of forward masking [23]. Prediction B has the form

$$AM(\Delta T, \Delta F) = AM(0, \Delta F) - \alpha' \log(\Delta T) \qquad (4)$$

with $\alpha' = AM(0, \Delta F)/\log(\Delta T_{0dB})$, ΔT_{0dB} being the ΔT-axis intercept, or 0-dB masking point, at which the forward masking functions converge. Given the parameters α and β determined by fitting (2) to the temporal masking data presented in Fig. 2, $\Delta T_{0dB} = 10^{-\beta/\alpha}$ (see Tab. 1). As for Prediction A, $AM(0, \Delta F)$ is determined from the spectral masking data. The mean masking patterns predicted with Prediction B for ΔT values of 5, 10, and 20 ms are depicted in Fig. 5 (filled diamonds, dashed lines). It can be seen that the shape of the masking patterns with Prediction B is more similar to the data than that with Prediction A. Nevertheless, it is clear that Prediction B overestimates the amount of masking in almost all conditions, the overestimation being particularly large for small frequency separations ($|\Delta F| \leqslant 2$ ERB units). Overall, both prediction schemes failed in accurately predicting TF masking data for Gaussian stimuli. This confirms that TF masking is not predictable by assuming a simple combination of temporal and spectral masking functions.

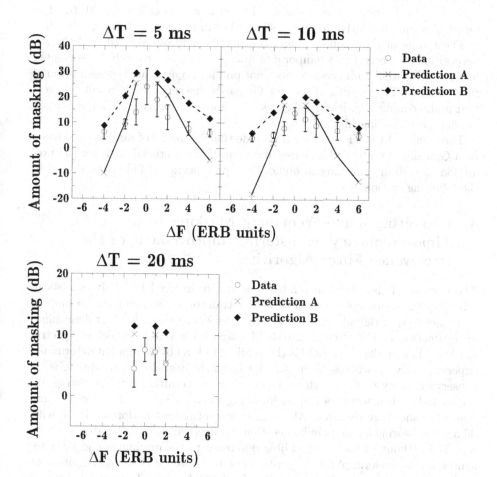

Fig. 5. Mean forward masking patterns for $\Delta T = 5$, 10, and 20 ms predicted with Prediction A (×, solid lines) and Prediction B (♦, dashed lines). Because only one point was measured for $\Delta F < 0$ and $\Delta T = 20$ ms, only symbols are used in the bottom left panel. Error bars show ±1 standard deviation.

2.4 Interim Summary

To obtain a measure of the TF spread of masking produced by a signal with maximal concentration in the TF plane, three experiments were conducted that involved Gaussian-shaped sinusoids with fixed bandwidth (ERB = 600 Hz) and duration (ERD = 1.7 ms) both as masker and target. In all experiments, the masker had a carrier frequency of 4 kHz and a sensation level of 60 dB. The target was shifted relative to the masker either in frequency, in time, or both.

The results of the frequency- and time-shift conditions showed that the superposition of spectral and temporal masking effects, as currently implemented in some perceptual audio codecs, does not provide an accurate representation of the measured TF masking effects for Gaussian maskers. These results suggest that audio coding algorithms using such an approach provide rather erroneous predictions of TF masking.

The results of the TF conditions provide the TF spread of masking produced by a Gaussian TF atom. These new data constitute a crucial basis for the prediction of auditory masking in audio TF representations. This is addressed in the following section.

3 Exploiting Time-Frequency Masking in a Time-Frequency Transform: Improvement of the Irrelevance Filter Algorithm

The concept of the irrelevance filter was first introduced in [3]. It consists in removing the inaudible atoms in a Gabor transform while causing no audible difference to the original sound after re-synthesis. The algorithm first determines an estimation of the masked threshold based on a simple model of spectral masking. The masked threshold is then shifted in level by an amount determined experimentally, which results in the "irrelevance threshold". This shift gives a conservative way to deal with uncertainty effects resulting from removing TF atoms and with inaccuracies in the masking model. Next, all TF atoms falling below threshold are removed. Although a perceptual test performed in [3] with 36 normal-hearing listeners indicated that, on average, 36% of the atoms can be removed without causing any audible difference to the original sound after re-synthesis, the irrelevance filter algorithm can be improved. The main limitations of the algorithm are the fixed resolution in the Gabor transform and the use of a simple spectral masking model to predict masking in the TF domain.

In this section, a preliminary version of the extended irrelevance filter is presented. Because the algorithm presented below differs from the original algorithm in many aspects, including signal representation, masking model, and irrelevance threshold calculation, no direct comparison can be established between the two versions. Moreover, because the new algorithm is still being developed, it has not been formally evaluated yet (*e.g.*, by conducting perceptual listening tests with natural sounds). Thus, we merely evaluate the performance of the new algorithm based on preliminary results with deterministic signals and informal listening by the authors.

3.1 Choice of the Signal Representation: Wavelet Transform

To mimic the spectral resolution of the human auditory system, a signal representation allowing a variable frequency resolution is required. The continuous wavelet transform (CWT) fulfills this requirement, unlike the Gabor transform that allows only a fixed TF resolution (e.g., [10]). Thus, the CWT was chosen as the TF analysis-synthesis scheme used in this paper. In the following we summarize some general theory on wavelets (for a more detailed description see, e.g., [4, 35]) and describe the practical implementation of the CWT used in our algorithm.

The CWT results from the decomposition of a signal into a family of functions that are scaled versions of a prototype function ("mother wavelet") $g(t)$ according to

$$g_a(t) = \frac{1}{\sqrt{a}} g\left(\frac{t}{a}\right) \quad (a \in \mathbb{R}^{*+}) \tag{5}$$

where a is a *scale factor* allowing to compress $(a < 1)$ or dilate $(a > 1)$ the mother wavelet $g(t)$ $(a = 1)$. This parameter defines the time and frequency resolution in the TF plane. The scale is linked to the frequency according to $\omega = \omega_0/a$ where ω_0 is the pulsation of the mother wavelet. Then, for any signal $x(t)$,

$$CWT_x(b, a) = \langle g_{a,b}, x \rangle$$
$$= \frac{1}{\sqrt{a}} \int_{-\infty}^{+\infty} x(t) \overline{g\left(\frac{t-b}{a}\right)} \, dt \tag{6}$$

provides a two-dimensional representation of $x(t)$ in the time-scale plane, $b \in \mathbb{R}$ being the time variable. Using Parseval's relation, (6) can also be written in the frequency domain

$$CWT_x(b, a) = \frac{\sqrt{a}}{2\pi} \int_{-\infty}^{+\infty} \hat{x}(\omega) \overline{\hat{g}(a\omega)} e^{jb\omega} \, d\omega \tag{7}$$

where $\hat{x}(\omega)$ and $\hat{g}_a(\omega)$ denote the Fourier transforms of $x(t)$ and $g_a(t)$, respectively. The CWT is invertible if and only if $g(t)$ fulfills the admissibility condition

$$C_g = \frac{1}{2\pi} \int_{-\infty}^{+\infty} \frac{|\hat{g}(\omega)|^2}{\omega} \, d\omega < \infty \tag{8}$$

which implies that $g(t)$ be of finite energy. This is usually fulfilled in practice since $g(t)$ must be a function oscillating in time (hence the name "wavelet"). Additionally, $g(t)$ must be of zero mean. Finally, the reconstruction formula is

$$x(t) = \frac{1}{C_g} \iint_{a>0, \, \mathbb{R}} CWT_x(b, a) \, g_{a,b}(t) \frac{da\,db}{a^2} \tag{9}$$

which reflects the "atomic" decomposition of $x(t)$ into wavelets.

The CWT has the properties of being linear and ensuring energy conservation. Another property is the "reproducing kernel", which states that

$$CWT(a',b') = \frac{1}{C_g} \iint_{\mathbb{R}} K_g(a',b',a,b)CWT(a,b)\frac{dadb}{a^2} \qquad (10)$$

where $K_g(a',b',a,b) = \langle g_{a,b}, g_{a',b'} \rangle$ is called the reproducing kernel. Equation (10) means that the reproducing kernel ensures a strong correlation between all components in the CWT. In other words, any component at location a',b' depends upon the remote component at location a,b through the reproducing kernel. This is reflected by the fact that the CWT is highly redundant.

The numerical implementation of the CWT requires the discretization of the time and scale variables b,a and the choice of the mother wavelet $g(t)$. In our implementation we chose the following discretization $(a_j, b_k) = (a_0^j, kb_0)$ where $a_0 = 2$ and $b_0 = 1/F_S$ (F_S being the sampling frequency) are two constants defining the size of the sampling grid. Furthermore, we opted for a sub-sampling of the scale in voices and octaves such that

$$a_0^j = 2^{\frac{m}{\mathcal{D}_v} + n} = a_{m,n}$$

where $m \in [0,\ldots,\mathcal{D}_v - 1]$, $n \in [0,\ldots,\mathcal{D}_o - 1]$, and $j \in [0,\ldots,\mathcal{D}_v\mathcal{D}_o - 1]$, $\mathcal{D}_v$ and $\mathcal{D}_o$ being the number of voices and octaves, respectively. This discretization yields scale factors $a_0^j \geqslant 1$ with increment steps of $2^{1/\mathcal{D}_v}$. Moreover, it provides two parameters, $\mathcal{D}_v$ and $\mathcal{D}_o$, for determining the total number of scales in the representation.

Regarding the choice of the mother wavelet, the accurate prediction of masking in the time-scale domain requires that the spectro-temporal characteristics of the wavelets match the spectro-temporal characteristics of the masker used in the psychoacoustical experiment. Thus, a straightforward solution for $g(t)$ was to use a Gaussian-shaped sinusoid similar to that defined in (1). Because the CWT was computed in the frequency domain according to (7), we defined the following function for the mother wavelet

$$\hat{g}(\omega) = \frac{1}{2i\sqrt{\Gamma}}e^{-\pi\left(\frac{\omega-\omega_0}{\Gamma}\right)^2} \qquad (11)$$

where $\Gamma = \mu f_0 = \mu\frac{\omega_0}{2\pi}$, μ being the shape factor of the Gaussian window. To provide a Γ value of 600 Hz at $f_0 = 4$ kHz as used in the psychoacoustical experiment (see Sec. 2), μ was set to 0.15. Note that $\hat{g}(\omega)$ corresponds to the positive-frequency components of the Fourier transform of $s(t)$ in (1).

The frequency of the mother wavelet (f_0) was set to $3F_S/8$. Because we used only scale factors $a_0^j \geqslant 1$ (i.e., we used only compressed versions of $\hat{g}(\omega)$), f_0 defines the highest center frequency in the signal representation. To cover the whole spectrum of audible frequencies (i.e., 0.02–20 kHz) while maintaining a large overlap between wavelets, thus to avoid loosing details in the signals, we used 108 scales split into 9 octaves ($\mathcal{D}_o = 9$) and 12 voices per octave ($\mathcal{D}_v = 12$). At $F_S = 44.1$ kHz and $\mu = 0.15$, the highest-frequency analysis filter had a center frequency $f_0 = 16.5$ kHz and a bandwidth of 2.5 kHz. The lowest-frequency filter had a center frequency $f_0/a_0^{\mathcal{D}_v\mathcal{D}_o-1} = 33.8$ Hz and a bandwidth of 5 Hz.

3.2   Implementation of the Irrelevance Filter

The gathered TF masking data were used to predict masking in the time-scale domain. More specifically, the TF masking function in Fig. 4 was used as a *masking kernel* in the time-scale domain. Accordingly, this function had to be discretized in time and scales. Because we conserved all time samples of the signal, the ΔT axis was sampled at F_S. The ΔF axis (in ERB units) had to be matched to the scale axis (in voices and octaves). Considering that the ERB of an auditory filter corresponds to approximately one third of octave [20] and the present analysis counts 12 voices per octave, one ERB unit was associated with 4 voices. The TF masking kernel in Fig. 4 covers a range of 15 ERB units (ΔF = -5 to +10). Thus, the ΔF axis should be divided into 61 voices. This was achieved by interpolating the ΔF axis at a sampling rate of 4 voices per ERB unit based on a two-dimensional cubic spline fit along the TF plane.

In the following, we denote by $X(a, b)$, $a = \{a_j; j = 0, \ldots, D_o D_v - 1\}$ the discrete wavelet transform (DWT) of the input signal $x(k)$, k being the discrete time variable such that $t = kT_S$ (all signals were sampled at $F_S = 44.1$ kHz). The representation from which components have been removed is referred to as $\tilde{X}(a, b)$. Accordingly, the output signal (reconstructed from $\tilde{X}(a, b)$) is referred to as $\tilde{x}(k)$. $\mathcal{M}(a, b)$ refers to the discrete masking kernel in dB.

The structure of the irrelevance time-scale filter is shown in Fig. 6. The algorithm includes three main steps:

1. Scale the modulus of the DWT in dB SPL. The difficulty in the SPL normalization is that the actual playback level remains unknown during the entire signal processing. We considered that an amplitude variation of ± 1 bit in the signal is associated with an SPL of 0 dB, while a full-scale signal is associated with an SPL close to 92 dB [32].
2. Identify local maskers, *i.e.*, local maxima in the transform that fulfill

$$|X(a, b)| \geqslant Tq(a, \cdot) + 60 \quad \text{(in dB SPL)}$$

   where $Tq(a)$ is an analytic function approximating the absolute threshold of a normal-hearing listener in dB SPL. It is given by [33]

$$T_q(a) = 3.64 \, (f_0/a)^{-0.8} - 6.5 \, e^{-0.6\left(\frac{f_0}{a} - 3.3\right)^2} + \frac{(f_0/a)^4}{1000}$$

   with f_0 in kHz. More precisely, Step 2 selects the components whose SPL exceeds the absolute threshold by 60 dB. This selection rule follows from the masker sensation level of 60 dB used in the experiment (see Sec. 2). Let Ω_M denote the set of maskers selected in Step 2.
3. Apply the masking kernel $\mathcal{M}(a, b)$ (in dB) to each masker in order of descending SPL and iteratively compute the output wavelet transform as

$$\tilde{X}(a, b) = \begin{cases} X(a, b) & \text{if} \quad |X(a, b)| \geqslant Tq(a, \cdot) + \mathcal{M}(a, b) \quad \text{(dB SPL)} \\ 0 & \text{otherwise} \end{cases}$$

   until Ω_M is empty.

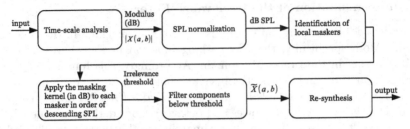

Fig. 6. Structure of the irrelevance time-scale filter

Note that a more straightforward approach could have consisted in applying $\mathcal{M}(a,b)$ to the whole time-scale domain, that is, without identifying local maskers in the transform (Step 2). However, we opted for a local application of $\mathcal{M}(a,b)$ because the amount of masking highly depends on level [20]. Thus, applying the TF masking kernel derived from data measured with an average masker SPL of 84 dB to components with SPLs below 84 dB is likely to result in an overestimation of masking. This would in turn result in the removal of *audible* components. To process all components in the transform, a level-dependent masking kernel is required.

3.3 Results

We present below the results obtained when the irrelevance filter was applied on deterministic and musical signals.[6] Two conditions measured in Exp. 3 were tested: one condition ("Condition 1": $\Delta F = +4$ ERB units, $\Delta T = 10$ ms, target SPL (L_T) = 50 dB) where the target is not masked and another condition ("Condition 2": $\Delta F = -2$ ERB units, $\Delta T = 5$ ms, $L_T = 15$ dB) where the target is masked. A test signal $x(t)$ composed of two Gaussians (see (1)) with time and frequency shifts was synthesized as follows:

$$x(t) = \underbrace{\mathfrak{g}_M(t)}_{\text{Masker}} + \underbrace{\mathfrak{g}_T(t - \Delta T)}_{\text{Target}} \tag{12}$$

with $\mathfrak{g}_l(t) = A_l \sin\left(2\pi f_l t + \frac{\pi}{4}\right) e^{-\pi(\Gamma t)^2}$, $l = \{M, T\}$ where A_l allows to control the signal SPLs[7]. Let $x_1(t)$ and $x_2(t)$ denote the test signals for Conditions 1 and 2, respectively. Their parameters are listed in Tab. 2.

Consider first $x_1(t)$. Because the target is not masked, the representation of $\mathfrak{g}_T(t)$ should not be removed from $X_1(a,b)$. Figure 7 depicts the original (Fig. 7a) and modified (Fig. 7b) representations of $x_1(t)$ in dB SPL. As expected, it can

---

[6] The sound files corresponding to each of the results can be downloaded as wav files at: http://www.lma.cnrs-mrs.fr/~kronland/cmmr2011.

[7] The SPL of the test signal was controlled by setting the signal amplitudes $A_l = 10^{(L_l-92)/20}$ where L_l is the desired SPL and 92 dB corresponds to the amplitude of a full-scale signal.

Table 2. Parameters used for test signals $x_1(t)$ and $x_2(t)$ to simulate experimental Conditions 1 and 2

	$x_1(t)$	$x_2(t)$
Γ	600	600
f_M (kHz)	4.0	4.0
L_M (dB SPL)	80	80
f_T (kHz)	6.3	3.2
L_T (dB SPL)	50	15
ΔT (ms)	10	5
Target status	*not masked*	*masked*

be seen that the target was not removed from $X_1(a,b)$. However, the representation of $\mathfrak{g}_M(t)$ was roughly altered by the filter. To evaluate the amount of components filtered out from $X_1(a,b)$, we computed the binary representations associated with $|X_1(a,b)|$ and $|\tilde{X}_1(a,b)|$. These representations (not shown) comprise pixels '1' where $|X_1(a,b)|$ (respectively, $|\tilde{X}_1(a,b)|$) > -10 dB SPL and pixels '0' elsewhere. Comparing the DWT of the input representation $X_1(a,b)$ and the output representation $\tilde{X}_1(a,b)$ indicated that about 45% components were removed. It has to be considered, however, that $|\tilde{X}_1(a,b)|$ in Fig. 7b is *not* the actual representation of $\tilde{x}_1(t)$. Because of the reproducing kernel (see (10)), reconstructing the signal from the modified representation restores some of the removed components. To illustrate this effect, the modulus of the DWT of $\tilde{x}_1(t)$, *i.e.*, the analysis of the reconstructed signal, is represented in Fig. 7c. It can be seen that the masker components removed by the filter were restored by the reproducing kernel. Informal listening revealed no perceptual difference between $\tilde{x}_1(t)$ and $x_1(t)$, and the reconstruction error $(\tilde{x}_1(t) - x_1(t))$ was $< 10^{-4}$.

Consider next $x_2(t)$. In this case the target is masked, and thus the representation of $\mathfrak{g}_T(t)$ should be removed from $X_2(a,b)$. This was the case, as depicted in Fig. 8b. Computations of the binary representations indicated that about 57% components were removed. As for $\tilde{x}_1(t)$, the reproducing kernel restored the masker components removed by the filter. Informal listening revealed no perceptual difference between $\tilde{x}_2(t)$ and $\mathfrak{g}_M(t)$.

Finally, we applied the irrelevance time-scale filter to a musical sound (referred to as $x_3(t)$), namely a clarinet sound representing the note A3. The results are depicted in Fig. 9. Computations of the binary representations indicated that about 50% components were removed. Although the reconstruction error was $< 10^{-4}$, in that case, informal listening revealed some perceptual differences between $\tilde{x}_3(t)$ and $x_3(t)$. More specifically, the filter altered the attack of the note, which became noisy.

3.4   Discussion

The preliminary results obtained with deterministic sounds indicated that the irrelevance time-scale filter removes information (as predicted from experimental

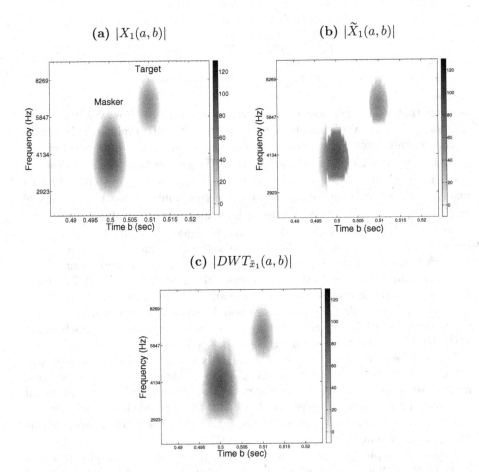

Fig. 7. Modulus of the DWT (in dB SPL) of test signal $x_1(t)$ (see Tab. 2) (a) at the input and (b) at the output of the irrelevance time-scale filter. (c) Modulus of the DWT (in dB SPL) of the reconstructed signal $\tilde{x}_1(t)$.

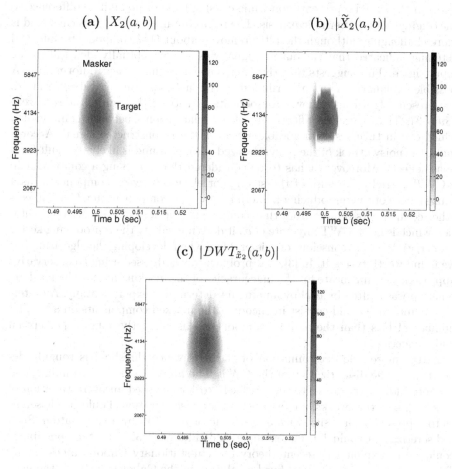

Fig. 8. As in Fig. 7 but for test signal $x_2(t)$

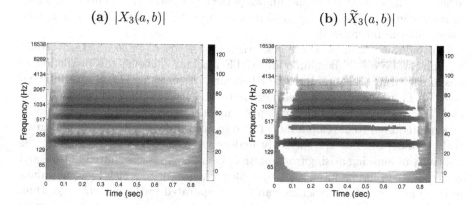

Fig. 9. As in Fig. 8 but for a musical sound ($x_3(t)$, clarinet note A3)

data) in the signal representation while causing little or no audible difference to the original sound after re-synthesis. The result obtained with a musical sound is more challenging: although the filter removed about 50% components, informal listening indicated that the output signal was not perceptually identical to the input signal. This suggests that the filter removed some *relevant* information. A possible explanation can be attributed to the methods employed itself. Indeed, the present algorithm removes components by setting their amplitudes to zero (Step 3). This operation affects the phase relationships between components, which can in turn result in audible effects in the reconstructed signal. Accordingly, the noisy attack of the re-synthesized clarinet sound is likely to result from phase effects. Moreover, it has to be considered that removing a component in a CWT is tricky. Because of the strong correlation between components (as a consequence of the reproducing kernel), removing a component in a CWT affects other components remote from that component and leads to a new representation which is not a CWT anymore (*i.e.*, it does not satisfy the reproducing kernel property). We were conscious of this problem when developing the algorithm but we found worth trying it. In [3], this problem was addressed using a conservative approach: to compensate for the inaccuracies of the masking model, the masking function was shifted in level by an amount determined experimentally. An alternative approach could consist in encoding the masked components on a smaller number of bits than the audible components, as currently done in perceptual audio codecs [32].

Furthermore, the determination of the irrelevance threshold is roughly dependent on the discretization of the CWT. The highly redundant sampling grid we opted for in the present study is likely to have caused an overestimation of masking. In future works, a more appropriate discretization should be chosen so as to represent a Gaussian with a shape factor $\mu = 0.15$ by a single atom. Such a discretization could be, for example, a dyadic grid [35]. Another possibility could be to exploit the recent theory on non-stationary Gabor frames [2, 15]. To overcome the limitation of fixed resolution in the Gabor transform, the non-stationary Gabor transform provides some freedom of evolution of resolution either in time or frequency and allows perfect reconstruction. This constitutes an interesting background for implementing our TF masking data and will be investigated in future works.

To avoid the constraint on the discretization, the discrete masking kernel could be replaced by an explicit function of TF masking allowing the prediction of masking for any TF coordinates. Furthermore, the masking kernel was designed based on TF masking data for a single Gaussian masker with fixed frequency and level. Because masking is highly dependent on frequency and level, additional data are required to develop a model able to accurately predict masking in real-world sounds. Studies are currently underway (*e.g.*, [19]) that investigate the additivity of masking arising from multiple Gaussian maskers shifted in time and frequency. It would be interesting to explore the extent to which these new data on the additivity of TF masking can be incorporated in the current algorithm. Combining data on the frequency- and level-dependency of spectral masking for

Gaussian atoms gathered in [23] and literature data on the level-dependency of temporal masking may allow designing a level-dependent TF masking kernel or function.

4 Summary and Conclusions

In this paper, the question of the development of a perfectly invertible audio signal representation being as close as possible to "what we see is what we hear" was addressed, with specific considerations to TF representations and auditory masking. The proposed approach consisted in predicting the audibility of each TF atom in the TF representations of sounds based on psychoacoustical data on TF masking. To achieve this approach, data on the spread of TF masking produced by a TF atom (*i.e.*, a signal with maximal concentration in the TF plane) were required. Because (i) a few psychoacoustical studies investigated TF masking and (ii) those studies used stimuli with temporally broad supports, their results could not be used to derive the spread of TF masking for one atom.

Therefore, three psychoacoustical experiments were conducted that involved Gaussian-shaped sinusoids with fixed bandwidth (ERB = 600 Hz) and duration (ERD = 1.7 ms) both as masker and target stimuli. The target was shifted either along the time axis, the frequency axis, or both relative to the masker. The same group or subgroup of listeners participated in all three experiments. The conclusions that can be drawn from our data are:

(i) The superposition of the temporal and spectral masking functions does not provide an accurate representation of the measured TF masking function for a Gaussian masker;

(ii) This suggests that audio coding algorithms using such an approach provide rather erroneous predictions of TF masking and that our data may allow to improve the estimation of TF masking in these systems;

(iii) These new data constitute a crucial basis for the prediction of auditory masking in the TF representations of sounds.

We proposed an algorithm (referred to as the "extended irrelevance filter") for removing the inaudible atoms in the wavelet transform of a sound while causing little or no audible difference to the original sound after re-synthesis. Preliminary results obtained with deterministic and musical signals are promising. Future works will include: development of a level-dependent model of TF masking, incorporation of the nonlinear additivity of masking, replacement of the CWT by the non-stationary Gabor transform, refinement of the methods to remove the inaudible components, and perceptual validation of the algorithm with calibrated natural sounds.

Acknowledgments. This work was supported by grants from Egide (PAI "Amadeus" WTZ 1/2006), the ANR (project "SenSons"), and the WWTF (project "MulAc" MA07025).

References

1. Agerkvist, F.T.: A time-frequency auditory model using wavelet packets. J. Audio Eng. Soc. 44(1/2), 37–50 (1996)
2. Balazs, P., Dörfler, M., Holighaus, N., Jaillet, F., Velasco, G.: Theory, implementation and applications of nonstationary Gabor frames. J. Comput. Appl. Math. 236(6), 1481–1496 (2011)
3. Balazs, P., Laback, B., Eckel, G., Deutsch, W.A.: Time-frequency sparsity by removing perceptually irrelevant components using a simple model of simultaneous masking. IEEE Trans. Audio Speech Lang. Process. 18(1), 34–49 (2010)
4. Daubechies, I.: Ten Lectures on Wavelets, 1st edn. CMB-NSF Lecture Notes nr. 61. SIAM, Philadelphia (1992)
5. Delgutte, B.: Physiological mechanisms of psychophysical masking: Observations from auditory-nerve fibers. J. Acoust. Soc. Am. 87(2), 791–809 (1990)
6. Duifhuis, H.: Consequences of peripheral frequency selectivity for nonsimultaneous masking. J. Acoust. Soc. Am. 54(6), 1471–1488 (1973)
7. Fastl, H.: Temporal masking effects: III. Pure tone masker. Acustica 43(5), 282–294 (1979)
8. Florentine, M.: Level discrimination of tones as a function of duration. J. Acoust. Soc. Am. 79(3), 792–798 (1986)
9. Glasberg, B.R., Moore, B.C.J.: Development and evaluation of a model for predicting the audibility of time-varying sounds in the presence of background sounds. J. Audio Eng. Soc. 53(10), 906–918 (2005)
10. Gröchening, K.: Foundations of time-frequency analysis, 1st edn. Birkhaüser, Boston (2001)
11. Hamdi, K.N., Ali, M., Tewfik, A.H.: Low bit rate high quality audio coding with combined harmonic and wavelet representations. In: Proceedings of the IEEE International Conference on Acoustics, Speech, Signal Processing (ICASSP 1996), Atlanta, GA, USA, vol. 2, pp. 1045–1048 (1996)
12. He, X., Scordilis, M.S.: Psychoacoustic music analysis based on the discrete wavelet packet transform. Res. Let. Signal Process. 2008(4), 1–5 (2008)
13. van der Heijden, M., Kohlrausch, A.: Using an excitation-pattern model to predict auditory masking. Hear. Res. 80, 38–52 (1994)
14. Huang, Y.H., Chiueh, T.D.: A new audio coding scheme using a forward masking model and perceptually weighted vector quantization. IEEE Trans. Audio Speech Lang. Process. 10(5), 325–335 (2002)
15. Jaillet, F., Balazs, P., Dörfler, M.: Nonstationary Gabor frames. In: Proc. of the 8th International Conference on Sampling Theory and Applications (SAMPTA 2009), Marseille, France (May 2009)
16. Jeong, H., Ih, J.: Implementation of a new algorithm using the STFT with variable frequency resolution for the time-frequency auditory model. J. Audio Eng. Soc. 47(4), 240–251 (1999)
17. Jepsen, M., Ewert, S.D., Dau, T.: A computational model of human auditory signal processing and perception. J. Acoust. Soc. Am. 124(1), 422–438 (2008)
18. Kidd Jr., G., Feth, L.L.: Patterns of residual masking. Hear. Res. 5(1), 49–67 (1981)
19. Laback, B., Balazs, P., Necciari, T., Savel, S., Meunier, S., Ystad, S., Kronland-Martinet, R.: Additivity of nonsimultaneous masking for short Gaussian-shaped sinusoids. J. Acoust. Soc. Am. 129(2), 888–897 (2011)
20. Moore, B.C.J.: An introduction to the psychology of hearing, 5th edn. Academic Press, London (2003)

21. Moore, B.C.J., Alcántara, J.I., Glasberg, B.R.: Behavioural measurement of level-dependent shifts in the vibration pattern on the basilar membrane. Hear. Res. 163, 101–110 (2002)
22. Moore, B.C.J., Alcántara, J.I., Dau, T.: Masking patterns for sinusoidal and narrow-band noise maskers. J. Acoust. Soc. Am. 104(2), 1023–1038 (1998)
23. Necciari, T.: Auditory time-frequency masking: Psychoacoustical measures and application to the analysis-synthesis of sound signals. Ph.D. thesis, University of Provence Aix-Marseille I, France (October 2010)
24. O'Donovan, J.J., Dermot, J.F.: Perceptually motivated time-frequency analysis. J. Acoust. Soc. Am. 117(1), 250–262 (2005)
25. Oxenham, A.J.: Forward masking: Adaptation or integration? J. Acoust. Soc. Am. 109(2), 732–741 (2001)
26. Patterson, R.D., Allerhand, M.H., Giguère, C.: Time-domain modeling of peripheral auditory processing: A modular architecture and a software platform. J. Acoust. Soc. Am. 98, 1890–1894 (1995)
27. Plack, C.J., Oxenham, A.J., Drga, V.: Linear and nonlinear processes in temporal masking. Acta Acust. United Ac. 88(3), 348–358 (2002)
28. Plack, C.J., Oxenham, A.J.: Basilar-membrane nonlinearity and the growth of forward masking. J. Acoust. Soc. Am. 103(3), 1598–1608 (1998)
29. Robles, L., Ruggero, A.: Mechanics of the mammalian cochlea. Physiol. Rev. 81(3), 1305–1352 (2001)
30. van Schijndel, N.H., Houtgast, T., Festen, J.M.: Intensity discrimination of Gaussian-windowed tones: Indications for the shape of the auditory frequency-time window. J. Acoust. Soc. Am. 105(6), 3425–3435 (1999)
31. Soderquist, D.R., Carstens, A.A., Frank, G.J.H.: Backward, simultaneous, and forward masking as a function of signal delay and frequency. J. Aud. Res. 21, 227–245 (1981)
32. Spanias, P., Painter, T., Atti, V.: Audio Signal Processing and Coding. Wiley-Interscience, Hoboken (2007)
33. Terhardt, E.: Calculating virtual pitch. Hear. Res. 1, 155–182 (1979)
34. Vafin, R., Andersen, S.V., Kleijn, W.B.: Exploiting time and frequency masking in consistent sinusoidal analysis-synthesis. In: Proceedings of the IEEE International Conference on Acoustics, Speech, Signal Processing (ICASSP 2000), Istanbul, Turkey, vol. 2, pp. 901–904 (2000)
35. Vetterli, M., Kovačević, J.: Wavelets and subband coding. Prentice Hall PTR, Englewood Cliffs (1995)
36. Zwicker, E.: Dependence of post-masking on masker duration and its relation to temporal effects in loudness. J. Acoust. Soc. Am. 75(1), 219–223 (1984)

Perceptual Control
of Environmental Sound Synthesis

Mitsuko Aramaki, Richard Kronland-Martinet, and Sølvi Ystad

Laboratoire de Mécanique et d'Acoustique, 31,
31, Chemin Joseph Aiguier
13402 Marseille Cedex 20
{aramaki,kronland,ystad}@lma.cnrs-mrs.fr

Abstract. In this article we explain how perceptual control of synthesis processes can be achieved through a multidisciplinary approach relating physical and signal properties of sound sources to evocations induced by sounds. This approach is applied to environmental and abstract sounds in 3 different experiments. In the first experiment a perceptual control of synthesized impact sounds evoking sound sources of different materials and shapes is presented. The second experiment describes an immersive environmental synthesizer simulating different kinds of environmental sounds evoking natural events such as rain, waves, wind and fire. In the last example motion evoked by abstract sounds is investigated. A tool for describing perceived motion through drawings is proposed in this case.

Keywords: perceptual control, synthesis, analysis, acoustic descriptors, environmental sounds, abstract sounds.

1   Introduction

The development and the optimization of synthesis models have been important research issues since computers produced the first sounds in the early sixties [20]. As computers became increasingly powerful, real-time implementation of synthesis became possible and new research fields related to the control and the development of digital musical instruments appeared. One of the main challenges linked to such fields is the mapping between the control parameters of the interface and the synthesis parameters. Certain synthesis algorithms such as additive synthesis [17,16,4] allow for a very precise reconstruction of sounds, but contain a large number of parameters (several hundreds in the case of piano synthesis), which makes the mapping between the control device and the synthesis model complicated. Other synthesis approaches such as global or non-linear approaches (e.g. frequency modulation (FM) or waveshaping [9,7]) are easier to implement and to control since they contain fewer synthesis parameters, but do not allow for a precise resynthesis. This means that the control device cannot be dissociated from the synthesis model when conceiving a digital musical instrument and even more, a genuine musical interface should go past the technical stage to integrate the creative thought [14]. So far, a large number of control

S. Ystad et al. (Eds.): CMMR/FRSM 2011, LNCS 7172, pp. 172–186, 2012.

devices have been developed for musical purposes [25], but only a few are being actively used in musical contexts either because the control is not sufficiently well adapted to performance situations or because they do not offer an adequate sound control. This means that the control of digital musical instruments is still an issue that necessitates more investigations. Nowadays, sounds are used in a large number of applications (e.g. car industry, video games, radio, cinema, medicine, tourism, ...) since new research domains where sounds are investigated to inform or guide persons (e.g. auditory display, sound design, virtual reality, ...) have developed. Researchers within these domains have traditionally made use of prerecorded sounds, but since important progress has been achieved concerning the development of efficient and realistic synthesis models, an increasing interest for synthesis solutions has lately been observed [8,29,33]. The control requirements related to such applications differ from musical control devices since the role of the sounds in this case is to provide specific information to the end users. Hence, a perceptual control that makes it possible to control sounds from semantic labels, gestures or drawings would be of great interest for such applications. Such control implies that perceptual and cognitive aspects are taken into account in order to understand how a sound is perceived and interpreted. Why are we for instance able to recognize the material of falling objects simply from the sounds they produce, or why do we easily accept the ersatz of horse hooves made by the noise produced when somebody is knocking coconuts together? Previous studies [6,28] have shown that the processing of both linguistic and non-linguistic target sounds in conceptual priming tests elicited similar relationships in the congruity processing. These results indicate that it should be possible to draw up a real *language of sounds*. A certain number of questions have to be answered before such a language can be defined, in particular whether the identification of a sound event through the signal is linked to the presence of specific acoustic morphologies, so-called invariants that can be identified from signal analyses [22]. If so, the identification of signal invariants should make it possible to propose a perceptual control of sound synthesis processes that enables a direct evocative control.

To develop perceptual control strategies of synthesis processes, it is in the first place necessary to understand the perceptual relevance of the sound attributes that characterize the sound category that is investigated. The sound attributes can be of different types and can either be linked to the physical behavior of the source [13], to the signal parameters [18] or to timbre descriptors obtained from perceptual considerations [21]. In this paper we focus on the perceptual control of environmental sounds and evoked motion by describing how such control can be defined from the identification of signal invariants obtained both from the considerations of physical behavior of the sound generating sources and the perceptual impact of the sounds on the listeners. The general approach proposed to obtain perceptual control strategies is shown in Figure 1.

In the first section of this article, we describe how the perceptual control of an impact sound synthesizer enabling the definition of the sound source through verbal labels can be defined. Then a tool for controlling 3D environmental

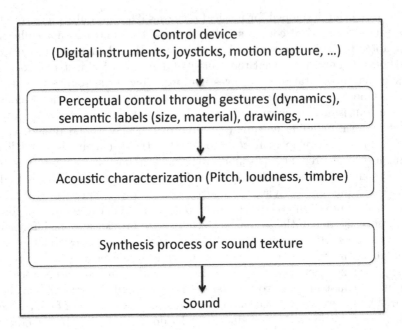

Fig. 1. Synoptics of the perceptual control strategy

immersive auditory scenes with verbal labels based on a synthesizer adapted to environmental sounds is described. Finally an investigation on perceived motion and how intuitive control parameters for this specific type of evocation can be defined is presented.

2   Impact Sound Synthesizer

From the physical point of view, impact sounds are typically generated by an object undergoing free oscillations after being excited by an impact, or by a collision with other solid objects. These vibrations are governed by a wave equation and the natural frequencies of the system are obtained from the solution of this equation. These natural frequencies correspond to the frequencies for which the objet is capable of undergoing harmonic motion. The wave propagation depends on the characteristics of the object that influences two physical phenomena, i.e. dispersion (due to the stiffness of the material) and dissipation (due to loss mechanisms). Dispersion results from the fact that the wave propagation speed varies with the frequency and introduces inharmonicity in the spectrum. Dissipation is directly linked to the damping of the sound and is generally frequency-dependent. The perceptual relevance of these phenomena and how they contribute to the identification of impact sounds will be discussed in the next section.

2.1   Invariant Sound Structures Characterizing Impact Sounds

Impact sounds have been largely investigated in the literature. In particular, some links between the physical characteristics of actions (impact, bouncing ...) and sound sources (material, shape, size, cavity ...) and their perceptual correlates were established (see [2,1] for a review). For instance, the perception of the hardness of a mallet impacting an object is related to the characteristics of the attack time. The perception of material seems to be linked to the characteristics of the damping that is generally frequency-dependent: high frequency components are damped more heavily than low frequency components. In addition to the damping, we concluded that the density of spectral components which is directly linked to the perceived roughness, is also relevant for the distinction between metal versus glass and wood categories [2,1]. The perceived shape of the object is related to the distribution of the spectral components of the produced sound. It can therefore be assumed that both the inharmonicity and the roughness determine the perceived shape of the object. From a physical point of view, large objects vibrate at lower eigenfrequencies than small ones. Hence, the perceived size of the object is mainly based on the pitch. For complex sounds, the determination of pitch is still an open issue. In some cases, the pitch may not correspond to an actual component of the spectrum and both spectral and virtual pitches are elicited [30]. However, for quasi-harmonic sounds, we assume that the pitch is linked to the fundamental frequency.

These considerations allowed us to identify signal morphologies (i.e. invariants) conveying relevant information on the perceived material, size, shape and type of impact on an object. A mapping strategy defining a link between synthesis parameters, acoustic descriptors and perceptual control parameters can then be defined, as described in the next section.

2.2   Control of the Impact Sound Synthesizer

To develop a perceptual control of impact sounds based on semantic description of the sound source, a mapping strategy between synthesis parameters (low level), acoustic descriptors (middle level) and semantic labels (high level) characterizing the evoked sound object was defined. The mapping strategy that was chosen is based on a three level architecture as seen in Figure 2) [5,3,2]. The top layer is composed of verbal descriptions of the object (nature of the material, size and shape, etc.). The middle layer concerns the control of acoustic descriptors that are known to be relevant from the perceptual point of view as described in section 2.1. The bottom layer is dedicated to the control of the parameters of the synthesis model (amplitudes, frequencies and damping coefficients of components). The mapping strategy between verbal descriptions of the sound source and sound descriptors is designed with respect to the previous considerations described in section 2.1. The control of the perceived material is based on the manipulation of damping but also that of spectral sound descriptors such as inharmonicity and roughness. Since the damping is frequency dependent, a damping law was arbitrarily defined and we proposed an exponential function:

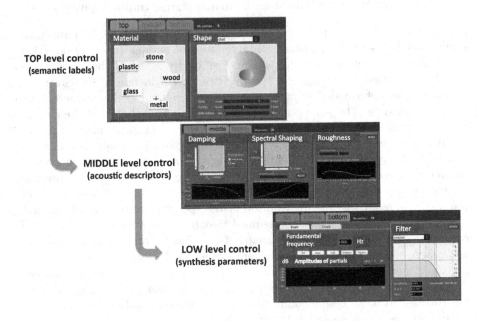

Fig. 2. Three level control strategy of impact sounds

$\alpha(\omega) = e^{(\alpha_G + \alpha_R \omega)}$ characterized by two parameters: a global damping α_G and a relative damping α_R. The choice of an exponential function enables us to reach various damping profiles characteristic of physical materials by acting on a few control parameters. Hence, the control of the damping was effectuated by two parameters. The perception of size is controlled by the frequency of the first component and the perception of shape by the spectral distribution of components defined from inharmonicity and roughness. As for damping, an inharmonicity law characterized by a few parameters was proposed. Some pre-defined presets give direct access to typical inharmonicity profiles, such as those of strings, membranes and plates. The roughness is created by applying amplitude and frequency modulations on the initial sound and can be controlled separately for each Bark band.

The mapping between sound descriptors and synthesis parameters is organized as follows. The damping coefficients of the components are determined from the damping law $\alpha(\omega)$ and their amplitudes from the envelope modulations introduced by the excitation point. The spectral distribution of components (frequency values) are defined from the inharmonicity law and the roughness. A direct control at low level allows for readjustments of this spectral distribution of components by acting separately on the frequency, amplitude and damping coefficients of each component. This mapping between middle and bottom layer depends on the synthesis model and should be adapted with respect to the chosen synthesis process.

What the control of action is concerned, the hardness of the mallet is controlled by the attack time and the brightness while the perceived force is related to the brightness: the heavier the applied force is, the brighter the sound. The timbre of the generated sound is also strongly influenced by the excitation point of the impact that creates envelope modulations in the spectrum due to the cancellation of modes presenting a node at the point of excitation. From a synthesis point of view, the location of the impact is taken into account by shaping the spectrum with a feed forward comb filter.

3   Immersive Environmental Sound Synthesizer

Impact sounds constitute a specific category of environmental sounds. In this section an immersive synthesizer simulating various kinds of environmental sounds is proposed. These sounds are divided in three main categories according to W. W. Gaver's taxonomy of everyday sound sources: vibrating solids (impact, bouncing, deformation ...) liquid (wave, drop, rain ...) and aerodynamic (wind, fire ...) objects [12,11]. Based on this taxonomy, we proposed a synthesizer to create and control immersive environmental scenes intended for interactive virtual and augmented reality and sonification applications. Both synthesis and spatialization engines were included in this tool so as to increase the realism and the feeling of being immersed in virtual worlds.

3.1   Invariant Sound Structures Characterizing Environmental Sounds

In the case of impact sounds, we have seen that physical considerations reveal important properties that can be used to identify the perceived effects of the generated sounds (cf. section 2.1). For other types of environmental sounds such as wave, wind or explosion sounds, the physical considerations involve complex modeling and can less easily be taken into account for synthesis perspective with interactive constraints. Hence the identification of perceptual cues linked to these sound categories was done by the analyses of sound signals representative of these categories. From a perceptual point of view, these sounds evoke a wide range of different physical sources, but interestingly, from a signal point of view, some common acoustic morphologies can be highlighted across these sounds. To date, we concluded on five elementary sound morphologies based on impacts, chirps and noise structures [32]. This finding is based on a heuristic approach that has been verified on a large set of environmental sounds. Actually, granular synthesis processes associated to the morphologies of these five grains have enabled the generation of various environmental sounds such as solid interactions and aerodynamic or liquid sounds. Sounds produced by solid interactions can be characterised from a physical point of view. When a linear approximation applies (small deformation of the structure), the response of a solid object to external forces can be viewed as the convolution of these forces with the modal response of the object. Such a response is given by a sum of exponentially damped sinusoids, defining the typical "tonal solid grain". Nevertheless, such a type of grain cannot itself account for all kinds of solid impact sounds. Actually, rapidly vanishing impact sounds or sounds characterized by a strong density of modes may rather be modelled as exponentially damped noise. This sound characterization stands for both perceptual and signal points of views, since no obvious pitch can be extracted from such sounds. Exponentially damped noise constitutes the so-called "noisy impact grain". Still dealing with physical considerations, we may design a "liquid grain" that takes into account cavitation phenomena occurring in liquid motion. Cavitation leads to local pressure variations that, from an acoustic point of view, generate time varying frequency components such as exponentially damped linear chirps. Exponentially damped chirps then constitute our third type of grain: the "liquid grain". Aerodynamic sounds generally result from complicated interactions between solids and gases. It is therefore difficult to extract useful information from corresponding physical models. The construction of granular synthesis processes was therefore based on heuristic perceptual expertise defining two kinds of aerodynamic grains: the "whistling grain" consisting in a slowly varying narrow band noise; and the "background aerodynamic grain" consisting in a broadband filtered noise. By combining these five grains using an accurate statistics of appearance, various environmental sounds can be designed such as rainy ambiances, seacoast ambiances, windy environments, fire noises, or solid interactions simulating solid impacts or footstep noises. We currently aim at extracting the parameters corresponding to these grains from the analysis of natural sound, using matching pursuit like methods.

3.2   Control of the Environmental Sound Synthesizer

To develop a perceptual control of the environmental sound synthesizer based on semantic labels, a mapping strategy that enabled the design of complex auditory scenes was defined. In particular, we took into account that some sound sources such as wind or rain are naturally diffuse and wide. Therefore, the control included the location and the spatial extension of sound sources in a 3D space. In contrast with the classical two-stage approach, which consists in first synthesizing a monophonic sound (timbre properties) and then spatializing the sound (spatial position and extension in a 3D space), the architecture of the proposed synthesizer yielded control strategies based on the overall manipulation of timbre and spatial attributes of sound sources at the same level of sound generation [31].

For that purpose, we decided to bring the spatial distribution of the sounds to the lowest level of the sound generation. Indeed, the characterization of each elementary time-localized sound component, that is generally limited to its amplitude, frequency and phase, was augmented by its spatial position in the 3D space. This tremendous addition leads to an increasing number of control possibilities while still being real time compatible thanks to an accurate use of the granular synthesis process in the frequency domain [34]. We then showed that the control of the spatial distribution of the partials together with the construction of decorrelated versions of the actual sound allowed for the control of the spatial position of the sound source together with the control of its perceived spatial width. These two perceptual spatial dimensions have shown to be of great importance in the design of immersive auditory scenes.

Complex 3D auditory scenes can be intuitively built by combining spatialized sound sources that are themselves built from the elementary "grain" structures (cf. section 3.1).

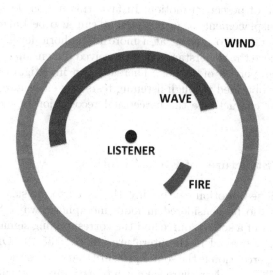

Fig. 3. Auditory scene of a windy day (wind source surrounding the listener) on a beach (wave coming towards the listener) and including a BBQ sound (fire located at the back right of the listener)

The fire is for instance built from three elementary grains that are a whistling grain (simulating the hissing), a background aerodynamic grain (simulating the background combustion) and noisy impact grains (simulating the cracklings). The grains are generated and launched randomly with respect to time using an accurate statistical law that can be controlled. A global control of the fire intensity, mapped with the control of the grain generation (amplitude and statistical law), can then be designed. The overall control of the environmental scene synthesizer is effectuated through a graphical interface (see figure 3) where the listener is positioned in the center of the scene. Then the user selects the sound sources to be included in the auditory scene among a set of available sources (fire, wind, rain, wave, chimes, footsteps ...) and places them around the listener by graphically defining the distance and the spatial width of the source. In cases of interactive uses, controls can be achieved using either MIDI interfaces, from data obtained from a graphical engine or other external data sources.

4   Synthesis of Evoked Motion

A third approach aiming at developing perceptual control devices for synthesized sounds that evoke specific motions is presented in this section. The definition of perceptual control necessitates more thorough investigations in this case than in the two previous cases due to the rather vague notion of perceived motion. Although physics of moving sound sources can to some extent give indications on certain morphologies that characterize specific movements [19], it cannot always explain the notion of perceived motion. In fact, this notion does not only rely on the physical displacement of an object, but can also be linked to temporal evolutions in general or to motion at a more metaphoric level. It is therefore necessary to improve the understanding of perceived dimension of motion linked to the intrinsic properties of sounds. Therefore, an investigation of perceived motion categories obtained through listening tests was effectuated before signal morphologies that characterize the perceptual recognition of motion could be identified.

4.1   Invariant Structures of Evoked Motion

As already mentioned, motion can be directly linked to physical moving sound sources, but can also be considered in more metaphoric ways. Studies on the physical movement of a sound source and the corresponding signal morphologies have been widely described in the literature [10,27,26,35,19]. One aspect that links physics and perception is the sound pressure that relates the sound intensity to the loudness. The sound pressure is known to vary inversely with the distance between the source and the listener. This rule is highly important from the perceptual point of view [27], and it is possibly decisive in the case of slowly moving sources. It is worth noting that only the relative changes in the sound pressure should be considered in this context. Another important aspect is the timbre and more specifically the brightness variations, which can be physically accounted for in terms of the air absorption [10]. A third phenomenon which is well known in physics is the Doppler effect which explains why frequency shifts can be heard while listening to the siren of an approaching police car [26]. Actually, depending on the relative speed of the source with respect to the listener, the frequency measured at the listener's position varies and the specific time-dependent pattern seems to be a highly relevant cue enabling the listener to construct a mental representation of the trajectory. Finally, the reverberation is another aspect that enables the distinction between close and distant sound sources [15]. A close sound source will produce direct sounds of greater magnitude than the reflected sounds, which means that the reverberation will be weaker for close sound sources than for distant ones.

  When considering evoked motion at a more metaphoric level, like for instance in music and cartoon production processes, signal morphologies responsible for the perceived motion cannot be directly linked to physics and must be identified in other ways, for instance through listening tests. The selection of stimuli for such investigations is intricate, since the recognition of the sound producing source might influence the judgement of the perceived motion. For instance, when the sound from a car is presented, the motion that a listener will associate to this sound will most probably be influenced by the possible motions that the car can make, even if the sound might contain other interesting indices that could have evoked motions at more metaphoric levels. To avoid this problem, we therefore decided to investigate motion through a specific sound category, so-called "abstract sounds" which are sounds that cannot be easily associated to an identifiable sound source. Hence, when listeners are asked to describe evocations induced by such sounds, they are forced to concentrate on intrinsic sound properties instead of the sound source. Such sounds, that have been explored by electroacoustic music composers, can be obtained from both recordings (for instance with a microphone close to a sound source) or from synthesized sounds obtained by for instance granular synthesis [23]. In a previous study aiming at investigating semiotics of abstract sounds [28], subjects often referred to various motions when describing these sounds. This observation reinforced our conviction that abstract sounds are well adapted to investigate evoked motion.

As a first approach toward a perceptual control of evoked motion, perceived motion categories were identified through a free categorization test [24]. Subjects were asked to categorize 68 abstract sound and further give a verbal description of each category. Six main categories were identified through this test, i.e. "rotating", "falling down", "approaching", "passing by", "going away", "going up". The extraction of signal features specific to each category revealed a systematic presence of amplitude and frequency modulations in the case of sounds belonging to the category"turning", a logarithmic decrease in amplitude in the category "passing" and amplitude envelopes characteristic of impulsive sounds for the category "falling". Interestingly, several subjects expressed the need to make drawings to describe the perceived motions. This tends to indicate that a relationship between the dynamics of sounds and a graphic representation is intuitive. This observation was decisive for our control strategy investigation presented in the next section.

4.2   Control of Evoked Motion

In the case of evoked motion the definition of a perceptual control is as previously mentioned less straightforward than in the case of impact sounds and environmental sounds. From the free categorization test described in the previous section, categories of motion were identified along with suitable signal invariants corresponding to each category. However, this test did not directly yield any perceptual cues as to how these evocations might be controlled in a synthesis tool. Therefore, to identify perceptually relevant control parameters corresponding to evoked dynamic patterns, further experiments were conducted in which subjects were asked to describe the evoked trajectories by drawings. Since hand made drawings would have been difficult to analyze and would have been influenced by differences in people's ability to draw, a parametrized drawing interface was developed, meaning that subjects were given identical drawing tools that required no specific skills. The control parameters available in the interface were based on the findings obtained in the free categorization test, and the accuracy of the drawing was limited to prevent the interface from becoming too complex to handle. The interface is shown in Figure 4.

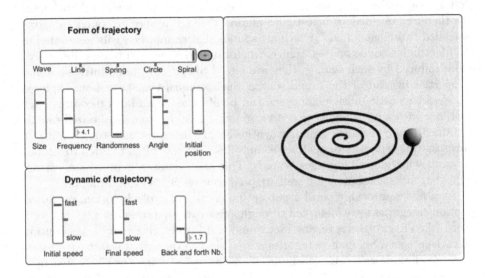

Fig. 4. Graphical User Interface

Two aspects, i.e. shape and dynamics, enabled the subjects to define the motion. Six parameters were available to draw the shape of the trajectory (shape, size, frequency oscillation, randomness, angle, initial position) and three parameters were available to define the dynamics (initial and final velocity and number of returns). Each time a sound was presented, the subject made a drawing that corresponded to the trajectory he or she had perceived. No time constraint was imposed and the subject could listen to the sound as often as he/she wanted. The dynamics was illustrated by a ball that followed the trajectory while the sound was played.

Results showed that although the subjects used various drawing strategies, equivalent drawings and common parameter values could still be discerned. As far as the shape was concerned, subjects showed good agreement on the distinction between linear and oscillating movements and between wave-like and circular oscillations. This means that these three aspects give a sufficiently exact control of the perceived shape of sound trajectories. As far as the orientation of the trajectory was concerned, only the distinction between horizontal and vertical seems to be relevant. While there was agreement among subjects about the distinction between the upward/downward direction, the difference between the left/right direction was not relevant. As far as the velocity was concerned, the subjects distinguished between constant and varying velocities, but they did not show good agreement in the way they specified the velocity variations they perceived. This might have been related to the graphical user interface which did not provide a sufficiently precise control of the dynamics according to several subjects.

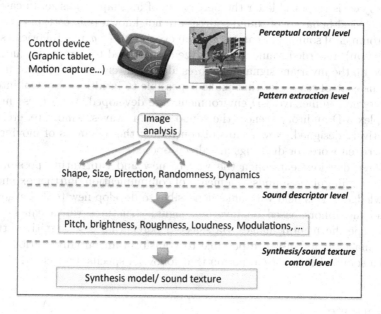

Fig. 5. Generic motion control

The identification of perceptually relevant parameters enabled the definition of a reduced number of control possibilities. Hence 3 kinds of shapes (linear, circular and regular), 3 different directions (south, north and horizontal), and various degrees of oscillation frequencies (high and low), randomness (non, little, much), size (small, medium, large) and dynamics (constant, medium an high speed) were found to be important control parameters that enabled the definition of perceived trajectories. Based on these findings, a generic motion control strategy could hereby be defined as shown in Figure 5. This strategy could be separated in three parts, i.e. a perceptual control level based on drawings, an image processing level dividing the drawings in elementary patterns (i.e. waves, lines, direction, etc) and a third level containing the synthesis algorithm or a sound texture.

5   Conclusion and Discussion

This article describes perceptual control strategies of synthesis processes obtained from the identification of sound structures (invariants) responsible for evocations induced by sounds. In the case of impact sounds, these sound structures are obtained by investigating the perceptual relevance of signal properties related to the physical behavior of the sound sources. Variations of physical phenomena such as dispersion and dissipation make perceptual distinctions possible between different types of objects (i.e. strings versus bars or plates versus membranes) or materials (wood, glass, metal,...). The spectral content of the impact sound, in particular the eigen-frequencies that characterize the modes of a vibrating object, is responsible for the perception of its shape and size. In cases where the physical behavior of sound sources are not known (*e.g.* certain categories of environmental sounds) or cannot explain evocations (*e.g.* metaphoric description of motion), recorded sounds are analyzed and linked to perceptual judgements. Based on the invariant signal structures identified (chirps, noise structures, ...), various control strategies that make it possible to intuitively control interacting objects and immersive 3-D environments are developed. With these interfaces, complex 3-D auditory scenes (the sound of rain, waves, wind, fire, etc.) can be intuitively designed. New means of controlling the dynamics of moving sounds via written words or drawings are also proposed.

These developments open the way to new and captivating possibilities for using non-linguistic sounds as a means of communication. Further extending our knowledge in this field will make it possible to develop new tools for generating sound metaphors based on invariant signal structures which can be used to evoke specific mental images via selected perceptual and cognitive attributes. This makes it for instance possible to transform an initially stationary sound into a sound that evokes a motion that follows a specific trajectory.

References

1. Aramaki, M., Besson, M., Kronland-Martinet, R., Ystad, S.: Timbre Perception of Sounds from Impacted Materials: Behavioral, Electrophysiological and Acoustic Approaches. In: Ystad, S., Kronland-Martinet, R., Jensen, K. (eds.) CMMR 2008. LNCS, vol. 5493, pp. 1–17. Springer, Heidelberg (2009)
2. Aramaki, M., Besson, M., Kronland-Martinet, R., Ystad, S.: Controlling the perceived material in an impact sound synthesizer. IEEE Transactions on Audio, Speech, and Language Processing 19(2), 301–314 (2011)
3. Aramaki, M., Gondre, C., Kronland-Martinet, R., Voinier, T., Ystad, S.: Imagine the Sounds: An Intuitive Control of an Impact Sound Synthesizer. In: Ystad, S., Aramaki, M., Kronland-Martinet, R., Jensen, K. (eds.) CMMR/ICAD 2009. LNCS, vol. 5954, pp. 408–421. Springer, Heidelberg (2010)
4. Aramaki, M., Kronland-Martinet, R.: Analysis-synthesis of impact sounds by real-time dynamic filtering. IEEE Transactions on Audio, Speech, and Language Processing 14(2), 695–705 (2006)
5. Aramaki, M., Kronland-Martinet, R., Voinier, T., Ystad, S.: A percussive sound synthetizer based on physical and perceptual attributes. Computer Music Journal 30(2), 32–41 (2006)
6. Aramaki, M., Marie, C., Kronland-Martinet, R., Ystad, S., Besson, M.: Sound categorization and conceptual priming for nonlinguistic and linguistic sounds. Journal of Cognitive Neuroscience 22(11), 2555–2569 (2010)
7. Le Brun, M.: Digital waveshaping synthesis. JAES 27(4), 250–266 (1979)

8. Bézat, M., Roussarie, V., Voinier, T., Kronland-Martinet, R., Ystad, S.: Car door closure sounds: Characterization of perceptual properties through analysis-synthesis approach. In: International Conference on Acoustics (ICA 2007), Madrid (2007)
9. Chowning, J.: The synthesis of complex audio spectra by means of frequency modulation. JAES 21(7), 526–534 (1973)
10. Chowning, J.: The simulation of moving sound sources. Journal of the Audio Engineering Society 19(1), 2–6 (1971)
11. Gaver, W.W.: How do we hear in the world? explorations in ecological acoustics. Ecological Psychology 5(4), 285–313 (1993)
12. Gaver, W.W.: What in the world do we hear? an ecological approach to auditory event perception. Ecological Psychology 5(1), 1–29 (1993)
13. Giordano, B.L., McAdams, S.: Material identification of real impact sounds: Effects of size variation in steel, wood, and plexiglass plates. Journal of the Acoustical Society of America 119(2), 1171–1181 (2006)
14. Gobin, P., Kronland-Martinet, R., Lagesse, G.-A., Voinier, T., Ystad, S.: Designing Musical Interfaces with Composition in Mind. In: Wiil, U.K. (ed.) CMMR 2003. LNCS, vol. 2771, pp. 225–246. Springer, Heidelberg (2004)
15. Jot, J.M., Warusfel, O.: A real-time spatial sound processor for music and virtual reality applications. In: Proceedings of the International Computer Music Conference (ICMC 1995), pp. 294–295 (1995)
16. Kleczkowski, P.: Group additive synthesis. Computer Music Journal 13(1), 12–20 (1989)
17. Kronland-Martinet, R.: The use of the wavelet transform for the analysis, synthesis and processing of speech and music sounds. Computer Music Journal 12(4), 11–20 (1989)
18. Kronland-Martinet, R., Guillemain, P., Ystad, S.: Modelling of natural sounds by time-frequency and wavelet representations. Organised Sound 2(3), 179–191 (1997)
19. Kronland-Martinet, R., Voinier, T.: Real-time perceptual simulation of moving sources: Application to the leslie cabinet and 3d sound immersion. EURASIP Journal on Audio, Speech, and Music Processing 2008 (2008)
20. Mathews, M.: The digital computer as a musical instrument. Science 142(3592), 553–557 (1963)
21. McAdams, S.: Perspectives on the contribution of timbre to musical structure. Computer Music Journal 23(3), 85–102 (2011)
22. McAdams, S., Bigand, E.: Thinking in Sound: The cognitive psychology of human audition. Oxford University Press (1993)
23. Merer, A., Ystad, S., Aramaki, M., Kronland-Martinet, R.: Exploring Music Contents. In: Abstract Sounds and Their Applications in Audio and Perception Research, pp. 269–297. Springer, Heidelberg (2011)
24. Merer, A., Ystad, S., Kronland-Martinet, R., Aramaki, M.: Semiotics of Sounds Evoking Motions: Categorization and Acoustic Features. In: Kronland-Martinet, R., Ystad, S., Jensen, K. (eds.) CMMR 2007. LNCS, vol. 4969, pp. 139–158. Springer, Heidelberg (2008)
25. Miranda, E.R., Wanderley, M.: New Digital Musical Instruments: Control And Interaction Beyond the Keyboard. A-R Editions (2006)
26. Neuhoff, J., McBeath, M.: The doppler illusion: the influence of dynamic intensity change on perceived pitch. Journal of Experimental Psychology: Human Perception and Performance 22(4), 970–985 (1996)
27. Rosenblum, L., Wier, C.C., Pastore, R.: Relative effectiveness of three stimulus variables for locating a moving sound source. Perception 16(2), 175–186 (1987)

28. Schön, D., Kronland-Martinet, R., Ystad, S., Besson, M.: The evocative power of sounds: Conceptual priming between words and nonverbal sounds. Journal of Cognitive Neuroscience 22(5), 1026–1035 (2010)

29. Sciabica, J., Bezat, M., Roussarie, V., Kronland-Martinet, R., Ystad, S.: Towards the timbre modeling of interior car sound. In: 15th International Conference on Auditory Display, Copenhagen (2009)

30. Terhardt, E., Stoll, G., Seewann, M.: Pitch of complex signals according to virtual-pitch theory: Tests, examples, and predictions. Journal of Acoustical Society of America 71, 671–678 (1982)

31. Verron, C., Aramaki, M., Kronland-Martinet, R., Pallone, G.: A 3d immersive synthesizer for environmental sounds. IEEE Transactions on Audio, Speech, and Language Processing 18(6), 1550–1561 (2010)

32. Verron, C., Pallone, G., Aramaki, M., Kronland-Martinet, R.: Controlling a spatialized environmental sound synthesizer. In: Proceedings of the IEEE Workshop on Applications of Signal Processing to Audio and Acoustics (WASPAA), New Paltz, NY, October 18-21, pp. 321–324 (2009)

33. Verron, C., Aramaki, M., Kronland-Martinet, R., Pallone, G.: Spatialized additive synthesis. In: Acoustics 2008, Paris, France (June 2008), http://hal.archives-ouvertes.fr/hal-00463365, oR 20 OR 20 CIFRE

34. Verron, C., Aramaki, M., Kronland-Martinet, R., Pallone, G.: Analysis/synthesis and spatialization of noisy environmental sounds. In: Proc. of the 15th International Conference on Auditory Display, Copenhague, Danemark, pp. 36–41 (2009)

35. Warren, J., Zielinski, B., Green, G., Rauschecker, J.P., Griffiths, T.: Perception of sound-source motion by the human brain. Neuron 34(1), 139–148 (2002)

Recognition of Assamese Phonemes
Using RNN Based Recognizer

Utpal Bhattacharjee

Department of Computer Science and Engineering, Rajiv Gandhi University
Rono Hills, Doimukh, Arunachal Pradesh, India, Pin-791 112
utpalbhattacharjee@rediffmail.com

Abstract. This paper discusses a novel technique for the recognition of Assamese phonemes using Recurrent Neural Network (RNN) based phoneme recognizer. A Multi-Layer Perceptron (MLP) has been used as phoneme segmenter for the segmentation of phonemes from isolated Assamese words. Two different RNN based approaches have been considered for recognition of the phonemes and their performances have been evaluated. MFCC has been used as the feature vector for both segmentation and recognition. With RNN based phoneme recognizer, a recognition accuracy of 91% has been achieved. The RNN based phoneme recognizer has been tested for speaker mismatched and channel mismatched conditions. It has been observed that the recognizer is robust to any unseen speaker. However, its performance degrades in channel mismatch condition. Cepstral Mean Normalization (CMN) has been used to overcome the problem of performance degradation effectively.

Keywords: RNN, MFCC, MLP, CMN.

1   Introduction

One of the basic assumptions about speech signal is that speech signal composed of many locally stationary but temporally related segments. These quasi-stationary speech segments or a concatenation of them corresponds to the basic phonetic units such as vowels and consonants. Therefore, modelling of a speech signal essentially deals with the concurrent aspects – static features of individual phonetic or sub-phonetic segments and temporal relation of these units. The incapability of artificial neural network to deal with speech dynamic hinders its application in speech recognition. Most of the artificial neural network models are good static classifier, but do not accept sequential or time varying input. An intuitive way to deal with speech dynamic is recurrent neural network. The recurrent neural network accepts sequentially arranged input vector U(1), U(2), U(3), ..., U(t), one at a time. In speech applications, these vectors typically contain the frame based spectral features. The internal state of RNN at time t is described by the state vector $X(t)=[x_1(t)\ x_2(t) ......x_N(t)]^T$, where $x_n(t)$ is the activation level of the nth neuron and N is the total number of neurons. At each time instant, the present network state x(t) is a non-linear function of current input vector U(t) and pervious state X(t-1), i.e.,

S. Ystad et al. (Eds.): CMMR/FRSM 2011, LNCS 7172, pp. 187–196, 2012.

$$X(t) = \Gamma(U(t), X(t-1)) \tag{1}$$

where $\Gamma(.)$ depends on the network architectures of individual neurons. Usually, a subset of the N neurons are used as the output neuron whose activation level forms the output vector $Y(t)$. As a result, a sequence of output vectors $\{Y(t)\}$ is produced. Unlike static neural network classifier whose decision is given solely by instantaneous output vector, the RNN utilizes the entire output sequence to discriminate the input sequence from others.

A variety of methods have been proposed to accomplish this phoneme segmentation [1][2][3]. Most of the methods rely heavily on a series of acoustic phonetic rules. Since the rules are difficult to generalized, their performance degrades in real world applications. In order to overcome these problems a neural network based approach has been used in this paper. The neural network based approach has advantage over the rule-based approach due to the fact that it is a non-parametric method and produces robust performance under unexpected environmental conditions. Many neural network based attempts has been made for phoneme segmentation and some encouraging result has been reported [4][5][6]. In this paper a MLP-based segmentation method has been utilized.

MFCC is extensively used and has proven to be successful for Automatic Speech and Speaker Recognition system. In the present work, MFCC has been used as feature vector. To avoid excessive computational load for feature extraction, the same feature set has been used for both segmentation and recognition purpose. In the present study, a new feature set has been derived from the original MFCC feature set to use it as input to the phoneme segmenter. This feature set is based on the difference between the feature vectors extracted from two consecutive frames. Differences in the feature values extracted from five consecutive frames have been considered as a single block of input feature for the phoneme segmenter. The feature vector for both phoneme segmenter and phoneme recognizer has been normalized between 0-1 due to the fact that artificial neural network gives better performance with normalized data.

2   Assamese Language and Its Phonological Features

The Assamese is the major language in the North Easter part of India with its own unique identity, culture and language through its origins root back to Indo-European family of language. Assamese is the easternmost member of the New Indo-Aryan (NIA) subfamily of languages spoken in Assam and many part of North-Eastern India. Some of the unique features of Assamese language are cited below [7]:

- A unique feature of the Assamese language is a total absence of any retroflex sounds. Instead the language has a whole series of alveolar sounds, which include oral and nasal stops, fricatives, laterals, approximants, flaps and trills, unlike other Indo-Aryan and Dravidian languages.
- Another striking phonological feature of the Assamese language is the extensive use of velar nasal /ŋ/. In other New Indo Aryan languages this /ŋ/ is always attached to a homorganic sound like /g/. In contrast it is always used singly in Assamese.

- The voiceless velar fricative /x/ is a distinct characteristic of Assamese language which is not to be found in any language in the entire country. It is similar to the velar sound in German of Europe. It may be an Indo-European feature, which has been preserved by Assamese.

The Assamese phonemic inventory consists of eight oral vowel phonemes, three nasalized vowel phonemes and twenty-two consonant phonemes. The phonemes of the Assamese language are given below[8]:

Table 1. Vowels of Assamese Language

		Front	Central	Back
Oral Vowel	High	i		u
	High-mid			ʊ
	Mid	e		o
	Low-mid	ɛ		ɔ
	Low		a	
Nasalized Vowel	High	i)		u)
	Low		a)	

Table 2. Consonants of Assamese Language

	Labial	Alveolar	Velar	Glottal
Voiceless stops	p	t	k	
	pʰ	tʰ	kʰ	
Voiced stops	b	d	g	
	bʰ	dʰ	gʰ	
Voiceless fricatives		s	x	h
Voiced fricatives		z		
Nasals	m	n	ŋ	
Approximants	w	ɹ		
Lateral		l		

3   System Description

The system developed during the present study consists of three major units – Feature Extractor, MLP based Phoneme Segmenter and RNN based Phoneme Recognizer. The description of each unit is given below:

3.1   The Feature Extractor

The speech signal has been directly digitized in WAV PCM format and sampling at 16 KHz frequency with 16 bit mono quantization. A pre-emphasis filter $H(z)=1-0.95z^{-1}$ has been applied before framing. Each frame is multiplied with a 30 ms Hamming window shifted by 10ms. From the windowed frame, FFT has been computed and the magnitude spectrum is filtered with a bank of 29 triangular filters spaced on Mel-scale. The log-compressed filter outputs are converted to cepstral coefficients by DCT giving 29 Mel Frequency Cepstral Coefficients (MFCC). However, in the present study we have considered only the coefficient from 1 to 23 because it covers the frequency range that is used by human in normal conversation. The 0th cepstral coefficient is not used in the cepstral feature vector and replaced with log of energy of the frame calculated in the time domain. To capture the time varying nature of the speech signal, the first order derivative of the Cepstral coefficients are also calculated. Combining the MFCC coefficients with its first order derivative, we get a 48-dimensional feature vector.

3.2   MLP Based Phoneme Segmenter

Multi-layer perceptron (MLP) with error-back propagation training have been successfully applied in a variety of pattern recognition problems [9][10][11]. They have good discrimination capability and can generate complex nonlinear decision boundaries. All the properties are very useful for speech recognition and phoneme segmentation. MLP may have any number of hidden layers, although additional hidden layers tend to make training slower, as the terrain in weight space becomes more complicated. To train the MLP, a modified version of well-known Back Propagation Algorithm [12] has been used. To avoid the oscillations at the local minima, a momentum constant has been introduced which provides optimization in the weight updating process.

   In the present study, a new feature set has been derived from the original MFCC based feature set. Inter-frame differences between two consecutive frames have been calculated and it is normalized between -1 to +1. Inter-frame differences obtained from 5 consecutive frames have been considered as a single input feature block for the phoneme segmenter. Each block consists of 192 parameters. A MLP-based phoneme segmenter with 192 input nodes, 28 hidden nodes and one output node has been used for the segmentation of the phonemes. The decision on 28 hidden nodes has been taken experimentally. The output node will return 1 if the 3rd frame of the original feature vector is a phoneme boundary, in all other cases it will return 0. In each pass the feature vector will slide by one frame.

3.3   Recurrent Neural Network Based Phoneme Recognizer

A fully connected recurrent neural network is used to construct the speech model. This network architecture was described by Williams and Zipser [13] and also known as Williams and Zipser's model. Let the network have N neurons and out of them k are used as output neurons. The output neurons are labelled from 1 to k and the hidden neurons are labelled from $k+1$ to N. Let P_{mn} be the feed-forward connection weight from m^{th} input component to the nth neuron and w_{nl} be the recurrent connection weight from the lth neuron to the nth neuron. At time t, when an M-dimensional feature vector $U(t)$ is presented to the network, the total input to the nth neuron is given by

$$Z_n(t) = \sum_{l=1}^{N} w_{nl}x_l(t-1) + \sum_{m=1}^{M} P_{nm}U_m(t) \qquad (2)$$

where $x_l(t-1)$ is the activation level of the lth neuron at time $t-1$ and $U_m(t)$ is the mth component of $U(t)$. The resultant activation level $X_n(t)$ is calculated as

$$X_n(t) = f_n(Z_n(t)) = \frac{1}{1+e^{-Z_n(t)}}, 1 \le n \le N \tag{3}$$

To describe the entire network response at time t, the output vector $Y(t)$ is formed by the activation level of all output neuron, i.e.

$$Y(t) = [x_1(t)x_2(t) \ldots \ldots \ldots x_k(t)]^T \tag{4}$$

Following the conventional winner-take-all representations, one and only one neuron is allowed to be activated each time. Thus, k discrete output states are formed. In state k, the kth output neuron is most activated over the others. Let $s(t)$ denote the output state at time t, which can be derived from $Y(t)$ as

$$S(t) = \underset{j=1}{\overset{k}{\arg\max}} \{x_j(t)\} \tag{5}$$

The RNN has been described so far only for a single time-step. When a sequence of input vector $\{U(t)\}$ is presented to the network, the output sequence $\{Y(t)\}$ is generated by eq. (2) – (4). By eq. (5), $\{Y(t)\}$ can be further converted into an output scalar sequence $\{s(t)\}$, and both of them have the same length as $\{U(t)\}$. $\{s(t)\}$ is a scalar sequence with integer value between 1 to n. It can be regarded as a quantized temporal representation of the RNN output.

The fully connected RNN described above performs time aligned mapping from a given input sequence to an output state sequence of the RNN. Each element in the state sequence is determined not only by the current input vector but also by the previous state of the RNN. Such state dependency is very important if the sequential order of input vector is considered as an indispensable feature in the sequence mapping.

In the present study, the recurrent neural network has been used to construct two phoneme recognizers. The first recognizer is named as "All in one speech model" and the second as "Class-based model". Both the models have been tested and their performances have been evaluated.

The Real Time Recurrent Learning (RTRL) algorithm [13] with sufficiently small learning rate has been used to train both the phoneme recognizer.

4   Database Description

A speech database has been developed for evaluation the performance of phoneme recognizer as well as to study the impact of channel and speaker variability on the performance of phoneme recognizer. The speech database consists of two sets one for each recording sessions. Each set consists of 30 speakers, with 20 speakers common in both sets. Speech data were recorded over three devices in parallel. Details of the devices used for recording are given below:

Table 3. Technical Details of the devices used for collecting speech data

Device Name	Device/sensor	Make/model	Sampling Rate	Recording format
Device 1	Headset mic	Zebronic Sports	16 kHz	wav
Device 2	Laptop	HP ProBook 4520s	16 kHz	wav
Device 3	DVR	TASCAM DR-100	44.1 kHz	mp3

Each set of the database consist of 1200 isolated Assamese words recorded in each device. The isolated words are selected from a set of 100 phonetically rich sentences collected from school book and recorded in parallel using all the three devices. From the recorded speech, the word of interest are manually isolated and considered as input to the system. The digital voice recorder speech data has been downsampled to 16 KHz and format has been converted to WAV PCM mono with 16 bit resolution. If the same speaker participates in two recording sessions, an interval of 10 days has been given between the recording sessions. The same number of words has been considered in both the sessions. At the time of selecting the isolated words, attempt has been made to keep two instances of each phoneme in each speaker voice in each recording session.

5   Experiment

In the present study, two RNN based recognizers have been used for recognizing the phonemes of Assamese language and a comparative study has been made between their performances. The comparison has been made in terms of recognition accuracy and convergence time. In both the recognizers, same set of MFCC features have been used. After identifying the phoneme boundaries, feature vector from each phoneme has been considered as a separate decision unit and they work as input to the RNN based phoneme recognizer to make a decision on the phoneme associated with that particular set of feature vector.

5.1   The All-in-One Phoneme Recognizer

In the present approach, a single RNN has been used to model 8 oral vowels and 22 consonants of Assamese language. The network consists of 48 input units, variable number of hidden units and 30 output units. The sequentially arranged input vector $\{U(1), U(2), U(3), \ldots\ldots\ldots\ldots, U(T)\}$, extracted from an utterance of a phoneme has been given as input to the speech recognizer. The 30 output units correspond to 30 phonemes of Assamese language. The decision on the number of hidden units is a crucial one since the number of hidden units has a direct effect on recognition accuracy and convergence time. With the increasing number of hidden nodes the recognition accuracy as well as convergence time increases. The system developed for the present study used 40 hidden units, which is found to be optimal in the model used for the recognition of 30 phonemes of Assamese language.

The feature vector extracted from each frame has been taken as input to the speech recognizer. The normalized feature vector having 48 elements for each frame has been taken as input. The first set of speech database has been considered for training the phoneme recognizer and the speech data from 20 common speaker in the second set has been considered for testing. Initially, the number of hidden nodes is kept at 20 and gradually it is increased to 60 in the steps of 10. The performance of the recognizer is summarized in the Table 4.

Table 4. Recognition accuracy of the recognizer (average of 300 experiments for each phoneme)

Number of Hidden Nodes →	10	20	30	40	50	60
Vowel	57.67	68.33	79.67	88.00	88.33	88.33
Consonant	55.67	66.33	77.00	82.33	82.33	82.33
Average	56.67	67.33	78.33	85.17	85.33	85.33

5.2 The Class Based Phoneme Recognizer

In class-based phoneme recognizer, the entire phoneme recognition task has been divided into two subtasks – (a) recognition of the phoneme class and (b) recognition of the phoneme within that class. All the phonemes of Assamese language have been divided into eight categories which are given in the Table 5.

Table 5. Classification of Assamese phonemes

Class	Phonemes
Vowel	[i], [e], [ɛ], [u], [ʊ], [o], [ɔ], [a]
Voiced Stops	[b], [bʰ], [d], [dʰ], [g], [gʰ]
Unvoiced Stops	[p], [pʰ], [t], [tʰ], [k], [kʰ]
Voiced Fricatives	[z]
Unvoiced Fricatives	[s], [x], [h]
Nasals	[m], [n], [ŋ]
Approximates	[w], [ɹ]
Lateral	[l]

The first unit, i.e. phoneme classifier consists of 48 input units, 8 output units and 12 hidden units, which is found to be optimal. The second part, that is the phoneme identifier, consist of 48 input units, 1~8 output units and 12 hidden units. The system is trained and tested with database used in the previous experiment. The recognizer has been trained using RTRL algorithm. The results of the experiments are listed in the Table 6.

Table 6. Recognition accuracy of the individual classes and their average (Average of 300 experiments)

Category	Sub Category	Recognition Accuracy(in %)
Vowel	-	96.67
Consonant	Nasal	87.33
	Voiced Fricative	91.33
	Unvoiced Fricative	88.67
	Voiced Stop	92.67
	Unvoiced Stop	86.67
	Approximates	93.67
	Lateral	91.00
Average Recognition Accuracy (in %)		91.00

5.3   Experiment with Speaker Variability

To study the effect of speaker variability on the phoneme recognition system, the Class Based Phoneme Recognizer has been trained with speech data from the first set of the database and tested with the speech data from 10 speakers new to the second session. The performance of the system is given below:

Table 7. Recognition accuracy of the individual classes and their average for speaker mismatch condition (Average of 300 experiments)

Category	Sub Category	Recognition Accuracy (in %)
Vowel	-	95.33
Consonant	Nasal	87.00
	Voiced Fricative	91.67
	Unvoiced Fricative	84.00
	Voiced Stop	82.67
	Unvoiced Stop	93.00
	Approximates	92.00
	Lateral	92.00
Overall Recognition Accuracy		89.71

5.4   Experiment with Channel Variability

To study the effect of channel variability, the phoneme recognizer has been trained with speech data collected by one input device and tested with speech data collected by all the devices. To study the influence of channel variability only on the phoneme recognizer, the phoneme segmenter has been trained with the speech data collected by the same device whose performance is tested. The results of the experiments have been given below:

Table 8. Recognition accuracy of the Class Based Phoneme Recognizer for device matched and mismatched conditions (Average of 300 experiments)

Training Device	Testing Device		
	Device 1	Device 2	Device 3
Device 1	88.08	77.79	75.29
Device 2	78.08	85.13	75.29
Device 3	72.96	78.00	84.38

5.5   Cepstral Mean Normalization

It has been observed that the RNN based phoneme recognizer is robust in its performance to unseen speaker. However, the experiment result shows that performance of the phoneme recognizer degrades considerably with change in training and testing device. One method to minimize the effect of these differences on recognizer performance is Cepstral Mean Normalisation (CMN). CMN involves subtracting the cepstral mean, calculated across the utterance, from each frame. In the present study, CMN has been applied to the MFCC feature vector and performance has been evaluated.

Table 9. Recognition accuracy of the Class Based Phoneme Recognizer for device matched and mismatched conditions with CMN (Average of 300 experiments)

Training Device	Testing Device		
	Device 1	Device 2	Device 3
Device 1	92.08	90.29	75.29
Device 2	88.08	90.96	87.79
Device 3	89.23	87.17	91.43

6   Conclusion

In this paper, Recurrent Neural Network has been used for recognizing the phonemes of Assamese language. Two RNN based approaches have been used for recognizing the phonemes of the Assamese language. In the first approach, all the phonemes were recognized using the same RNN based recognizer. It has been observed that when a single recurrent neural network is used for the recognition of all phonemes of Assamese language, the computational time increases and recognition accuracy decreases. One way to cope with this problem is to use a class based phoneme recognizer. The Class-Based recognizer has two layers. The first layer classifies the phonemes and automatically activates the recognizer (i.e. the second layer) which is trained for recognizing that particular class of phonemes. As a result of this two layer architecture, the total computational cost reduces by nearly 26% in terms of convergence time compared to single level recognizer. Further, it has been observed that recognition accuracy for All in One model is 85.17% (for 40 hidden nodes) whereas the recognition accuracy for Class-Based model is 91%. Thus nearly 6% improvement in terms of accuracy has also been observed in Class-Based model. The Class Based Phoneme Recognizer has been tested

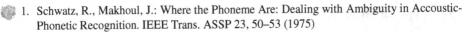

for unseen speaker and channel mismatched conditions. It has been observed that the recognizer is robust to unseen speaker but its performance degrades considerably with channel mismatched condition. To overcome this problem, Cepstral Mean Normalization has been used and a considerable improvement has been observed for the same channel as well as channel mismatched conditions.

References

1. Schwatz, R., Makhoul, J.: Where the Phoneme Are: Dealing with Ambiguity in Accoustic-Phonetic Recognition. IEEE Trans. ASSP 23, 50–53 (1975)
2. Zue, V.W.: The Use of Speech Knowledge in Automatic Speech Recognition. Proceedings of the IEEE 73, 1602–1615 (1985)
3. Weinsterin, C.J., McCandless, S.S., Mondehin, L.F., Zue, V.W.: A System for Acoustic Phonetic Analysis of Continuous Speech. IEEE Trans. ASSP 23, 54–67 (1975)
4. Suh, Y., Lee, Y.: Phoneme Segmentation of Continuous Speech using Multilayer Perceptron. In: Proc. ICSLP 1996, pp. 1297–1300 (1996)
5. Bhattacharjee, U.: Search Key Identification in a Spoken Query using Isolated Keyword Recognition. International Journal of Computer Applications 5(8), 14–21 (2010)
6. Buniet, L., Fohr, D.: Continuous Speech Segmentation with the Gamma Memory Model. In: Proc. of EUROSPEECH 1995, pp. 1685–1688 (1995)
7. Recourse Center for Indian Language Technology Solution, IIT Guwahati, http://www.iitg.ernet.in/rcilts/phaseI/asamiya.htm
8. Technology Development for Indian Language, Department of Information Technology, http://tdil.mit.gov.in
9. Box, G.E.P., Jenkins, G.M., Reinsel, G.C.: Time Series Analysis- Forecasting and Control, 3rd edn. Prentice-Hall, Englewood Cliffs (1994)
10. Sodanil, M., Nitsuwat, S., Haruechaiyasak, C.: Thai Word Recognition Using Hybrid MLP-HMM. International Journal of Computer Science and Network Security 10(3), 103–110 (2010)
11. Tuan, P.V., Kubin, T.: DTW-Based Phonetic Groups Classification using Neural Networks. In: Proc. ICASSP, pp. 401–404 (2005)
12. Gelenb, E. (ed.): Neural Network: Advances and Applications. North-Holland, New York (1991)
13. Williams, R.J., Zipser, D.: A learning algorithm for continually running fully recurrent neural networks. Neural Computation 1, 270–280 (1989)

A System for Analysis of Large Scale Speech Data for the Development of Rules of Intonation for Speech Synthesis

Asoke Kumar Datta[1] and Arup Saha[2]

[1] BOM Public Charitable Trust
3/3 Girish Ghose Street, Kolkata 700035
dattashoke@yahoo.com
[2] C-DAC, Kolkata, Salt Lake, Kolkata
arupmtech@gmail.com

Abstract. For providing naturalness in synthesized speech it is imperative to give appropriate intonation on the synthesized sentences. The problem is not with synthesis engines but with the fact that comprehensive intonation rules of natural intonation are not available for any of the major spoken language of India. The knowledge available in this area is primarily subjective with the risk of unintentional personal bias. It lacks plurality in the sense that these do not reflect the natural intonation of common people. It is imperative to derive intonation rules through analysis of large amount of sentences spoken by common people. Manual processing is time consuming and extremely cumbrous. The present paper describes briefly an automated approach for such a task. A pilot study on about 1000 complex and interrogative sentences spoken by five female and four male native speakers is presented. 93% accuracy is obtained for the desired objective.

Keywords: Concatenative speech synthesis, intonation, epoch synchronous overlap add.

1 Introduction

Intonation plays an important role in providing both intelligibility and naturalness in synthesised speech. In addition to its important function in communicating linguistic information concerning emphasis, sentence structure and discourse structure, it is also important in the transmission of paralinguistic and non-linguistic information such as speaker's intention, emotion and idiosyncrasy [1]. Since the naturalness of the synthesized speech output of a text-to-speech (TTS) system depends predominantly on its intonation, it is necessary to construct models or rules, which will relate the native intonation of output speech and the linguistic content of the text [1]. For this it is necessary to analyze a large corpus of spoken sentences. For analysis of such a large data, which includes an examination of dynamic pattern of the pitch contour extracted from spoken sentences, correlating them with the syntax, parts of speech and sometimes even emphasis, is so massive that some short of automation appears to be very

S. Ystad et al. (Eds.): CMMR/FRSM 2011, LNCS 7172, pp. 197–206, 2012.

198   A.K. Datta and A. Saha

welcome. Furthermore the pitch contour of natural speech contains small perturbation without any contribution to the perceived intonation. These need to be removed resulting in a much needed data compression.

One may note that SLP is quite different from NLP. Spoken language is a natural language quite different from the artificial textual language. Analysis in NLP is a top-down process and follows a well specified grammar. The grammar for spoken language, on the other hand, cannot be so well specified. It is so because unlike writing where one has to know the grammar beforehand, when one speaks one does not, generally, have to follow a specified grammar strictly. However it does not mean that speech does not have a grammar. It seems that the grammar of speech evolves through intercourse between the members of the dialect community. Such a natural grammar, as opposed to the artificial grammar formulated by wise men, is likely to be fuzzy in nature. In actual practice we do not have an incorrect spoken sentence. The syntax and order seem to be ill-defined because of the spontaneity of speech communication. Over and above the dimensions of acoustic phonetics (corresponding to the graphemes, the only dimension, in NLP) other dimensions like intonation (related to pitch), stress, focus (related to pitch, duration and loudness), rhythm (related primarily to time and duration) come into play. It makes formal language theoretic approach more complex as the symbols are n-tuples. To build a grammar for SLP one needs the bottom-up approach and for this analysis of large volume of free speech collected from a large number of speakers of the dialect is imperative. The need for automation comes in here.

The emphasis of the present study is not to find appropriate intonation and prosody rules for Bangla but on the development of an automatic procedure to extract relevant parameters for the purpose corresponding to appropriate linguistic segments like syllable, word, clause, phrase and sentences. However to see how the automation helps researcher to find rules some examples with Bangla read sentences is included The result of such analysis with only average pitch contour along with the correlation of syllable marking reveals existence of prosodic groups and clause /phrase segmentation with about 93% accuracy. It also reveals characteristic signatures of statements as opposed to interrogation.

The present paper describes an algorithmic approach for studying basic intonation patterns of a large number of sentences with the objective of providing a rule base for speech synthesis. The emphasis is on developing a processing scheme for quickly analyzing large audio database from spoken sentences. The analysis process includes extraction of pitch, estimation of syllabic contours using linear or non-linear estimation, automatically selected based on the nature of the data and later associating them with different linguistic elements like emphasis, prosodic groups, etc. The average pitch value of a syllable instead of the actual pitch contour is important parameter for general analysis as it has been reported that the contour patterns in syllables are not cognitively relevant in cognition of intonation [2]. This also reduces avoidable microstructure in pitch contour and consequent complexity of analysis. This pilot study uses complex affirmative sentences and interrogative sentences from the corpus of C-DAC, Kolkata [3], as these are likely to reveal most of the general trends of intonation patterns involving clauses, phrases and prosodic groups. The corpus provides the wave files tagged in terms of phonemes, syllables and words. The number of different complex sentences selected for the purpose is 46. This is read by five female and four native Bangla educated adult informants. After rejecting the misread sentences the total number of complex sentences analyzed are 447. That for interrogative sentences is 683.

2   Methodology

As early as 1980 Prof. Fujisaki proposed a model for intonation study primarily based on neuro-motor control impulses depending upon the grammatical structure of sentences [1]. The model is intended for extracting intonation rules in the context of speech synthesis and relied heavily on existing grammar of the textual language. This applies only to speech communication which is well thought beforehand and when the speaker is well conversant with the artificial textual grammar of the corresponding dialect. In the present case the intention is look for rules pertaining not to the formal speech of educated speakers but to day to day communication of common people of a particular dialect. It is already pointed out in section 1 that spoken language has its own grammar and it is not available for Indian dialects. It is therefore necessary to find intonation rules directly the spoken data base for which analysis of really large amount of data files must be handled in relation to the transcript of the speech data.

The primary processing for this purpose is done using state-phase analysis of the speech signal described in detail elsewhere [4]. The output of the state-phase analysis $p=\{p_1,p_2,\ldots, p_n)$ is actually a sequence of pitch values corresponding to individual periods in the signal where p is a function of time $p=f(t)$, and $t_i = t_{i-1}+(1/p_n)$. As the procedure uses the signal file along with the associated tag file pitch contours for each syllable are obtained at the output.

As one may like to look at the pitch contour at syllabic level and as the pitch contours are usually rough there is a need for simple representation. In the present approach regression lines for seemingly linear contours and sinusoidal curves for nonlinear contours are contemplated. Linearity was decided on the basis of R-square value of the regression line.

If a sequence is closely linear it can be represented by a equation of the type $p=mt+k$, where m can be estimated by the equation 1

$$m = \frac{N \sum_{n=1}^{N} (p_n t_n) - \sum_{n=1}^{N} p_n \sum_{n=1}^{N} t_n}{N \sum_{n=1}^{N} t_n^2 - \left(\sum_{n=1}^{N} t_n \right)^2} \qquad (1)$$

and the constant k is calculated by the equation 2

$$k = \frac{(\sum_{n=1}^{N} p_n \sum_{n=1}^{N} t_n^2) - (\sum_{n=1}^{N} t_n \sum_{n=1}^{N} p_n t_n)}{N \sum_{n=1}^{N} t_n^2 - \left(\sum_{n=1}^{N} t_n \right)^2} \qquad (2)$$

The closeness of the fit of the sequence of the line is determined by R^2

$$R^2 = \frac{(N\sum_{n=1}^{N} p_n t_n - \sum_{n=1}^{N} p_n \sum_{n=1}^{N} t_n)^2}{(N\sum_{n=1}^{N} t_n^2 - (\sum_{n=1}^{N} t_n)^2)(N\sum_{n=1}^{N} p_n^2 - (\sum_{n=1}^{N} p_n)^2)} \tag{3}$$

If R^2 value is greater than 0.2 it is taken to suggests non-linearity and it would be represented by either a hill or a valley. Let us consider the value

$$\theta = \Sigma(p_i - ((p_{max} + p_{min})/2) \tag{4}$$

If θ is positive the sequence is represented by a hill when it is negative the sequence is a valley.

Each sequence is divided into two segments by the position (time) of the extreme value. Both the hill and the valley are represented by a pair of appropriate sine and cosine curves.

The hill is estimated by the following equation:

$C_n = p_{start} + [(p_{max} - p_{start})*\sin((n/N-1)*(\pi/2))]$, for $0<n<N-1$,
$C_n = p_{start} + [(p_{max} - p_{start})*\cos((n/(E-N-1))*(\pi/2))]$, for $N-1<n<E$,

where N is the position of the extreme value and E is total number of pitch points.

The valley is estimated by the following equation:

$C_n = p_{start} - [(p_{max} - p_{start})*\sin((n/N-1)*(\pi/2))]$, for $0<n<N-1$,
$C_n = p_{start} - [(p_{max} - p_{start})*\cos((n/(E-N-1))*(\pi/2))]$, for $N-1<n<E$,

where N is the position of the extreme value and E is total number of pitch points.

3   Experimental Procedures

The digital recording of the speech signal is done at 22050/16/mono mode. The wave files of the sentences along with the text files tagged with syllable segment and phoneme markers are used for the processing. Pitch is extracted using state-phase [4] approach which includes necessary correction and smoothing procedure for each syllable. The example of the pitch contour of a complex sentence is given in Figure 1. The raw pitch contour appears to quite complex in character because of the small local perturbation caused by the non-linearity of mucosal layers over vocal cord muscles. These local small perturbations are known to be of little importance in cognition of intonation [2].

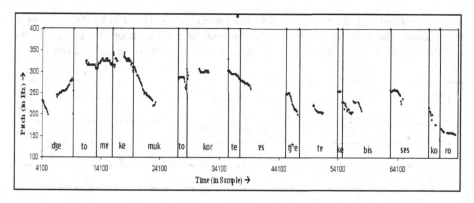

Fig. 1. Pitch contour of a sentence

The program automatically correlates the pitch contour with the syllable, phrase, and clause marker for the sentence using the tag file. The syllable contours are then examined to see whether they are reasonably linear or not. This is performed through linear regression analysis. R^2 statistics is used for the purpose. If R^2 is greater 0.2, the contour is taken to be linear. If linear estimation is not suitable the segment is estimated using a pair of sine and cosine functions.

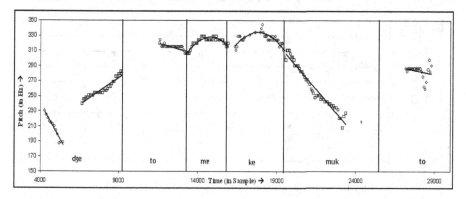

Fig. 2. Contour of the original pitch along with the estimations of a part of the sentence

Figure 2 gives an example of the estimation. In the figure the original pitch contour of the syllables are shown alternatively by open squares and circles in order to distinguish between two consecutive syllables. The fitted curves are demonstrated by solid lines. The estimation appears to quite close.

Though elaborate listening tests were not performed a number of different categories of sentences were examined by the authors themselves for the efficacy. The re-synthesized sentences both from the original pitch contour and the estimated contour were found to be cognitively inseparable.

The programme also provides average values of pitch of the syllable (figure 3-4). The figures show hills separated by valleys. Interestingly these hills when properly defined, referred to hereafter as prosodic groups, appears to have potential to be considered as new elements of SLP directly obtainable from speech data. This will be discussed in a later section. The arrow in the figure indicates minima in the contour. It is taken to indicate the end of a prosodic group if this or the preceding syllable is the end of a word.

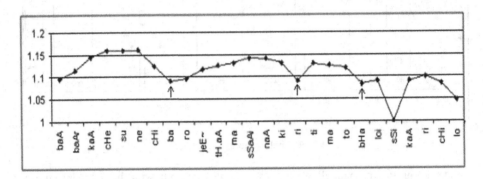

Fig. 3. Contour of average syllabic pitch of a long sentence

Figure 4 represents the prosodic groups separated by silence in a short spoken sentence. First one is a clause. The second is a single verb and the third is again a clause.

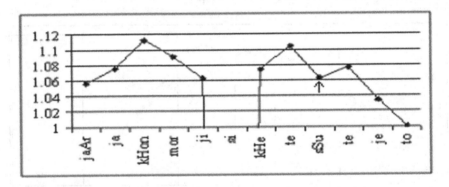

Fig. 4. Contour of average syllabic pitch of a short sentence

4   Results

As already mentioned the main program takes as input the speech signal corresponding to a sentence and the annotation file thereof. The output provides the following information for each syllable:

1. Average power,
2. Average duration,
3. Average pitch,
4. Nature of the pitch contour (whether approximately linear, hill or valley)
5. Slope of pitch contour (in case of linear ones)
6. Trend lines

Results from running the program on 447 complex sentences containing 8223 syllables and 3881 words reveal that peaks and valleys consists of respectively 11% and 19% of the total number of syllables. Of the rest 70% approximately linear syllabic contours 63% show positive slope and the rest 37% negative slope. The hills and valleys were manually checked and found to be mostly associated with some sort of focuses used by the speakers. It is possible to include in the program sub-programs to indicate the relative position of the each syllable within the word to help linguists gather overall picture from large databases automatically.

85% of the trend lines (in place of declination) for the complex sentences (figure 5) show negative slopes. The unusual 15% with positive slope can be easily segregated by the program for critical examination by the linguists. The aforesaid data is obtained in a few minutes of computation thus relieving analysts of significant labor and time for manual examination.

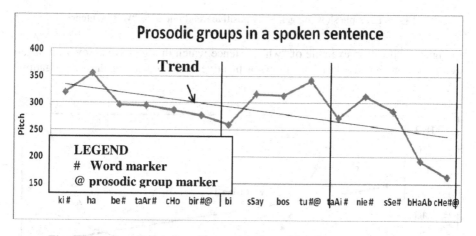

Fig. 5. Example showing prosodic groups and trend line for a Complex sentence

The same program was run on interrogative sentences of the type 'wh' (348 in number) and 'y/n' (335 in numbers). The trend lines show interesting departure from those of complex affirmative sentences. Interestingly the trend line in case of wh sentences have +slope in 67% cases. If we add to this the sentences which have +ve trend lines for the last half this increases to 85%.

Figure 6 shows an example of the general positive slope observe for "wh" sentence. The two extreme hills are prosodic group while the middle one represents the single word which is a post position. Incidentally the prosodic groups are clauses, last one being an interrogative word.

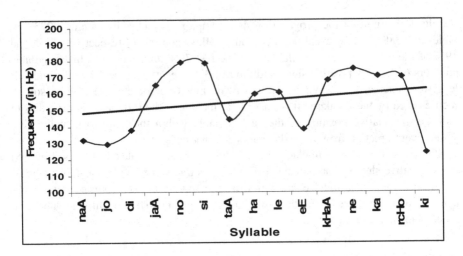

Fig. 6. Example showing generally positive trend line for a "WH" sentence

Figure 7 shows an example of "wh" sentence which though have an over all negative trend line but the last half shows a positive trend indicating the interrogation.

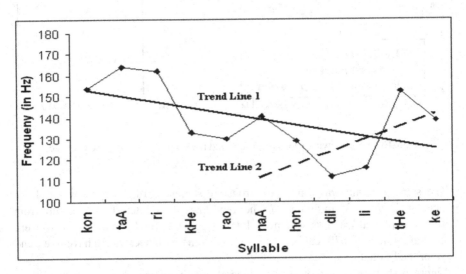

Fig. 7. Example showing a "WH" sentence having a positive trend line for the last half

In the case of 'y/n' sentences, however these figures are 46% and 61% respectively.

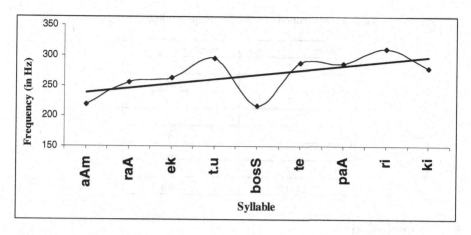

Fig. 8. Example showing generally positive trend line for a "y/n" sentence

Figure 8 shows an example of the general positive slope observe for "y/n" sentence. The two hills are prosodic groups. The prosodic group is a interrogative clauses.

Figure 9 shows an example of "y/n" sentence which though have an over all negative trend line but the last half shows a positive trend indicating the interrogation. All these parameters are obtained from the software.

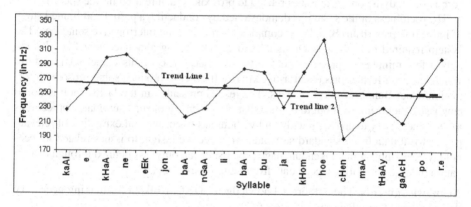

Fig. 9. Example showing a "y/n" sentence having a positive trend line for the last half

A second program uses only the average pitch value for syllables in the sentence considered in the study at present. A set of complex affirmative sentences spoken by seven female and five male speakers consists of the data base. There are 447 sentences containing 8223 syllables and 3881 words. The program finds minima in the sequence of average pitch and logically establishes a group relation with an accuracy of 93%. It breaks the sequence into groups, what will be referred to as prosodic groups (Figure 5). Altogether 1686 prosodic groups of different sizes shown in table below are found. All the groups of size more than one are found to be either a noun or a verb phrases.

Table 1. Distribution of prosodic groups for different sizes

Size	number
1	840
2	584
3	214
4	35
5	10
6	2
7	1
Total	1686

5   Conclusion

A simple data driven model to represent comprehensively the intonation patterns in speech is presented. It allows significant data reduction while re-synthesis of the speech from the compressed intonation pattern is seen to be cognitively inseparable from the original utterance. The program extracts all information seemingly necessary for the study of prosody and presents them in easily readable form. The endeavor is to develop a system for quickly and automatically extract parametric information from large speech corpus for studying prosodic issues related to prosodic structure used in free speech.

The usefulness of the system is demonstrated by conducting a partial and limited study of intonation patterns in Bangla for complex affirmative and interrogative sentences. The system required only the speech signal and corresponding annotated text files. It took only a few minutes to process about 1100 sentences. The results came out in a form which has been further processed using Microsoft excel to produce some prosodic information about Bangla within two days. The results presented in the last section is not to emphasize the result itself but to the fact that development of such automated procedures are very necessary to arrive, quickly and without hassles of manual extraction of relevant parametrical data using standard software. An objective insight to issues related to technology development in spoken language processing can only be obtained through examination of large amount of speech data from multiple speakers.

Acknowledgments. The authors acknowledge C-DAC, Kolkata for making necessary data available from their speech corpora.

References

1. Fujisaki, H.: Prosody, Models, and Spontaneous Speech. In: Sagisaka, Y., Campbell, N., Higuchi, N. (eds.) Computing Prosody, pp. 27–42. Springer, New York (1996)
2. Chowdhury, S., Datta, A.K., Chaudhuri, B.B.: Intonation Patterns for Text Reading in Standard Colloquial Bengali. Journal of the Acoustical Society of India 30, 160–163 (2002)
3. http://www.cdackolkata.in/html/txttospeeh/corpora/corpora_ma in/MainB.html
4. Chowdhury, S., Datta, A.K., Choudhury, B.B.: Pitch detection Algorithm using State Phase Analysis. J. Acous. Ind. 28, 247–250 (2000)

Adaptive and Iterative Wiener Filter
for Oriya Speech Processing Applications

Sanghamitra Mohanty[1] and Basanta Kumar Swain[2]

[1] Department of Computer Science and Application,
Utkal University, Bhubaneswar-751004, India
Sangham1@rediffmail.com
[2] Department of Computer Science and Engineering,
Government College of Engineering Kalahandi, Bhawanipatna-766001, India
technobks@yahoo.com

Abstract. This paper addresses the performance enhancement of speech processing applications like speech recognition, speaker identification and language identification in the presence of additive noise with help of proposed adaptive and iterative Wiener filter. This paper deals with the problem of single microphone, frequency domain speech enhancement in noisy environments using Wiener filter in iterative and adaptive manner based on the speech signal statistics (mean and variance). The algorithm achieves good temporal resolution while maintaining formant and harmonic trajectories. The results of implementation of such a structure will demonstrate significant improvements in Oriya isolated word recognition, Oriya continuous digit recognition, speaker identification and language identification performance under noisy conditions. The accuracy of all above applications is increased by 3% to 8% in average due to the proposed speech enhancement technique incorporation in our ongoing research works.

Keywords: Speech enhancement, Adaptive and iterative Wiener filter, Speech recognition, Speaker identification, Language identification.

1 Introduction

Speech processing is used widely in every day's applications that most people take for granted, such as network wire lines, cellular telephony, telephony system and telephone answering machines. But speech processing applications in man-machine communications start to degrade when noise gets added with original speech signal [1], [2]. Due to its popularity and increase in demand, engineers are trying various approaches for improving the process. Speech enhancement is a common approach to address the effects of degradation due to noise and channel contamination. This approach is intended to suppress unwanted signal and recover the clean speech which increases the robustness of the systems and improves quality, listening comfort and intelligibility. However, the subtraction-type algorithms have a serious draw back that the enhanced speech is accompanied by unpleasant musical noise artifact which is characterized by tones with random frequencies[3]. Apart from being extremely

S. Ystad et al. (Eds.): CMMR/FRSM 2011, LNCS 7172, pp. 207–214, 2012.

annoying to the listeners, the musical noise also hampers the performance of the speech-coding algorithms largely. In this paper, we present a novel approach, based on an adaptive and iterative Wiener filter by considering speech statistics, i.e., mean and variance. The proposed adaptive and iterative Wiener filter is used as preprocessing operation in Markov model based Oriya isolated speech recognizer, continuous Oriya digit recognition using bakis model of HMM, speaker identification using DTW for Oriya language and language identification using SVM. From this research work, we found that the adaptive and iterative Wiener filter increases the accuracy to a great extent. The accuracy rate of Markov model based isolated word speech recognizer, continuous Oriya digit recognition using Bakis Model of HMM, speaker identification using DTW and language identification using SVM are increased from 76.23% to 84.23%, 73.54 % to 77.54 %, 70 % to 80%, 78.4% to 84.6 % respectively. In the next section, we formulate adaptive and iterative Wiener filter. In the third section, we experimentally demonstrate the effectiveness of the proposed technique in the field of robust Oriya speech recognition (isolated word and continuous digit), speaker identification and language identification. Finally, we give our conclusions on the basis of our findings.

2   The Proposed Adaptive and Iterative Wiener Filter

Monaural speech x[n] corrupted by additive noise b[m] which lead to generate the noisy signal y[n] that may be modeled by the discrete-time equation as

$$y[n] = x[n] + b[m] . \tag{1}$$

The goal is to estimate x[n] from knowledge of y[n] alone. Lone approach to recovering the desired signal x[n] relies on the additivity of the power spectra, i.e.,

$$S_y(w) = S_x(w) + S_b(w) . \tag{2}$$

The Wiener filter is a popular alternative technique that has been used in many signal enhancement methods for recovering clean signal x[n] corrupted by additive noise b[m] shown in equation (1), is to find a linear filter h[n]. Under the condition that the signals x[n] and b[m] are uncorrelated and stationary, the frequency solution to this stochastic optimization problem gives the following filter transfer function [4], [5]:

$$H_s(w) = \frac{S_x(w)}{S_x(w) + S_b(w)} . \tag{3}$$

$S_x(w)$ and $S_b(w)$ are the power spectral densities of the clean and the noise signals, respectively. We can similarly express the time varying Wiener filter as

$$Hs(pL, w) = \frac{\hat{S}_x(pL,w)}{\hat{S}_x(pL,w) + \hat{S}_b(w)} . \tag{4}$$

This definition can be incorporated to the Wiener filter equation as follows

$$H_s(pL, w) = 1 + \frac{1}{SNR(pL,w) + \hat{S}_b(w)} . \tag{5}$$

An adaptive and iterative implementation of the Wiener filter derives the required benefits from the varying local statistics of the speech signal. In this approach, the estimated speech signal mean m_x and variance σ^2_x are exploited. It is assumed that additive noise b[m] is zero mean and has a white nature with variance of σ^2_b. Thus, the power spectrum $S_b(w)$ can be approximated by

$$S_b(w) = \sigma_b^2. \tag{6}$$

Suppose a signal y[n] is short-time processed at frame interval L samples and we have available an estimate of the Wiener filter on frame p-1, denoted by Ĥs $((p-1)L,w)$. We assume, as before the background b[m] is stationary and that its power spectrum, $S_b(w)$, is estimated by averaging spectra over a known background region. For a non-stationary clean signal x[n], one approach to obtain an estimate of its time-varying power spectrum on the pth frame uses the past Wiener filter Hs$((p-1)L,w)$ to enhance the current frame. This operation yields an estimated STFT on the pth frame

$$\hat{X}(pL,w) = Y(pL,w)\hat{H}_s((p-1)L,w), \tag{7}$$

which is used to update the Wiener filter:

$$H_s(pL,w) = \frac{|\hat{X}(pL,w)|^2}{|\hat{X}(pL,w)| + \hat{S}_b(w)}. \tag{8}$$

This can be also represented as

$$H_S(pL,w) = \frac{\sigma_b^2}{\sigma_x^2 + \sigma_b^2}. \tag{9}$$

The filter equation (9) can vary rapidly from frame to frame as with spectral subtraction, the result is a noise residual with fluctuating artifacts. One approach to slow down the rapid frame to frame movement of the object power spectrum smoothing on the pth frame by $\hat{S}_x(pL,w)$. Then the smooth power spectrum estimate is obtained as

$$\hat{S}_x(pL,w) = \tau \hat{S}_x((pL-1),w) + (1-\tau)\hat{S}_x(pL,w), \tag{10}$$

where τ is smoothing constant. Our goal is to make the adaptive Wiener filter more responsive to the presence of the desired signal without sacrificing the filter's capability to suppress noise. This is accomplished by using the recursive smoothing constant in equation (10). A time varying smoothing constant is selected to reflect the degree stationary of the waveform which is obtained through a spectral derivative measure. The derivative measure defined for the pth frame as

$$\Delta Y(pL) = \sqrt{\frac{1}{\pi}\int |Y(pL,w) - Y((p-1)L,w)|^2\ dw}. \tag{11}$$

It is temporally smoothed as

$$\Delta \hat{Y}(pL) = f_\Delta[p] * \Delta Y(pL), \tag{12}$$

$f_\Delta[p]$ is a non-causal linear filter. The smooth spectral derivative measure is then mapped to a time- varying smoothing constant as

$$\tau(p) = E\left[1 - 2\Delta\hat{Y}(pL) - \Delta\hat{Y}(pL) - \Delta\hat{Y}\right], \tag{13}$$

where

$$E(x) = \begin{cases} 0, & x < 0 \\ x, & 0 \le x \le 1 \\ 1, & x > 1 \end{cases}$$

Where $\Delta\hat{Y}$ is the average spectral derivative over the known background region. Subtraction of $\Delta\hat{Y}$ and multiplication by 2 in the argument of E are found empirically to normalize $\tau(p)$ to fall roughly between zero and unity. The resulting smooth clear signal spectrum is given by

$$\hat{S}_x(pL, w) = \tau(p)\hat{S}_x(((p - 1)L - 1), w) + (1 - \tau(p))\hat{S}_x(pL, w). \tag{14}$$

3   Experiment and Result

Experiment 1: Experiments have been made with speech signal corrupted by background noise, collected from more than one hundred Oriya-speakers of Orissa state in the shopping mall environment. The parameters of speech sample buried in noise are considered for testing of the algorithms were-variable time duration, PCM 16 kHz, 16 bit mono sample with background noise. Fig. 1 shows the waveform and spectrogram of noisy speech signal recorded from a female speaker. Fig. 2 shows the enhanced waveform and spectrogram of aforesaid noisy speech signal after passing through the adaptive and iterative Wiener filter with 25 ms analysis window,10 ms frame interval, and overlap-add synthesis are applied.

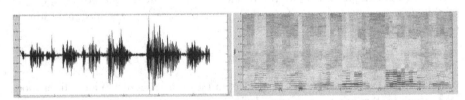

Fig. 1. The waveform and spectrogram of noisy speech signal recorded from a female speaker

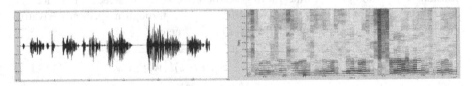

Fig. 2. Enhanced waveform and spectrogram of above said noisy speech signal after passing through the adaptive and iterative Wiener filter

The signal to noise ratio (SNR) results for different enhancement algorithms are compared and shown in Fig. 3.

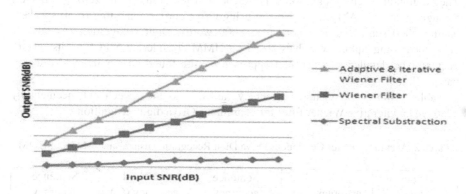

Fig. 3. SNR results for noise at -10 dB to +35 dB SNR levels

Experiment 2: Markov Model Based Oriya Isolated Speech Recognizer

The implementation of Oriya isolated recognition system is based on hidden Markov model (HMMs) [6],[7]. The training phase of the system is carried out by employing data collected from 30 speakers and another data set of 5 people is used in test model for evaluating the recognition accuracy of the system. The vocabulary of the speakers was collected in the form of isolated word of Oriya language looking into the contexts of closed ended questions types such as fill in the blanks questions, dichotomous questions, ranking scale questions, multiple questions and rating scale questions. The system recognizes spoken answers in Oriya in the context of an assessment of students based on closed ended questions task. Thirteen dimensional MFCC values are being used as features in both training as well as testing stage. The detail of experimental approach can be found in our research paper mentioned in [7].

Here, we have mentioned the accuracy rate of Markov model based Oriya isolated speech recognizer before and after implementation of adaptive and iterative Wiener filter in Table 1.

Table 1. Accuracy rate of Markov Model based Oriya isolated speech recognizer

Types of data	Word accuracy (%) before speech enhancement	Word accuracy (%) after speech enhancement by adaptive and iterative Wiener filter
Seen data	76.23	84.23
Unseen data	58.86	63.12

Experiment 3: Continuous Oriya Digit Recognition Using Bakis Model of HMM

The continuous digit recognition experiment with ten digits from "zero" ("SUNA") through "nine" ("NA") was performed using Oriya corpus consisting of 50 speakers having 2000 sentences and more than 8000 words. Digit recognition system was developed using Sphinx which is based on HMM considering MFCC as its feature vectors. The detailed experimental approach can be found on our indexed research paper [8].

Table 2 shows the changed accuracy rate due to the speech enhancement by adaptive and iterative Wiener filter for continuous Oriya digit recognition.

Table 2. Accuracy rate for Continuous Oriya Digit Recognition using Bakis Model of HMM

Types of data	Word accuracy (%) before speech enhancement	Sentence accuracy (%) before speech enhancement	Word accuracy (%) after speech enhancement by adaptive and iterative Wiener filter	Sentence accuracy (%)after speech enhancement by adaptive and iterative Wiener filter
Seen data	94.72	73.54	98.80	77.54
Unseen data	78.23	57.83	82.12	60

Experiment 4: Language Identification Using Support Vector Machine

The role of language identification is to find out the language using the transformed digitized speech of uttered sound from a speaker by the computer. Language identification solves many real life problems by allowing human computer dialogue in audio mode. As speech is the more natural and easy mode of communication among the human being, it is essential that computer should well interpret the language used by the all the human beings in order to respond to the users. Language identification is carried out using Support Vector Machine with radial basis function (RBF) kernel as a pattern recognition classifier. The corpus used in this research work is gathered from 35 speakers for five language category such as *Oriya, Hindi, Indian English, Sanskrit and Nepali*. Jitter and shimmer are used as acoustic feature parameters during training and testing stage. The detailed of the experimental approach can be found from our research paper [9].

Table 3 shows the accuracy rate before and after implementation of adaptive and iterative Wiener filter in vowel domain, syllable domain and word domain.

Table 3. Accuracy rate for Language Identification using Support Vector Machine

Domain Feature	Vowel (%) before speech enhancement	Syllable (%) before speech enhancement	Word (%) before speech enhancement	Vowel (%) after speech enhancement by adaptive and iterative Wiener filter	Syllable (%) after speech enhancement by adaptive and iterative Wiener filter	Word (%) after speech enhancement by adaptive and iterative Wiener filter
Jitter	78.4	73.3	76.6	84.6	77.3	81.72
Shimmer	79.1	73.8	76.9	85.7	77.6	82.15

Experiment 5: Speaker Identification Using DTW for Oriya Language

Dynamic time-warping is one of the prominent techniques to accomplish the speaker identification task. DTW is a cost minimization matching technique, in which a test signal is stretched or compressed according to a reference template. Dynamic time warping (DTW) is used to calculate the distance between the feature matrix of the input signal and the reference patterns. The pattern corresponding to the minimum distance is treated as the identified speaker. We have used fundamental frequency and first four formants as feature vectors in speaker identification task. The fully experimental details can be found in our research paper [10]. Table 4 shows the accuracy rate due to the incorporation of adaptive and iterative Wiener filter as preprocessing block in speaker identification task.

Table 4. Accuracy rate for Speaker Identification using DTW for Oriya Language

USER DECISION	Genuine user before speech enhancement (%)	Imposter before speech enhancement (%)	Genuine user after speech enhancement by adaptive and iterative Wiener filter (%)	Imposter after speech enhancement by adaptive and iterative Wiener filter (%)
Accept	70	40	80	33
Reject	30	60	20	67

4   Conclusions

In this paper, we have used additive and iterative Wiener filter as preprocessing operation in our ongoing Oriya speech processing research works such as Markov Model Based Oriya Isolated Speech Recognizer, Continuous Oriya Digit Recognition using Bakis Model of HMM, Language Identification using Support Vector Machine and Speaker Identification using DTW for Oriya language. By applying all these applications we found that the additive and iterative Wiener filter plays an important role in increasing the accuracy rate which is necessary for implementation of speech processing applications in day to day activities. As a result of which the accuracy rate of Oriya speech processing applications are increased from 3 % to 8% due to the incorporation of additive and iterative Wiener filter. It is also found that the additive and iterative Wiener filter performs better as compared to Spectral subtraction and Wiener filter.

References

1. Vaseghi, S.V.: Advanced Digital Signal Processing and Noise Reduction, 3rd edn. Wiley and Sons
2. Berouti, M., Schwartz, R., Makhoul, J.: Enhancement of speech corrupted by acoustic noise. In: Proc. IEEE Int. Conf. Acoust., Speech Signal Processing, pp. 208–211 (1979)
3. Boll, S.F.: Suppression of acoustic noise in speech using spectral subtraction. IEEE Trans. Acoust., Speech, Signal Processing ASSP 27, 113–120 (1979)
4. Ifeachor, E.C.: Digital Signal Processing A Practical Approach, 2nd edn. Pearson Education
5. Quatieri, T.F.: Discrete-Time Speech Signal Processing Principles and Practice, Third Impression. Pearson Education (2007)
6. Rabiner, L.R., Schafer, R.W.: Digital Processing of Speech Signals, 1st edn. Pearson Education (2004)
7. Mohanty, S., Swain, B.K.: Markov Model Based Oriya Isolated Speech Recognizer-An Emerging Solution for Visually Impaired Students in School and Public Examination. Special Issue of IJCCT 2(2,3,4) (2010)
8. Mohanty, S., Swain, B.K.: Continuous Oriya Digit Recognition using Bakis Model of HMM. International Journal of Computer Information Systems 2(1) (2011)
9. Mohanty, S., Swain, B.K.: Language Identification using Support Vector Machine, http://desceco.org/O-COCOSDA2010/proceedings/paper_43.pdf
10. Mohanty, S., Swain, B.K.: Speaker Identification using DTW for Oriya Language. In: International Symposium on Frontier of Research of Speech and Music (FRSM 2009), December 15-16 (2009)

On the Role of Formants in Cognition of Vowels and Place of Articulation of Plosives

Asoke Kumar Datta[1] and Bhaswati Mukherjee[2]

[1] BOM Public Charitable Trust, 3;3 Girish Ghose Street, Kolkata 700035, India
dattashoke@yahoo.com
[2] Department of Applied Psychology, Calcutta University
bhaswati.mukherjee@live.in

Abstract. The paper examines the general notion that place of articulation of vowels and plosives are primarily cognized by the formant frequencies and the transitions thereof respectively. A brief status report on the objective classification of vowels based on formant frequencies is presented including an experimental study of relevant parameters of formant frequencies for machine classification of plosives from correctly spoken VCV syllables by native speakers. The paper contains details of the test for cognitive assessment of the aforesaid general notion. For this normal speech signals are altered using digital tools. The test bed is Bangla isolated vowels and plosives in nonsense VCV syllables. 30 native educated listeners are used. The result of the listening test is reported which shows that, in general, neither the frequencies (for vowel cognition) nor the transitions of the first two formants (for plosives) are necessary or sufficient for the cognition of the places of articulation.

Keywords: Vowels, plosives, formants, formant transitions, machine recognition, human cognition.

1 Introduction

The places of articulation of vowels, plosives are generally believed to be perceived on the basis of the formant frequencies, particularly of the first two formants [1-3]. This belief has gained ground because of our proneness to analyze and characterize sound in terms of the properties of the sinusoidal components. The elegant and formal mathematical tool of Fourier Transforms provided a very convenient and robust way for analysis. The spectrograms of speech revealed distinctive formant structures for voiced region. Automatic speech recognition studies mostly used these spectral features with useful results. Elegant theories of speech production using models of each physiological organ produced spectacular results [4]. At the physiological and neural end of speech cognition large array of resonators (approximately 30,000 fibers) in cochlea were found [5-10]. There have been experiments to show that firings from the associated nerve fibers can give a conforming description of the formant structure of the input sound. Also the firing appears to phase lock to formant frequencies over a large range of sound intensities and harmonics not near the formants are suppressed.

S. Ystad et al. (Eds.): CMMR/FRSM 2011, LNCS 7172, pp. 215–234, 2012.
© Springer-Verlag Berlin Heidelberg 2012

The net result is enhancement of formants so that very close formants could also be resolved [6]. It is reported that the excitation pattern of the auditory nerves over the cochlea produces some patterns which may be called auditory spectra of the signal [7]. All these led to the present belief that the perception processes are based primarily on the formant structure of the signal. Contradictory evidence to this omnipotence of formants in cognition of place of articulation of some phonemes began appearing in early 90's [11], wherein it is claimed with specially synthesized signals formants are neither necessary nor sufficient for cognition of vowels and unvoiced unaspirated plosives. Bangla, like most of the major Indian languages, have a large number plosive/stop sounds, around 20 in number. These are organized into four groups based on place of articulation, generally named as velar, alveolar (retroflexed in most language), dental and labial. Each group again has five different manners of production namely unaspirated-unvoiced, aspirated-unvoiced, unaspirated-voiced, aspirated-voiced- and nasal (Table 1).

Table 1. Manner and place of articulation of Bangla Plosives

	Unaspirated unvoiced	Aspirated unvoiced	Unaspirated voiced	Aspirated voiced	Nasal murmur
velar	/k/	/kʰ/	/g/	/gʰ/	/ŋ/
palatal	/t/	/tʰ/	/d/	/dʰ/	/n/
alveolar	/t/	/tʰ/	/d/	/dʰ/	/n/
labial	/p/	/pʰ/	/b/	/bʰ/	/m/

There has been a considerable interest in the recognition of place of articulation since early fifties for both human cognition and ASR [12-16]. It is now generally agreed that transition of the adjoining vowel formants cause by the co-articulatory influence of the plosives are the most important cues for cognition of the place of articulation of the plosives/stops. The unvoiced-unaspirated manner is used for the present study.

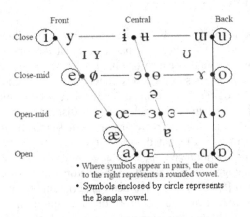

Fig. 1. Bangla Vowels in IPA Chart [19]

There are seven major vowels in Bangla, namely /u/, /o/, /ɒ/, /ɛ/, /æ/, /e/, /a/ and /i/. The formant structure, particularly the first two formants are well studied and reported [17]. Figure 1 presents Bangla vowels and their corresponding positions in the vowel diagram of IPA symbol chart. Figure 2 presents the distribution of Bangla vowels in the F1 – F2 plane. A total of 400 segments of each of the most frequently used words Bangla embedded in a neutral carrier sentence spoken by 4 male and 4 female native informants was taken for this study. The ellipses represent broadly the areas of [13, 14, 16].

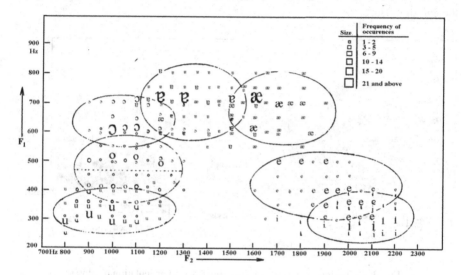

Fig. 2. Bangla Vowels in F1-F2 Plane for data pooled for both sexes

This paper presents a new study of various parameters associated with the dynamic behavior of the formants in objectively discriminating different categories of plosives. Finally this paper also presents a detailed cognitive study to test whether the aforesaid formant related parameters generally used for machine recognition is cognitively relevant. For this purpose the hypothesis that the first two formants are necessary and sufficient for human cognition of a) the place of articulation of plosives are determined by the transition of the first two formants and b) the place of articulation of vowels are determined by the steady state values of the first two formants is tested. Specially prepared signals from actual speech sounds are used for the purpose. The technique of preparation is described in detail. Listening tests are conducted with 30 native listeners.

2   Machine Identification of Place of Articulation of Plosives

Figure 3 shows the definition of the different basic parameters examined for their roles in objective categorization of place of articulation of selected plosives. It may be noted that though the VC and CV transitions are parts of the vowel these parts have separate identities both on the physical and cognitive domain and therefore need to be separated in the present context. The other parts in the above figure are the plosive itself which constitutes of occlusion and the burst. It is generally observed that the steady states of vowels in syllables are not so steady after all. In the present case, therefore, the terminations of the steady states are defined as the time where the transition ends for the first two formants. Such transitory phenomena are associated with a corresponding fade in or fade out of the amplitude of the signal. Whenever amplitude transition extends beyond formant transition the end of this transition is taken as the terminal point, the beginning and the end of closure.

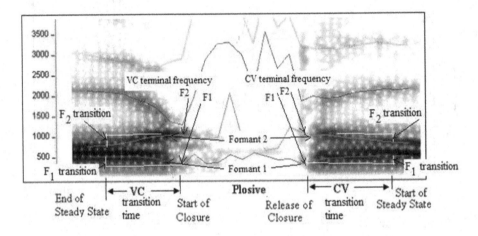

Fig. 3. Definition of segments in transition during articulation of plosive

While ASR studies in this area often use data from sense words used in continuous speech these are not always correctly pronounced. In the present study nonsense words of the form /cvcvcvcv/ are used and accuracy of pronunciation is assured through a listening test by experts.

The effectiveness of the cues is investigated separately for each vowel as well when the data for all vowels are pooled together. This is likely to reveal if the vowels have significant co-articulatory influence on the place of articulation or the structure of the oral cavity at the time of release or closure. To examine these as well as their relative merits for categorization of the places of articulation of plosives in the context of adjoining vowels VCV syllables has been used. For this purpose in the following parameters are selected:

1) Values of F1 and F2 at the time of closure (referred to as terminal frequency)
2) Values of F1 and F2 at the time of release (referred to as terminal frequency)
3) Values of transition of F1 and F2 due to closure
4) Values of transition of F1 and F2 due to release
5) Times of CV and VC transition.

2.1   Experimental Procedure

Utterances of altogether 15 native speakers of Bangla of both sexes in the form /cvcvcvcv/ where vowels 'v' span over /o,u,ɔ,ɐ,æ,e,i/ and consonants 'c' span over /k, ʈ,t,p/ were recorded with a Shure dynamic microphone in a quiet laboratory room. Only those were used for the study which were judged correct by three experts. Altogether 28 utterances were recorded for each informant. As the first syllable in Bangla is usually stressed, the first CV is neglected and the other three VCV segments are separated from each utterance (figure 4).

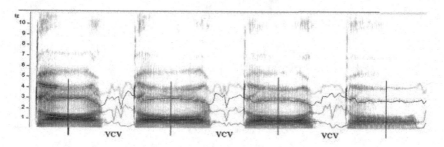

Fig. 4. Segmentation of /ʈɔʈɔʈɔʈɔ/ into separate vcv syllables

Figure 4 presents the spectrographic representations of the utterance /ʈɔʈɔʈɔʈɔ/ and corresponding segmentation into VCV segments for parameter extraction. The definitions of different transitional parameters are illustrated in the figure. The parameter values are manually obtained using the software 'Wavesurfer'.

2.2   Results

It seems pertinent to present the distribution of different parameters separately for all the vowels before we embark upon the ANOVA tests (Figure 5a and 7b) shows the mean values and the range (mean ± s.d.) of the parameters to have feel of the distribution of the different parameters used. It may be noted that transition time as defined is the same for both the formants.

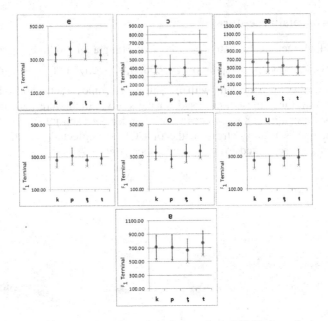

Fig. 5a. The range of VC terminal frequencies of F1 for four plosives

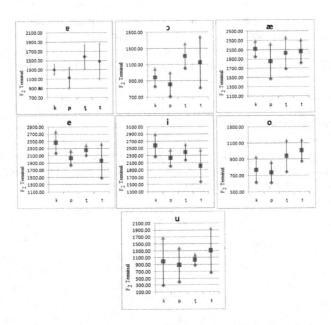

Fig. 5b. The range of VC terminal frequencies of F1 for four plosives

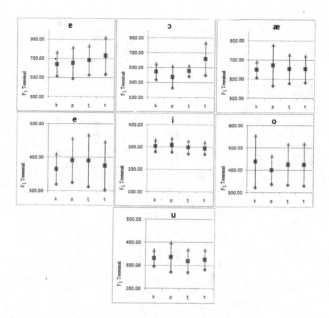

Fig. 6a. The range of VC terminal frequencies of F1 for four plosives

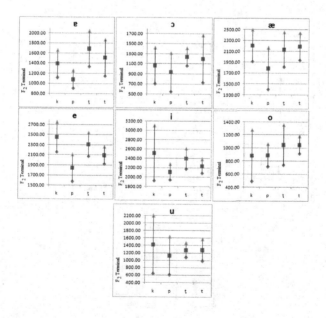

Fig. 6b. The range of CV terminal frequencies of F2 for four plosives

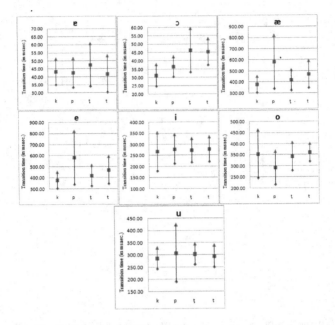

Fig. 7a. The range of VC transition times for four plosives

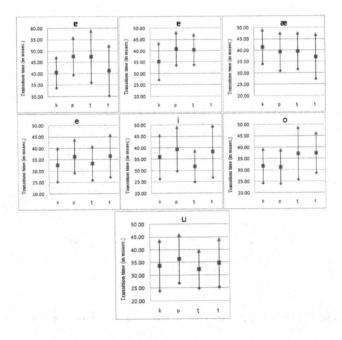

Fig. 7b. The range of CV transition times for four plosives

A visual examination of the means and standard deviations reveal that while some parameters for some vowels show differentiability other seem to be highly mixed up. To have a more comprehensive objective evaluation one-way ANOVA tests are performed and the results are tabulated in tables 2 – 9. The four plosives k, ʈ, t, and p constitutes the four classes. The hypothesis taken is that the values of the parameters for different classes come from the same population. The acceptance of the hypothesis (indicated by 'A' in the decision column) means that the parameter cannot differentiate between the classes with the degree of confidence with which the F-test is performed. Rejection indicated by 'R' means that the parameter can distinguish at least two classes. The degree of confidence with which the present tests are performed is at 0.05 level.

It may be seen from table 2 that of the 8 frequency related parameters 5 shows differentiability in the context of vowel 'ɐ', particularly all the parameters related to formant 2 exhibits this character.

Table 2. Results of F-test when data for vowel ɐ

Vowel	Parameter	Degrees of freedom		F-stat	F-critical	Decision
		between group	within group			
	VCterminal F1	3	76	1.1529	2.725	A
	VCtrans F1	3	76	3.0745	2.725	R
	VCterminal F2	3	76	1.1405	2.725	A
	VCtrans F2	3	76	1.4344	2.725	A
	CVterminal F1	3	76	11.367	2.725	R
ɐ	CV trans F1	3	76	8.1460	2.725	R
	CVterminal F2	3	76	15.286	2.725	R
	CV trans F2	3	76	6.6086	2.725	R
	VCtrans_time	3	76	1.0821	2.725	A
	CV_trans_time	3	74	3.0334	2.728	R

Table 3. Below reveals that of the 8 formant related parameters 6 reveals differentiability for vowel 'ɔ'

Vowel	Parameter	Degrees of freedom		F-stat	F-critical	Decision
		between group	within group			
ɔ	VC terminal F1	3	107	2.1943	2.696	A
	VC trans F1	3	107	47.791	2.696	R
	VC terminal F2	3	107	22.914	2.696	R
	VC trans F2	3	107	14.076	2.696	R
	CV terminal F1	3	107	3.5924	2.696	R
	CV trans F1	3	107	1.7116	2.696	A
	CV terminal F2	3	107	13.307	2.696	R
	CV trans F2	3	107	15.067	2.696	R
	VC_trans_time	3	107	7.8390	2.696	R
	CV_trans_time	3	107	1.8639	2.696	A

Table 4. Results of F-test when data for vowel æ

Vowel	Parameter	Degrees of freedom		F-stat	F-critical	Decision
		between group	within group			
æ	VC terminal F1	3	110	0.3935	2.696	A
	VC trans F1	3	110	0.6515	2.696	A
	VC terminal F2	3	110	1.8381	2.696	A
	VC trans F2	3	110	9.2015	2.696	R
	CV terminal F1	3	110	3.3988	2.696	R
	CV trans F1	3	110	1.1505	2.696	A
	CV terminal F2	3	110	1.2081	2.696	A
	CV trans F2	3	110	1.5867	2.696	A
	VC_trans_time	3	110	0.7364	2.696	A
	CV_trans_time	3	110	1.3647	2.696	A

For 'æ' however, of the 8 formant related parameters only 2 show any differentiability (table 4). In the context of vowel 'e' again, 5 out of 8 formants related parameters show differentiability (table 5).

Table 5. Results of F-test when data for vowel **e**

Vowel	Parameter	Degrees of freedom		F-stat	F-critical	Decision
		between group	within group			
	VC terminal F1	3	98	0.8960	2.697	A
	VC trans F1	3	98	0.2807	2.697	A
	VC terminal F2	3	98	8.8266	2.697	R
	VC trans F2	3	98	16.403	2.697	R
	CV terminal F1	3	98	5.3334	2.697	R
e	CV trans F1	3	98	0.3447	2.697	A
	CV terminal F2	3	98	5.1201	2.697	R
	CV trans F2	3	98	7.5367	2.697	R
	VC_trans_time	3	98	0.5566	2.697	A
	CV_trans_time	3	98	0.2468	2.697	A

Table 6. Results of F-test when data for vowel **i**

Vowel	Parameter	Degrees of freedom		F-stat	F-critical	Decision
		between group	within group			
	VC terminal F1	3	98	0.4281	2.697	A
	VC trans F1	3	98	1.9452	2.697	A
	VC terminal F2	3	98	2.3977	2.697	A
	VC trans F2	3	98	1.9114	2.697	A
	CV terminal F1	3	98	0.7930	2.697	A
i	CV trans F1	3	98	1.3911	2.697	A
	CV terminal F2	3	98	0.2359	2.697	A
	CV trans F2	3	98	0.6202	2.697	A
	VC_trans_time	3	98	0.7733	2.697	A
	CV_trans_time	3	98	0.6317	2.697	A

Interestingly table 6 revels that none of the parameters show differentiability for any the parameters tested for the vowel 'e'.

Table 7. Results of F-test when data for vowel **o**

| Vowel | Parameter | Degrres of freedom | | F-stat | F-critical | Decision |
		between group	within group			
	VCterminal F1	3	105	0.6596	2.696	A
	VC trans F1	3	105	58.523	2.696	R
	VCterminal F2	3	105	19.911	2.696	R
	VC trans F2	3	105	4.3334	2.696	R
	CVterminal F1	3	105	0.7599	2.696	A
o	CV trans F1	3	105	78.194	2.696	R
	CVterminal F2	3	105	5.4302	2.696	R
	CV trans F2	3	105	5.4588	2.696	R
	VC_trans_time	3	105	6.6176	2.696	R
	CV_trans_time	3	105	2.4234	2.696	A

Table 8. Results of F-test when data for vowel 'u'

| Vowel | Parameter | Degrres of freedom | | F-stat | F-critical | Decision |
		between group	within group			
	VCterminal F1	3	106	3.2057	2.696	R
	VC trans F1	3	106	1.8752	2.696	A
	VCterminal F2	3	106	7.4848	2.696	R
	VC trans F2	3	76	3.1451	3.117	R
	CVterminal F1	3	106	1.4689	2.696	A
u	CV trans F1	2	76	0.3300	3.117	A
	CVterminal F2	3	106	3.1182	2.696	R
	CV trans F2	2	76	7.1325	3.117	R
	VC_trans_time	3	106	2.7999	2.696	R
	CV_trans_time	3	106	2.9151	2.696	R

While for vowel 'o' 6 out of 8 (table 7) formant related parameters show differentiability, it is 5 out of 8 for the vowel 'u' (table 8). It is interesting to note that when data for all vowels are pooled together the ANOVA tests reveal differentiability of the parameters tested with almost the same percentage (nearly 70%) as when the data are taken separately for different vowels (table 9). This is different from the general notion obtained from automatic speech recognition [18] (ASR) studies. Of course here the data consists of tested well- pronounced ones whereas in case of ASR studies they are usually taken from normal conversational speech. The other notable feature is that except for vowel 'u' terminal frequency of formant 1 does not show differentiability between classes.

Table 9. Results of F-test when data for all vowels are pooled together

Vowel		Degrres of freedom		F-stat	F- critical	Decision
		between group	within group			
	VCterminal F1	3	729	0.4523	2.696	A
	VC trans F1	3	729	7.8952	2.696	R
	CVterminal F1	3	729	1.4448	2.696	A
	CV trans F1	3	699	2.5579	2.696	A
	VCterminal F2	3	729	2.5667	2.696	A
Pooled	VC trans F2	3	702	12.924	2.696	R
	CVterminal F2	3	729	4.8346	2.696	R
	CV trans F2	3	698	7.5056	2.696	R
	VCtrans_time	3	729	5.2267	2.696	R
	CVtrans_time	3	725	3.1829	2.696	R

3   Cognitive Study

The speech signals are understood to be produced by the repeated resonating of the pharyngeal cavities by a train of acoustic impulses coming from trachea. It is well known in the physics of sound that each of impulsive resonances must have their own fundamental frequency depending on the structure of the resonator like, for example the sound of a plucked string instrument. However, strangely in contrast, in the physics of speech the fundamental frequency refers to the repetition rate of the incoming trains of impulses coming from the glottis. Incidentally the Fourier transform reveals the spectral structure commensurate with this fundamental frequency and not the fundamental frequency dictated by the physics of a resonating system activated by an impulse. Again the second pulse interrupts before the resonance due to the first pulse die out. It is therefore bound to produce some sort of discontinuity at the point of interruption. However the inertia of the resonating system smoothes out the discontinuity to a large extent. Furthermore the phonemes are categorized primarily on the basis of the configuration of the pharyngeal cavity at the time of articulation. But even for normal voice more than 50% of a period the bronchial tubes remain acoustically connected with the pharynx. This will influence the spectral signature of the pharyngeal cavity to a large extent. This raises some doubt about the robustness of spectral structure normally so much theoreticall y highlighted. As reported in the introduction doubts about necessity and sufficiency of formants in cognition began appearing in early 90s [11]. This section is devoted to the testing of this traditional notion.

3.1   Manipulation of the Signals

The aforesaid facts together with the report that the perception of phonetic quality depends only on a small segment (about 1.5 msec) of the pitch-period measured from the epochs is used for preparing the test signals[20, 21]. It is shown therein that if any portion, equal to a period, from the steady portion of a vowel utterance is selected and repeated the original vowel will be heard irrespective of the position of the selection. However if smaller window (of less than 2 msec.) is taken then the phonetic quality of the original vowel, of course with a higher pitch, will be heard only when the beginning of the window is approximately aligned with the epoch of the period. This implies that the phonetic quality of the vowel resides within a small time from the epoch. Figure 4 indicates how an epoch is determined.

Figure 8 and 9 illustrate the first step in the process of preparing the test signals for vowel cognition. The first two periods represent one perceptual-pitch-period each from the vowels /ɔ/ and /e/. Each period has a length of approximately 8 msec. A is a window of length approximately 2 msec. the beginning of which is aligned with the epoch position so that the end coincides with a zero crossing. B is another window of approximately 6 msec such that the beginning is aligned the zero crossing of samedirection approximately after 2 msec from the epoch of the second signal. These signals are copied and then pasted one after the other to create a new period. Usually this will generate a signal, which has almost the quality of the first signal and approximately the spectral structure of the second signal. Patient retrial is necessary to obtain a satisfactory result. Finally the digital filters are used to fine-tune the spectral structure. The frequency components above the second resonance (formant) are removed.

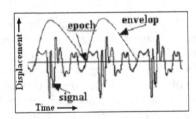

Fig. 8. Determination of the epoch

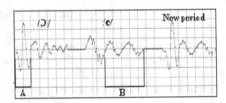

Fig. 9. Preparation of Test signals for vowels

For articulation of plosives the oral cavity is blocked by the tongue making firm contact with the upper palate thus making a compete closure of the air path causing air pressure in the back chamber to increase. This process divides the oral cavity into two separate chambers of sizes different for different place of articulation. During the period of occlusion the point of contact may or may not slide. The place of articulation is the place where the tongue sharply releases the closure causing a burst. As the frequency of formants depends on the shape and size of the two cavities the formant frequencies at the time of release is strongly correlated with the place of articulation. From the release to the attaining of the articulatory configuration for the following vowel the dynamics of the tongue movement is mapped on to the transition of formants. A similar phenomenon happens in the reverse order for the VC transition. As there is a possibility of adjustment of the tongue position during the period of occlusion the terminal positions of the formant frequencies in VC transition may not accurately reflect the articulatory configuration at the time of release. It may be noted that as the first formant is related to the height of the tongue and as the tongue is always at the highest point at the time of release the transition of first formant may not be strongly related to the place of articulation. The transitions of the formants depend much on the adjoining vowels. For example if the vowel is front and high, /i/, the dental plosives is not likely to show large transition of the second formant. Similar is the case of /k/ with vowel /u/.

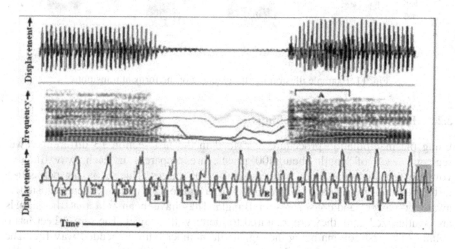

Fig. 10. Illustration of signal preparation with VCV utterance / ɐʈɐ /

Figure 10 illustrates the method of straightening the transitions of formants, which is said to be the primary cognitive cue of the place of articulation of a plosive. The upper two sections in the figure are the waveform and the 3-D spectrogram with formant display of a /vcv/ utterance. This was drawn using Wave Surfer.

The portion marked A in the middle section represents the CV transition. The lowermost section in the figure is the expanded picture of the waveform corresponding to the part 'A'. For each of the perceptual-pitch-periods about 2 msec is taken to be significant for the cognitive categorization of the plosive. The rest marked as B in the figure carries the information of spectral transition. The shaded portion of the last waveform is taken to be perceptually neutral and is most significant for spectral estimation leading to formant extraction. In the present altering of the signal all B's are carefully replaced by the shaded portion. All the while necessary amplitude adjustments are done. Finally FFT filter is used for fine-tuning. Finally the occlusion period and the burst are de-amplified to the value of zero. All these are done using Cool-Edit Pro. Figure 11 shows the effect of manipulation. One can see that the all transitions are significantly straightened.

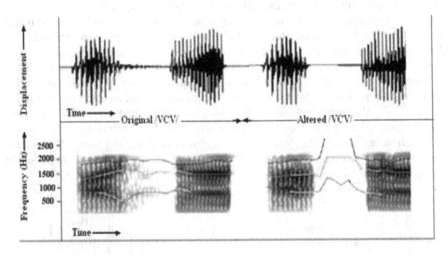

Fig. 11. Example illustrating straightening of the formant transitions

3.2   Preparation of the Listening Set

Using the manipulation procedure described in the last section 13 different vowel segments each of length about 400 msecs. are prepared. In each .wav file one vowel is repeated five times with a gap of 500 msecs. This set is for perception test related to vowels and is presented to a set of 30 native educated listeners aware of vowels and consonants in Bangla. They have been told that the signals are synthesized and they are required to identify the vowel. The score sheet has 6 columns the first column being the signal file number with embedded wav file. The next five columns were for ticking the choice amongst five vowels namely, /u/, /a/, /ae/, /e/ and /o/. The two extremevowels are omitted as the corresponding altered signals could not be prepared.

Further 22 VCV utterances are used to prepare 22 separate altered sound files. Those VCV are chosen which normally reveal large transitions. As stated earlier the altering consisted of flattening the formant transitions as well as normalization of the occlusion period and removal of the burst as indicated in the last section. As before each .wav file contains five repetitions of the /vcv/ utterances with a gap of 500 msecs. The same set of native listeners as in the case of vowels was used.

4   Results and Discussions

Table 10 presents the results of the vowel listening test along with the measured formants of the signals used for listening tests. The listening scores are given in ratios. As there are five categories expected ratio for random choice is 0.2. The scores, which are greater than or equal to 0.6, are shown in bold figures. Files having a star against the serial are the altered ones. Columns 7 and 8 gives the measured formants. Column 9 gives the phoneme as dictated by the latest data on extensive study on acoustic phonetics of Bangla [19] (table 11). Weighted Euclidean distance was used to determine the category of the vowel.

Table 10. Results of vowel listening test

File No	Listening score					Measured Formants		Vowel dictated by	
	/ɔ/	/a/	/ae/	/e/	/o/	F1	F2	Measured Formants	Listening tests
1	**0.67**	0.33				656	1116	/ɔ/	/ɔ/
2*	0.17	**0.83**				656	1116	/ɔ/	/a/
3	0.33		0.17		0.5	624	906	/ɔ/	/ɔ/,/o/
4*	0.5		0.17		0.33	656	906	/ɔ/	/ɔ/,/o/
5*				**1.0**		602	2326	/æ/	/e/
6*	0.17		0.17	**0.67**		602	2326	/æ/	/e/
7*	0.17		**0.6**		0.23	430	2325	/e/	/ae/
8	0.33			**0.67**		430	2325	/e/	/e/
9*				0.28	**0.72**	430	2497	/e/	/o/
10*	0.17	0.17	**0.67**			775	2239	/æ/	/æ/
11		0.17	**0.67**	0.17		775	2325	/æ/	/æ/
12	0.17			**0.6**	0.23	327	1938	/e/	/e/
13*			0.2	0.2	**0.6**	327	1938	/e/	/o/

The values in the said table represent the proportion/frequency. For testing its statistical significance we have used non-parametric test like Chi-Square test table 13). The results of the chi-square test show the obtained values are significant at 99% level of confidence.

There are few important points to note from the table. One is that even from almost the same values for formant 1 and 2 two separate vowels are distinctly perceived (files 1/2, 7/8/9 and 12/13). The other point is that the signals with F2 as high 2000 and n2500 KHz were perceived as /o/ (signals 9 and 13). All the altered signals are perceived different from the category dictated by the formant frequencies. Table 12 presents the results of listening test for cognition of place of articulation of there are four categories in plosive listening test, a random proportional score of 0.25 is expected in each category if auditory perception cues are not present in the signal. In the table when a proportional score of more than 0.5 is observed in only one category the score is presented in bold letters. Out of 22 audio files noticeable preference (score ≥ 0.5) are observed in 17 cases. Of these 14 cases audio files show reasonably good categorization with proportional score of more than 0.67. The file six shows listeners are equally divided between two adjoining categories. For consonants also the Chi-square was done (table 13). The results of the chi-square test show the obtained values are significant at 99% level of confidence. The results of cognition tests for vowels and plosives clearly show that even without the cues of formant transition human beings can effectively identify place of articulation for vowels and plosives in Bangla.

Table 11. Mean and Standard deviation of Bangla vowels [9]

Bangla Vowels		Female		Male		Total	
		F1	F2	F1	F2	F1	F2
/u/	Average	349.8	1033.7	325.5	1035.7	338.6	1034.6
	SD	51.5	169.7	44.2	154.6	49.8	162.8
/o/	Average	473.8	1058.6	378.2	1015.8	426.8	1037.5
	SD	85.5	175.8	48.8	178.3	84.7	335.8
/ɔ/	Average	692.4	1122.4	543.7	1020	633.6	1081.9
	SD	124.4	174.6	113.9	153.6	140.6	173.9
/a/	Average	907.2	1508.7	866	1530.6	886.7	1519.6
	SD	125.7	195.8	289.4	329.5	223.7	270.9
/æ/	Average	862.5	2108.3	591.8	1846.2	742.9	1992.5
	SD	91.4	188	97.7	176.9	164.2	224.6
/e/	Average	452.9	2423.4	383.3	1978.6	412.3	2163.8
	SD	82.1	190.8	52.6	144.7	74.8	274.7
/i/	Average	331.2	2583	309.4	2131.9	319.9	2349.2
	SD	53.2	216.3	38.4	146	47.3	290.5

Table 12. Results of listening test for cognition of place of articulation of plosives

Signal	Velar	Palatal	Dental	Labial
File 1	/ɐgu/ (0)	/ɐdu/	/ɐdu/	/ɐbu/ (0)
File 2	/ɐgu/	/ɐdu/	/ɐdu/ (0.6)	/ɐbu/ (0)
File 3	/ɐkɐ/(0.1	/ɐţɐ/	/ɐtɐ/	/ɐpɐ/ (0)
File 4	/ɐkɐ/(0)	/ɐţɐ/	/ɐtɐ/	/ɐpɐ/ (0)
File 5	/ɐkɐ/ (0)	/ɐţɐ/	/ɐtɐ/ (0)	/ɐpɐ/
File 6	/ɐkɐ/	/ɐţɐ/ (0.5)	/ɐtɐ/ (0)	/ɐpɐ/ (0)
File 7	/ɐku/ (0)	/ɐţu/ (1.0)	/ɐtu/ (0)	/ɐpu/ (0)
File 8	/ɐku/	/ɐţu/	/ɐtu/ (0.5)	/ɐpu/ (0)
File 9	/ikɐ/	/iţɐ/ (0)	/itɐ/ (0.33)	/ipɐ/(0)
File 10	/ikɐ/	/iţɐ/ (0)	/itɐ/(0)	/ipɐ/
File 11	/ike/	/iţɐ/ (0.17)	/ite/ (0)	/ipe/
File 12	/ike/	/ite/ (0)	/ite/ (0)	/ipe/
File 13	/ikɐ/ (1.0)	/iţɐ/ (0)	/itɐ/ (0)	/ipɐ/ (0)
File 14	/ogɐ/ (0)	/odɐ/	/odɐ/ (0.4)	/obɐ/
File 15	/ogɐ/	/odɐ/ (0.8)	/odɐ/ (0.1)	/obɐ/ (0)
File 16	/ɔgi/ (0)	/ɔdi/ (0)	/ɔdi/ (0)	/ɔbi/ (1.0)
File 17	/ɔgi/	/ɔdi/ (0)	/ɔdi/ (0)	/ɔbi/
File 18	/ægu/ (0)	/ædu/	/ædu/ (0)	/æbu/ (0)
File 19	/ægu/ (0)	/ædu/	/ædu/	/æbu/ (0)
File 21	/æka/(0.3	/æţɐ/(0.33)	/æta/(0.33)	/æpa/(0)
File 22	/æka/(0.3)	/æţɐ/(0.4)	/æta/(0)	/æpa/(0.3

Table 13. Result of Chi-square test

Category of Stimuli	Value	Degress of Freedom	Confidence	Remarks
Vowels	637.33	29	0.01	Significant at 0.01 level.
Consonants	926.76	29	0.01	Significant at 0.01 level.

5   Conclusion

The study shows that though the formants are consistent acoustic parameters related to speech signal corresponding to different places of articulation for vowels and plosives, they are neither necessary nor sufficient for human cognition. However the tests do not signify that they are not used by human cognitive mechanism in this discriminatory task.

234   A.K. Datta and B. Mukherjee

References

1. Chistovitch, L., Sheiken, R., Lublinskaya, V.: Center of gravity and spectral peaks as the determinants of vowel quality. In: Lindblom, B., Ohman, S. (eds.) Frontiers of Speech Communication Research, pp. 143–157. Academic Press (1970)
2. Dellatre, P.C., Liberman, A.M., Cooper, F.S.: Acoustic loci and Transitional cues for consonants. JASA 27, 769–773 (1955)
3. Stevens, K., Blumstein, S.E.: Invariant cues for place of articulation in stop consonants. JASA 64, 1358–1368 (1978)
4. Fant, G.: Acoustic theory of speech production. Moulton & Co., s-Gravenhage (1960)
5. Spoendlin, H.: Innervation densities in Cochlea. Acta Otolar 73, 235–248 (1972)
6. Dellugate, B., Kiang, N.: Speech coding in auditory nerve. JASA 75, 866–978 (1984)
7. Young, E., Barter, P.: Rate responses to auditory nerves to tones in noise near masked threshold. JASA 70, 426–442 (1986)
8. Sachs, M., Young, E., Miller, M.: Speech encoding in Auditory Nerve: Implication for cochlear implans. In: Parkins, C., Anderson, S. (eds.) Cochlear Prosthesis, pp. 94–113. Annals NY Academy of Sciences (1983)
9. Siney, D., Geisler, C.: Comparison of responses of auditory nerve fibers to consonant-vowel syllabus with prediction from linear models. JASA 76, 116–121 (1884)
10. Sachs, M., Young, A.D.: Effects of non-linearity in speech encoding in auditory nerve. JASA 68, 858–875 (1986)
11. Datta, A.K.: Do Ear Perceive Vowels through Formants? In: Proc. 3rd European Conference on Speech Communication and Technology, Genova, Italy, September 21-23 (1993); also in Proc., PC Mahalanobis Birth Centenary, vol. IAPRDT3, Indian Statistical Institute, Calcutta
12. Datta, A.K., Ganguly, N.R., Ray, S.: Recognition of Unaspirated Plosives: A Statistical Approach. IEEE Trans. Acous. Speech and Sig. Process. ASSP 28(1), 85–91 (1980)
13. Datta, A.K., Ganguli, N.R., Ray, S.: Transition – A Cue for Identification of Plosives. Jour. Acous. of Ind. VI(4), 124–131 (1979)
14. Datta, A.K., Ganguly, N.R., Mukherjee, B., Ray, S., Dutta Majumder, D.: Formant Transition as a Cue for Automatic Recognition of Plosives. In: Proc. All India Interdisciplinary Symposium on Recent Trends of Res. and Dev in Digital Technique and pattern Recognition, ISI, Cal. (February 1978)
15. Datta, A.K., Ganguly, N.R., Dutta Majumder, D.: Acoustic Features of Consonants; a Study Based on Telugu Speech Sounds. Acustica 47(2) (1981)
16. Datta, A.K., Ganguly, N.R.: Terminal Frequencies in CV Combination in Multisyllabic Words. Acustica 47(4), 314–324 (1981)
17. Datta, A.K.: Acoustic Phonetics of Non-Nasal Standard Bengali Vowels: A Spectrographic Study. JIETE 34 (1988)
18. Advance Speech Processing Group, Technical Report on Objective Verification of Place and Manner of Articulation of Bangla Phonemes, C-DAC, Kolkata (2009)
19. Pal, S.K., Datta, A.K., Dutta Majumder, D.: Self- supervised Vowel Recognition System. Pattern Recog. 22, 27–32 (1980)
20. Dan, T., Mukherjee, B., Datta, A.K.: Temporal Approach for Synthesis of Singing (SopranoI). In: Proc. Stockholm Music Acous. Conf (SMAC 1993), pp. 282–287 (1993)
21. Datta, A.K., Ganguly, N.R., Mukherjee, B.: Intonation in Segment-Concatenated Speech. In: Proc. ESCA Workshop on Speech Synthesis, Autrans, France, pp. 153–156 (September 1990)

Author Index